PURPLE ROSES

Northwestern's Glorious March to Pasadena

Tim Cronin

Sagamore Publishing Inc.
Champaign, Illinois

©1996 Timothy W. Cronin

All rights reserved.

Book cover and interior design: Michelle R. Dressen
Editor: Susan M. McKinney
Cover photos: Scott Strazzante

ISBN: 1-57167-072-6

We have made every effort to trace the ownership of copyrighted photos. If we have failed to give adequate credit we will be pleased to make changes in future printings.

Printed in the United States.

To my mom, a longtime fan of the purple and white.

And to long-suffering Wildcat fans everywhere who always deserved a winner!

CONTENTS

Acknowledgments vi
Foreword vii
Introduction viii

Chapter 1: The Vision 2
Chapter 2: The Legacy of Losing 10
Chapter 3: The Struggle 18
Chapter 4: High Hopes in Kenosha 30
Chapter 5: The Upset of the Century 38
Chapter 6: Recognition without Respect 48
Chapter 7: The Teflon Bandwagon 54
Chapter 8: Back on the Flight Path 64
Chapter 9: A Successful Conference Call 72
Chapter 10: The Defense Never Rested 82
Chapter 11: Footsteps in the Night 94
Chapter 12: Full-house Domination 102
Chapter 13: Driven to Victory 112
Chapter 14: They Didn't Play Possum 122
Chapter 15: A Red-Letter Game 134
Chapter 16: Champions! 144
Chapter 17: A Tale of Two Cities 154
Chapter 18: Reflection and Reward 162
Chapter 19: Honor Without Glory 170
Chapter 20: A Bright Future 188

ACKNOWLEDGMENTS

It is almost too obvious to mention, but I believe it worth mentioning anyway. This book would not have been possible without the on-field efforts of the Northwestern Wildcats, a tireless and amazing group, and a brilliant coaching staff. They gave the Big Ten, in its centennial season, a champion for all time.

If the Cats didn't beat Notre Dame, and then Michigan, and then Wisconsin, and then Penn State, there may have been an over-.500 season, and even a bowl, but there would never have been a book. Conversely, If they had gone 10-1, and had been uninteresting subjects, this book would have been all the poorer.

But the 1995 Wildcats, from ever-quotable head coach Gary Barnett to his players, are not only a great team, but a lively group, witty and expressive and original and friendly and honest. It has been a pure joy hanging around them, listening to their thoughts, laughing at their one-liners and soaking up the atmosphere as they met goal after goal. Postgame interviews were good and Mondays at the Nicolet Center were better. Every writer should be lucky enough to fall into a story like this at least once.

Three people believed in this book from the outset. Mike Pearson, the University of Illinois' able sports information director, thought enough of the idea mentioned to him over lunch in Memorial Stadium's Varsity Room to call Peter Bannon of Sagamore Publishing across town.

Peter was enthusiastic about it, as was Joe Bannon, and *Purple Roses* was suddenly more than a pipe dream. Mike, Peter and Joe, the next lunch is on me.

There were two big backers at the *Daily Southtown*. Editor Michael J. Kelley and new sports editor Mike Waters gave the thumbs-up instantly and wholeheartedly. Their support and encouragement is deeply appreciated.

Many of my *Daily Southtown* colleagues helped in more ways than they know. John Hector, the sports editor until midseason (when he traded jobs in the newsroom with Mike Waters, a transaction that unaccountably didn't make the AP wire), has always been a source of great advice, wise counsel and corny puns. Thanks, John.

Likewise, a tip o' the hat to Gerry Ahern and Mike Deacon, who covered Northwestern on the weeks I was off at Notre Dame and Illinois, and to Phil Arvia, for putting up with my constant chatter during games.

Many of the photos herein are from *Daily Southtown* staffers. David Banks, Larry Ruehl, Scott Strazzante and Art Vassy all helped bring this book into sharp focus. Likewise, thanks to veteran photographer Ray Foli, who dug deep into his files for pictures of Northwestern's bad old days.

Northwestern's sports information department was hard-pressed to keep up with the largest onslaught of media requests in school history, but Brad Hurlbut, Lisa Juscik, Mark Simpson and Chris Hughes always came through like champs. I have a hunch it will only get busier in years to come, gang. Hope the phone system holds up.

The work of former Northwestern SIDs Greg Shea, Rob Grady, Tim Clodjeaux, Sharon Miller, Mike Nemeth, Jim Vruggink, Susie Prichard, Jerry Ashby, George Beres and the late Walt Paulison, keepers of the Wildcat flame over the years, was vital to the background chapters. It pays to never throw away a media guide!

There's competition in the press box, but also comradeship. Wildcat beat regulars Bill Jauss of the *Chicago Tribune* (on NU's freshman squad the last time the Wildcats went to the Rose Bowl), Len Ziehm of the *Chicago Sun-Times* and Larry Watts of *Pioneer Press*, three guys who had seen many Wildcat losses and interviewed many unhappy people over the years, really deserved a winning season. They're always fun to hang out with, as are Timm Boyle, Bob Logan and Mark Alesia of the *Daily Herald,* Chris Krug of the *Northwest Herald,* and fellow Lindsey Nelson imitator Rick Gano of Associated Press. Logan, known to one and all as "Lefty," predicted "a hard-fought tussle between two evenly-matched squads" when NU played this season, and he was right.

The production crew at Sagamore, beginning with Michelle Dressen and Susan McKinney, was top-rate at guiding a first-time author through book publishing's maze.

Alex Sarkisian's marvelous foreword proves that the Northwestern spirit can never be extinguished.

Dean Spiros, Reid Hanley, John Leptich and Chris Andersen, authors all, told me I could do it when I thought there was too little time and too many words remaining.

Kelly Sullivan, the most enthusiastic person I have ever known, believed and provided encouragement right from the start. Thanks, Kell.

Speaking of believing, yes, Kenmar Jauss, I believe. Doesn't everybody now?

—Tim Cronin

FOREWORD

By Alex Sarkisian
Captain, 1949 Rose Bowl Team

The story told here is the beginning of a love affair made of trust, hard work, and respect for one another.

Allow me to reflect back on my first meeting with Coach Gary Barnett. A group of men interested in the fortunes of Northwestern University football, and willing to help in any way for the program to become successful, sat down with him. Coach Barnett told us his needs, other than athletes. Some needs were met. Others are being addressed at this time.

Each year, Coach Barnett has done what others were unable to do, and that is, to improve the program. This year, 1995, Northwestern won the Big Ten championship and a trip to the Rose Bowl.

Those of us on the 1948 Wildcats team that played in the 1949 Rose Bowl always had a wish. Speaking for my teammates, Coach Barnett, you have enabled us to achieve that joyous wish, which is to sit in the Rose Bowl and cheer another Northwestern team in the Granddaddy of Them All, the Rose Bowl Game!

It was a wish we thought was only a wish, but you have taken that wish and made it reality. You made us truly proud to say, "We are Northwestern men!"

To Coach Barnett, his staff, the 1995 Big Ten champions, and any and all athletic department staff that has made this possible, we say thank you very much from the 1949 Rose Bowl team.

P.S. Go Cats!

INTRODUCTION

It was just over two hours before Northwestern's game at Purdue, a game that would see the Wildcats clinch a share of their first Big Ten championship in 59 years, was to begin. Only a few early-arriving reporters in search of free pop and donuts were in the press box at Ross-Ade Stadium in West Lafayette, Indiana.

Down in the first row, Boilermaker play-by-play announcer Joe McConnell was remembering the year he had broadcast Wildcats football, the 2-8-1 season of 1988. There weren't many basketball wins for the always-enthusiastic McConnell to get excited about either.

"Enjoy the magic carpet ride," said McConnell with a smile before going to his radio booth.

That's exactly what Northwestern's season had become. It was a fantastic trip to a place Wildcat followers hadn't seen in decades: first place. And, as a reward, a final stop in Pasadena.

In my years covering sports, I've been fortunate enough to see some of the great events in recent years, and to visit some memorable places. I've stood inside Turn One at the start of the Indianapolis 500. I've been at Augusta National and watched the legendary Arnold Palmer leading the Masters. I've covered the traveling circuses that are the Final Four, NBA Finals and Stanley Cup Final. I was at Notre Dame the day the wind died and Harry Oliver, a kid with a bartender's build, kicked a 51-yard field goal as time expired to beat Michigan.

I've watched No. 1 play No. 2, followed the leaders in the U.S. Open, been awed by the pageantry of the World Cup and reported on countless Hall of Famers, from Stan Mikita to A.J. Foyt.

But I've never seen a story like this one. Along the way, it became more than just a charming early-season surprise. With an inexplicable twist—a loss to Miami of Ohio under the most bizarre circumstances imaginable—it became the best sports story in the country.

Here was Northwestern, the football team that hadn't won in decades, that, the experts said, couldn't ever win again in the big-time, big-money era of college sports, winning week after week after week. And magic had nothing to do with it. NU was earning those wins.

Here were the Wildcats, wild again, and everybody wild about them. Here, now, they were at Purdue, about to win at least a share of the Big Ten championship in the conference's centennial year. It was too good to be true.

But it was true. And when Michigan beat Ohio State the next week, it was better. The Wildcats were sole champions and headed for the Rose Bowl, where only once before a Northwestern team had ventured.

The following pages tell the amazing story of the 1995 Northwestern Wildcats, the team that believed in itself and proved that long odds mean nothing.

Enjoy the magic carpet ride!

Coach Gary Barnett watches with breathless anticipation the Ohio State-Michigan game that would decide the Wildcats' Bowl fate. (David Banks/Daily Southtown)

Chapter 1
THE VISION

"We'll take the Purple to Pasadena."
—Gary Barnett, on January 11, 1992

GARY BARNETT was hired as the 27th football coach at Northwestern University on December 18, 1991. To true college football experts, he was known as an up-and-coming assistant coach, one working at a program of national renown. To everyone else—and everyone else comprised the great majority of sports fans inside and outside NU—he was unknown.

In the next few weeks, Barnett began to assemble a staff, and started to recruit. He talked to writers and gave radio and TV interviews, but what he didn't do was make any large-scale public appearances.

Thus, when he stood at center court at Welsh-Ryan Arena on January 11, 1992, and spoke to the sellout crowd of 8,117 at halftime of the basketball game between the Wildcats and Ohio State, none of the Northwestern community—to say nothing of Chicago sports fans at large—knew quite what to expect of 45-year-old Gary Barnett.

He came from a fine program in Colorado, one that had won a national championship. He was the offensive coordinator his last year there after previously coaching the quarterbacks and running backs, and had coached some notable players there, including quarterback Sal Aunese and running back Eric Bieniemy.

Seemed personable. Seemed lively. But coaches like that had arrived at Northwestern with high hopes before. John Pont, the George Washington look-alike. Rick Venturi, an NU grad. Dennis Green, the first black coach in the school's history. Francis Peay, Barnett's immediate predecessor. All of them had good qualities, good reputations, good intentions. Some wanted to run the ball. Some wanted to pass the ball. All of them had lost.

Was Barnett different? Those in Welsh-Ryan who weren't crowding the concession stands at halftime found out he was. They found out he dared to dream.

"We'll take the Purple to Pasadena," he said.

Pasadena. As in the Rose Bowl. As in Big Ten champions. As participants, not spectators.

Less than four years later, Barnett's vision had become reality. In 1995, Northwestern's football program went from being putrid to the pinnacle. Only one bizarre loss to Miami of Ohio marred an otherwise perfect season, one that began with an exhilarating upset of the Fighting Irish at Notre Dame, and along the Big Ten trail, included a gritty win at Michigan, a dominating victory over Wisconsin, a come-from-behind triumph over Penn State, a revenge-minded beating of Iowa, and, finally, a romp over Purdue in West Lafayette, where Barnett's first

Northwestern squad had first tasted victory.

The 8-0 conference slate guaranteed Northwestern at least a share of a Big Ten title for the first time in 59 seasons. For an undisputed crown, the Wildcats needed help. Guys like Darnell Autry and Pat Fitzgerald and Rob Johnson and Sam Valenzisi and Matt Rice had done their jobs.

Now, they needed Michigan to beat heavily-favored Ohio State. As if by magic, they got that help. The Wolverines did their part, posting a 31-23 victory over their arch-rivals. The Wildcats were smelling Roses and were Pasadena-bound, off to play Southern California in the most anticipated and unexpected Rose Bowl in ages.

On that cold night in 1992, though, nobody was smelling roses. On the contrary, they were wondering if Barnett knew what he had gotten into.

The Purple to Pasadena? Talk like that not only hadn't been heard in Evanston for decades, the idea hadn't even been considered. Respectability was the goal. Work toward a .500 season, maybe sneak into a bowl game somewhere down the line. The Liberty Bowl, maybe. The Independence Bowl, perhaps. Who wouldn't want to be in Shreveport for the holidays?

The Rose Bowl? That was inconceivable. To go to the Rose Bowl, the Wildcats would have to not only become a good team, they'd have to become a great team, one that could rise up and beat the Michigans and Penn States and Ohio States of the world. They'd have to become a team capable of winning the Big Ten, which, year-in and year-out, vied with the Southeastern Conference for the honor of being college football's toughest league.

Northwestern hadn't beaten Ohio State since 1971. It hadn't beaten Michigan since 1965. It still hadn't played conference newcomer Penn State and nobody was complaining. Longtime Wildcat observers didn't have to think for more than a millisecond about what the outcome of a NU-Penn State game would be. It took longer to estimate how many ambulances would be needed to cart injured Wildcats off to Evanston Hospital.

Northwestern's school colors, purple and white, should have been black and blue, said wags. The nickname should be changed to Mildcats. Some headline writers did it on their own. Potential spectators, be they students, alumni or just plain fans, voted with their feet and didn't come to home games. Dyche Stadium was the home field, but there was no advantage to it.

NU was the Big Ten's doormat, its rag doll. The conference loved having the school, the loop's only private institution, in the league, so the theory went, because of its superior academic reputation and the Chicago television market. Wildcat football provided television households and generated academic All-Americans. Nothing more.

NU's last winning football season was 1971. Way back when, back on New Year's Day 1949, Northwestern had actually been in the Rose Bowl, and even won it, posting a 20-14 victory over California in the closing minutes, but the Wildcats were there only because Michigan had repeated as conference champs, and the Big Ten had a no-repeat rule to spread the bowl experience around. That was a long, long time ago. And the school's last Big Ten title came in 1936, so far back the University of Chicago was still a member of what was known as the Western Conference.

So here was Barnett, saying hello, and at the same time, putting his neck on the line.

"Take the Purple to Pasadena."

Barnett had said it. He said it with feeling. He said it out loud.

Now, the fans knew what they had in this Barnett fellow. They had a risk-taker in their midst.

Risk-takers were precisely who Barnett was looking for when he went recruiting. He didn't want run-of-the-mill players who were sharp enough to qualify at NU. He didn't want solid players who could make the grade but didn't want to take a chance on a program that hadn't won consistently in a generation.

He wanted people willing to take the dare of going to Northwestern and turning the program around with him. Find enough of those, and losses would begin to turn into wins. Wouldn't they?

Above all, along with people who were talented on the field and in the classroom, Barnett wanted players who'd pull together, not pull apart.

"The whole secret comes down to one simple word that can be turned upside down and read, and the wrong thing will happen to you," he explained midway through the 1995 season. "If it's read the right way, the right thing will happen to you.

"That's if it's a 'we' thing and not a 'me' thing. If your team is thinking 'we,' and your talent level is up, then it can work together. But if you've got a 'me' team, I don't care what your emotion and talent level is. You're gonna lose more than you're gonna win."

And he wanted players with class who would go to class.

"The fit here has to be that you've really got to want to be a good student, you've got to want to work hard academically. That isn't true of everybody (in college football). It really isn't.

"We get hammered in recruiting, because other schools will recruit against you, saying, 'Do you really want to go work that hard someplace for four years, when it should be fun?' So we have to find someone who will stand up to that and say, 'Yeah, I do.'

"There's enough of those guys out there. We just have to find them. They're just not all in one location, unfortunately."

Emma Lazarus, in her poem, "The New Colossus," written for the dedication of the Statue of Liberty, wrote of "huddled masses yearning to breathe free." Barnett's job was tougher. He was looking for men to put in a huddle who yearned to win.

He found his risk-takers. He found them in Chicago and in Chicago's suburbs. He found them from southern California to Framingham, Massachusetts. He lured players from the warmth of Florida, noting somewhere in his recruiting speech that Northwestern's mile-long Evanston campus was on the shore of Lake Michigan. He pulled in players from the flatlands of Iowa and Nebraska, from the deep South, but began his recruiting search his first year in an old Wildcat hotbed that had always paid dividends: Ohio.

Barnett's first risk-taker, the first recruit of his first recruiting season, was Justin Chabot of Oxford, Ohio. Growing up as a star lineman for Talawanda High School, and considering his family background, it would have been natural for Chabot to stay in Oxford and go to college at Miami of Ohio.

It didn't seem natural, or comfortable, to Chabot.

"I had a lot of connections with Miami," said Chabot. "My father's chairman of the English department. My brother was already there, the '94 team captain and team MVP. My sister-in-law now, her father is defensive coordinator. Every kind of connection you can imagine, I had there.

"That's great and I love Oxford and I'm friends with their team, and I have respect for their players and coaches, but I had to get away. I had to build something for myself. I didn't want to be Prof. Chabot's son. I didn't want to be Jeff Chabot's little brother. I wanted to be Justin Chabot.

"That's no one's fault. That was the role I had in Oxford. It was something I felt and wanted to get out of."

Aside from Miami, only Northwestern and West Virginia offered Chabot a scholarship.

"I wasn't highly recruited," Chabot said. "I was a skinny guy, about 215 pounds, when coach Barnett came by. I knew I had to put on weight, but he didn't question me about it. He was confident I could do it.

"He came into my house about four years ago. He just has a confidence about himself. When he says something, you believe it, and he believes it. You can tell he's not just throwing you a line, that he really believes he can do things.

"He told me that Northwestern had so much to offer. 'You'd have the great city of Chicago, the best football conference in America, one of the greatest academic institutions in the land,' he said. 'You'd have so much going for you. We just have to get a couple guys in there, or a bunch of guys who want to win. Once we start to get people in there with the right attitude, we will win.'

"The first two or three years, our record didn't necessarily improve, but I know every one of these guys can say our attitude on the team did, and we became a closer team.

"We knew it was going to happen. We thought it was going to happen last year, and it didn't, for whatever reason, but we kept believing, and it's happened now. When you have someone leading you that is confident in himself, that gives you confidence in yourself as well."

Chabot was in the end-zone stands at Welsh-Ryan the night Barnett was introduced to NU fans. He heard him talk about "taking the Purple to Pasadena." He loved it.

"It kinda gave me chills," Chabot recalled. "I think everyone cheered, thinking that was a great thought, and wouldn't that be great, but I know coach Barnett believed that. I could hear it in his voice and I could see it in his eyes.

"It made me believe it as well. I wanted to be a part of it. To say that, it takes a lot of confidence. You just can't go up there and say that. I don't think people necessarily believed it, but I think the people who have come here to play believed it. He said it, and we backed it up, with a lot of credit going to him."

In Barnett's first three seasons, Northwestern lost 24 games, winning just eight and tying one. To outside observers, whether they were fans, alumni or reporters, there was no way to tell that his fourth season would be the rousing campaign it turned out to be. Yes, the Wildcats were improving. Yes, the players were bigger, a shade faster. Yes, the Wildcats were more competitive. But they still got blown out in the second half of most games.

Barnett never wavered in his aim. And when the team set goals for 1995, they were considerable.

The first was "Great attitude and chemistry."

The second was "Relentless team," which happen to be two of Barnett's favorite words, melded into one of his favorite phrases.

The third was "Winning season."

The fourth was "Bowl game."

The fifth was the ultimate goal: "Rose Bowl."

The goals were posted on a sign in the meeting room of the John C. Nicolet Football Center, across the driveway from Dyche Stadium.

For Barnett, goal-setting was nothing new. Nor what others perceived as his relentless—to use that word once more—optimism. In almost every circumstance, his attitude is positive.

"I think, if you grow up an athlete, or as much of an athlete as I could be, that's what you learn," Barnett said before the Rose Bowl. "It's a mentality that an athlete has. The glass is always half-full. The only play is the next play. It starts to permeate your entire attitude in everything that you do. You'd have to ask my wife, but I think that's probably the way I am. I'm maybe a little meaner than that.

"Determination is maybe, in describing me, a better word than positive. I think it just comes from always being involved in sports, in coaching.

If you're going to coach it, you have to live it. Those things that you believe that your players should do, and things that you say to your players that are important, then you have to live that same way, and if you don't, then they don't see how it works. They don't get the connection.

"If that's what you truly believe, then it's easy to live that way."

And easy to decide to come to Northwestern, leaving a solid Colorado program for the great unknown.

"There were just too many positives when we came here and looked at it to think it couldn't be done," Barnett said.

Nevertheless, Barnett needed a bit of prodding from Bill McCartney, who had hired him at Colorado in 1984.

"I'd always been a little bit enamored of Northwestern," Barnett recalled. "I knew the president, Arnold Weber, and the vice president of financial affairs. Weber hired Bill McCartney when he was at Colorado. I knew where they stood."

But Barnett was unsure, even after the interview process had gone so well and he was offered the job.

"I wasn't really going to take the job even after the interview," he said. "But Mac told me these jobs just didn't come along all the time. It was open, I knew the people, it was the Big Ten, and my daughter wanted to go to Northwestern.

"Mac was right. It was a risk worth taking."

Barnett believed he and his well-chosen group of assistants couldn't instill the determination to succeed in the team on their own, and looked for outside help for reinforcement. He found a fresh voice in an old friend.

"We started three years ago with a gentleman by the name of Steve Musseau," Barnett explained. "Steve's a former junior college coach, high school coach. He's 74 years old, he's had three quadruple bypasses, he's got a heart defibrillator, he's had cancer and he's also a diabetic. So he knows a little bit about adversity.

"He's worked with our kids over the last three years, and he worked with 'em at Kenosha, and the first game, the Notre Dame game. He still writes them and calls.

"Steve just sort of represented someone else saying what we were trying to say. He introduced 'High Hopes,' the song, this year for us.

"Our first meeting this year was right in this room," Barnett said in the Nicolet Center auditorium. "We had 100 guys here, and in walks this guy with a robe on, and a beard, and long hair and a cane.

"I didn't know he was coming, and I said, 'Coach Musseau!' and he said, 'No. Moses.' He says, 'I've been walking around for 40 years, and we're going to the Promised Land.'

"He's sort of like a Gandhi to our players."

Gandhi with a twist, that is.

"He's a crazy old man," said offensive guard Ryan Padgett with a smile. "One of the memorable things was, he was talking to us about negative thoughts. He told us, don't think of a circus elephant. The first thing you thought of was a circus elephant.

"That relates to, if you keep bad thoughts in your head, like, if you're running back, think, 'I can't fumble,' then that's the first thing you're gonna do. You have to constantly be saying, 'I'm going to have a 10-yard run,' or 'I'll have a great block here.' "

"He teaches you how to think, how to think to get things done," center Rob Johnson concurred. "Especially in the adverse situation that we faced here at Northwestern. You have so many negative vibes coming at you from every different direction. You've got to get everything out of your head and you've got to focus on what you can do, be focused on bringing our team together, having a team instead of a bunch of individuals."

Northwestern certainly became a team. Barnett was working toward that from the start.

Coach Gary Barnett, coaching the Cats from the sidelines, inspired his team to "Expect Victory" in an effort to "Take the Purple to Pasadena." (Hans Scott)

He was no less bold, no less determined, in 1992.

"We're in better shape in many ways than we were at Colorado in 1984," Barnett said in the summer of 1992, remembering his first year on Bill McCartney's staff. "Facility-wise, player-wise, attitude-wise, energy-wise, all those things, on paper, we're at an advantage here. And in recruiting.

"Here's what we told our players. We said that chemistry and attitude are the keys to winning, no matter what the talent level. As soon as our attitude is where it needs to be and our chemistry is where it needs to be, we're going to win games.

"We've set a goal to have a winning season," Barnett said prior to that first season. "That's what our goal's gonna be. We want to do that. We haven't had one since 1971 or '72, I can't remember that far. It's been a while. It's been a drought.

"So that's our goal. That's what we're going to go out and work for. I think most people shoot too low and hit rather than aim too high and miss. It'll always be our philosophy (to aim high). I'm not afraid to do that."

It took four years for Barnett's original goal, a winning season, to be reached. When it did, the other goals fell like dominoes. Big purple and white dominoes. There's a line of them stretching from here to, well, you know.

"We'll take the Purple to Pasadena," Barnett had blurted out. Now, they were going. What many believed was fantasy was now fantastic reality.

—A 10-1 season, the best in school history!
—An 8-0 record in the Big Ten!
—A nine-game winning streak!
—And a trip to Pasadena! For Northwestern!

The improbability of it happening at a school whose football team required question marks rather than exclamation points in the past helped capture the fascination of a nation. Smart people could play championship-caliber football.

"Take the Purple to Pasadena." That line, even more than his "Expect Victory" slogan, which NU used as a promotional catch phrase for the first two seasons, including funny TV spots he starred in, has stayed with Gary Barnett.

Every year, those words are included in his biography in the school's football media guide. It wasn't until the 1995 Wildcats clinched the Big Ten title and Rose Bowl berth that goes with it that he explained it came from his first lunch with Northwestern people, downtown at the Davis Street Market.

"When I was interviewing for the job here, one of the people on the committee, John Yale, said to me that he just had this dream of taking the purple to Pasadena.

"I just really liked it, so I opened my mouth at a basketball game one night, and out it came! So I was stuck. There it was; I'd laid it out.

"I thought it was sorta catchy. Sounded good at the time. Sounds real good right now."

Call it a risk well-taken.

Michigan's Rob Lytle bulls through the Wildcat defense for a score in the second quarter of a 38-7 Wolverine win in 1976. (Ray Foli)

Chapter 2
THE LEGACY OF LOSING

"We can be a winner."
—Bruce Corrie, then-NU athletic director upon firing Francis Peay

GARY BARNETT talked a good game upon his arrival, which is more than the Wildcats had played for the previous 20 years. He knew the last winning season at Northwestern was a 7-4 campaign in 1971, one that saw the senior-dominated Wildcats go 6-3 in the Big Ten to inspire a brief case of Rose Bowl fever on campus and guarantee a second-place league finish.

Northwestern had finished third in the Big Ten in 1970, during which senior Mike Adamle won the *Chicago Tribune* Silver Football as the Big Ten's Most Valuable Player. Finishing second in '71, a year highlighted by a 14-10 win at Ohio State, allowed fans who even then were long-suffering to dream of a trip to Pasadena in 1972.

After all, if a second-place finish followed a third-place finish, shouldn't a title follow a runner-up year?

No, not if the key players, including All-Big Ten quarterback Maurie Daigneau, whose 1,733 passing yards set a standard unsurpassed until Mike Kerrigan came along nearly a decade later, had already graduated. And they had.

Three other All-Big Ten players from 1971 were gone: defensive back Eric Hutchinson (a two-time all-league selection), offensive guard Tom McCreight and flanker Barry Pearson. With the bench bare, Agase's 1972 outfit was shut out three times and struggled to a 2-9 record. Nobody knew it at the time, but the Wildcats' losing spiral had begun.

Agase bolted for Purdue soon after the season when the Boilermakers offered him a fat contract. He was replaced by John Pont, who was replaced by Rick Venturi, who was replaced by Dennis Green, who was replaced by Francis Peay, who was fired on November 25, 1991. A month later, Barnett arrived on the scene.

When Barnett said Northwestern could have great football teams, few got excited. There wasn't a run on season tickets. The school library didn't have to shorten working hours. After all, the tune had been played before, under the direction of a quartet of orchestra leaders. There was no reason to think Barnett would have any more success than Pont or Venturi or Green or Peay, all of whom worked long hours and ended up banging their heads against the wall. From 1972 through 1991, a span of 220 games, NU went 38-179-3, a winning percentage of .179.

Only twice from 1972 through 1994 would the Wildcats win as many as four games. There were four winless seasons. Northwestern set a record for college football futility with 34 straight losses. (Columbia, the perennial Ivy League

Wildcat defenders Keith Sprouse (48) and Guy Knafelc (6) try to figure out how Charles Nash of Arizona scored in a 1976 game at Dyche Stadium. (Ray Foli)

doormat, came along a few years later to lose 44 straight, setting the standard for Division I-A or I-AA.)

Losing? NU players majored in it. The school offered a doctorate in defeat for the price of a football ticket.

The Wildcats won three games — total — from 1976 through 1981. They went five years— an 0-38-1 stretch — without a win in the Big Ten.

They didn't win a game in the 1980s until Sept. 25, 1982, when an unsuspecting Northern Illinois team became the streak-breaking victim. A Huskie squad comprised greatly of players who would grab the Mid-American Conference title a year later ventured into Dyche Stadium and was clobbered. The Wildcats captured a 31-6 victory, and what few students there were in the gathering of 22,078 diehards tore down the north goal post, marched the pieces out of Dyche, went east down Central Street, and dumped them into the lake.

Smelling a victory over a lesser opponent, reporters from New York to Los Angeles showed up to see The Streak put to rest. Highlights ran on the networks. Finally, NU was in the spotlight for winning.

Not, though, for long. For the rest of those 20 years, NU football was a local story, and an ugly one.

Pont's first teams showed promise, to a degree. His first team opened with a win over Michigan State and finished 4-7 overall and 4-4 in the Big Ten, winning two of the last three games. There were also a pair of two-point losses, which optimists pointed to as close calls. Of course, there was also a 44-0 hammering at Notre Dame and a 60-0 pounding at Ohio State. Woody Hayes remembered the surprise NU had pulled in Columbus two years earlier.

Reality began to set in in 1974. The Wildcats allowed 49 points or more on four occasions and scored a touchdown or less five times. Somehow, they snuck away with a 3-8 record and back-to-back conference wins over Minnesota and Indiana.

In '75, Pont's third team opened with two wins in a row, which hadn't happened since 1964, Agase's rookie year. The Wildcats stood 3-2 going into the October 18, 1975 game with Michigan in Ann Arbor.

They were fortunate to leave that charming town in one piece. Michigan's 69-0 rout on October 18, 1975, was the worst loss handed Northwestern since 1913, and did more than count for one defeat in the standings. It was the first boulder in the avalanche of losses the Wildcats would sustain until this season.

Beginning with that game, NU would:

—lose 15 straight games;
—come up short in 26 of 27;
—and drop 71 of 75. Northern Illinois, as if sent from Heaven rather than DeKalb, was opponent No. 76.

Pont, a fine fundamental coach who had maneuvered surprising Indiana into the 1968 Rose Bowl, tired of losing during the 1977 season, and fired himself before finishing the year with a win over Illinois, staying on as athletic director. He hired Rick Venturi. It seemed like a good idea at the time. Venturi had played at NU in the mid-1960s, and had been an assistant at NU, Purdue and Illinois. He knew the situation.

The Legacy of Losing 13

What he didn't have was players, nor anything resembling good recruiting classes, save for one player, offensive guard Chris Hinton, who would be a first-rounder in the 1983 NFL Draft.

Evanston had long vanished from Venturi's rear-view mirror by then. He lasted only three years as head coach, his 1-31-1 record the worst of any NU mentor who stayed for more than one season. (Lou Saban, never one to outstay his welcome anywhere, rang up a cool 0-8-1 mark in 1955 and made a quick exit.)

Venturi's career opened with a hint of what was to come: a 0-0 tie with the Fighting Illini in Champaign. It was a game that neither school likes to remember, what with seven turnovers and three missed field-goal attempts along the way.

"We really didn't expect a 0-0 tie," said Venturi.

"We really didn't expect a 0-0 tie," said Illini head coach Gary Moeller.

They got a 0-0 tie. For what it was worth, NU had a two-game unbeaten streak, thanks to the win over Illinois at the end of the previous season. It wasn't worth much. The Cats would lose the next 11, with Venturi getting his only win as Northwestern's head coach in the second game of the 1979 season, a 27-22 win over Wyoming.

And that was it. The following week, Syracuse came to Dyche and administered a 54-21 pasting. It was loss No. 1 in what would become known as The Streak.

Along the way, Northwestern would give up 1,370 points, an average of 40.29 per game, and score just 340. In other words, the average score in the 34-game trip through the wilderness was 40-10.

Not all the games were average. In 1980, when the Cats managed to lose all 11, their finest hour came in a 17-10 loss in Ann Arbor to Michigan, a game that had originally been slated for Dyche Stadium. The Wolverines, expecting to coast, had to play their first-team offense and defense for 60 minutes.

That was the bright spot in Venturi's last campaign. The next four weeks, NU was outscored 199-49, with the final straw a 63-0 loss to Ohio State on Homecoming. Northwestern's Homecoming.

No Wildcat team had ever been drubbed so decisively at home. Ohio State quarterback Art Schlichter scored on a 1-yard plunge 2:49 into the game. Everything else was gravy for the Buckeyes. There was a lot of gravy.

There was also, on Northwestern's side, internal acrimony. Less than 48 hours before the game, a group of 32 black players, members of Black Athletes Uniting for the Light, had com-

Northwestern back Malcolm Hunter is beaten by Arizona's Keith Hartwig for a 23-yard score in a 1976 loss. (Ray Foli)

plained to Pont, Venturi and the chancellor of student affairs that blacks had been treated unfairly. Allegations of racial epithets on the practice field and improper medical treatment were made.

The group insisted that the majority of their complaints didn't deal with racial issues, but that was what was most publicized.

They rewrote the complaint, eliminating references to race or gender. University president Robert Strotz then supported BAUL's proposals concerning injuries, dismissals, recruiting and academic counseling near the end of the season.

The fate of both Venturi and Pont was sealed. They were dumped three days after the season ended, the morning after the annual season-ending banquet, at which Venturi said, "I won't quit. I believe in this program and in what we've done."

Dennis Green, the first black head coach in Big Ten history, was Venturi's replacement, while Doug Single, skilled at fund-raising, took over as athletic director.

Single went about improving NU's plant, including remodeling McGaw Hall and sprucing up Dyche Stadium. He directed programs that raised $30 million for NU athletics, and in his tenure, the Wildcats won 60 percent of their games and 12 Big Ten titles in all sports.

Football was not one of those sports. Single had the easy job compared to Green's. What Green couldn't do, at least at the outset, was replace the losing attitude. While he was bubbly and enthusiastic, the aftermath of the allegations against Venturi hung in the air like a heavy fog. Recruiting, never easy at NU, became even tougher.

The lack of quality starters and a virtual absence of depth showed on the scoreboard. The 1981 Wildcats were shut out five times and outscored 505-82, and statistically, and artistically, were the worst team in Northwestern history. Only Indiana, which edged NU 21-20 in the opener, was challenged by the Wildcats. Every other team on the schedule toyed with the Cats, winning by an average of 42.2 points.

That's six touchdowns! No wonder The Streak had reached, by the end of that campaign, 31 games.

The legacy of losing continued through the first three games of 1982. A 49-13 whipping at Illinois. A 30-0 loss to Indiana. A 27-13 defeat by Miami of Ohio, which hadn't lost to NU since 1963.

Many thought the Wildcats would beat the Redskins. Instead, Miami won going away, handing the Wildcats consecutive loss No. 34, 16 of them at home. The Cats were 3-71-1 starting with that 69-0 pounding by Michigan in '75.

With the Big Ten season looming and NU's last conference win five seasons distant, the September 25 game with Northern Illinois now became the last, best chance to avoid another 0-11 campaign.

As noted, the Wildcats prevailed, and in convincing fashion. The hardy few who would have taken a one-point squeaker in NU's favor were treated to a 31-6 romp over the Huskies. Ricky Edwards scored four touchdowns, matching the school record set by Otto Graham and equaled by Mike Adamle, and ran for 177 yards. There hadn't been a 100-yard game by an NU back in two seasons.

Greg Boykin of Northwestern is snared by Notre Dame's Willie Fry in the Irish's 48-0 win in 1976. (Ray Foli)

"We knew it would happen, and we knew when it happened, it would happen big," said Green, in charge for The Streak's last 14 losses.

Hinton, a freshman outside linebacker the last time Northwestern had won, played at his by-then customary offensive tackle spot against the Huskies.

"I felt it on the first offensive drive," said Hinton, who would go on to have an outstanding pro career.

"We created a monster," said NIU head coach Bill Mallory. "They were a pack of wolves. Our kicking game stunk, our offense stunk, our defense stunk.

"We just stunk."

Northwestern didn't smell another victory for two weeks, losing in-between to Iowa, but its 31-21 win over Minnesota snapped another streak: 38 straight losses in the Big Ten. The Cats beat Michigan State on the next-to-last week of the season for their third win of the year, equaling the number of wins they'd managed in the previous six seasons. That, by NU's standards, was a great turnaround, and reporters concurred. Green was named the Big Ten's coach of the year. There was a glimmer of hope on campus.

As least, there was among those on campus who were still paying attention. During the way-down years, interest in the program had collapsed. Attendance sunk to embarrassing depths, averaging an announced 19,975 in the four-year period from 1977 to 1980.

The bottom had fallen out late in the 1976 season, when a pair of games against Minnesota and Michigan State barely drew over 15,000. The low of 15,183 came against the Golden Gophers. Even more telling, top-ranked Michigan visited Dyche Stadium on October 16, 1976, and generated only 28,045 paid admissions. Michigan AD Don Canham said NU would be better off selling its home games against the Wolverines to Michigan.

Pont concurred. Northwestern's 1980 home game with the Wolverines was shifted to Michigan. Rather than have to pay the conference guarantee of $100,000 to Michigan, and likely have less than that in gate receipts left over, NU raked in nearly $300,000 from U-M. The Wildcats played in Ann Arbor in 1979, 1980 and 1981.

Only because Notre Dame visited Dyche in the fall of '76—the last visit of the Fighting Irish to Evanston—was NU's average 25,305. And most in that crowd of 44,936, a non-sellout, were rooting for the Irish.

Media interest also suffered. *The Chicago Tribune* and *Chicago Sun-Times* were, along with reporters from *The Daily Northwestern*, the only newspapers to cover most road games until the recent resurgence in interest. The school had to scramble to get game broadcasts on the AM dial after WMAQ, a 50,000-watt powerhouse, dropped its coverage of Wildcat football. WJJD was the outlet for a few years, but after that, for seven seasons, the school's own student-run station, WNUR-FM, was easier to pick up in some areas than the low-powered AM outlet that succeeded WJJD. The call letters, aptly, were WAIT.

In 1988, highly-rated WGN grabbed the Cats. In 1990, WBBM-AM took over the broadcasts, with NU grad Dave Eanet calling the action, working first with Brian Davis, and more recently with Ted Albrecht.

Television? ABC came calling only when it absolutely had to. The Wildcats were on TV only four times in the 1970s, and only in the Big Ten area.

When Single took over as AD, he brought in marketing people, which was something new at NU. Their gambits helped. By 1983, attendance averaged over 30,000 again, though that year also saw the last sellout in 49,256-seat Dyche—when Rose Bowl-bound Illinois visited —until 1995. Crowds have averaged at least 28,000 a game in all but two of the last 13 years, with this year's figure of 38,230 the best average since 1968.

Among the antics designed to help draw fans was a 1980 visit by the San Diego Chicken for the Indiana game. With only 19,535 on hand, the Chicken's appearance laid an egg. So did NU, blowing a 10-point lead to lose 35-20.

Another idea was for longtime mascot Willie the Wildcat to be locked in a cage at the beginning of games. As soon as NU scored, Willie would be sprung to go about his mascot duties.

Great idea, except the Cats were not in the habit of scoring that often, much less early. Willie spent hours waiting in vain for an NU tally. Sympathetic cheerleaders finally vetoed the idea and gave Willie his freedom. The cage was abandoned.

16 PURPLE ROSES

Ara Parseghian, the last Northwestern coach to have a winning record, returned to Dyche Stadium in 1976 to coach the College All-Stars. (Ray Foli)

Fans had to provide their own amusements. In the student section, marshmallow fights became popular. Silly and harmless, they were a lot like the teams from that era.

If the teams were poor, there were more than a few standout players. Hinton collected NU's first All-Big Ten First Team selection in four years when he was voted to the squad in 1983. Safety Pat Geegan, in 1978, had been the last teamer, but Hinton's appearance started something.

Punter John Kidd was named best in the conference in 1983, defensive tackle Keith Cruise earned a spot in 1984, and in 1986, two Wildcats, tight end Rich Borresen and placekicker John Duvic, made the team, the first double-hit for NU in a decade.

Others made the NFL. Along with Hinton, Steve Tasker, Randy Dean, Steve Craig, and Mike Kerrigan had notable careers. Kerrigan, in fact, quarterbacked Hamilton to the CFL Grey Cup title in 1986, the first Wildcat signal-caller to lead his team to a pro championship since Otto Graham.

In terms of talent, the Wildcats were improving, even though the record rarely showed it. The 1982 season had made it appear the Wildcats had turned a corner. Instead, there were more corners to come. A 2-9 record in 1983. The same in 1984, after which Single mulled firing Green.

A 3-8 mark in 1985 included back-to-back wins over Missouri and Northern Illinois, the first such twin-killing in a decade. Otherwise, the beat, and the beatings, went on.

Green got out. Offered a job on the San Francisco 49ers staff by Bill Walsh in March of 1986, Green pondered his 10-45-1 record, his sour relationship with Single, and what he considered foot-dragging concerning improvement of facilities, and jumped at rejoining his one-time boss at Stanford, even though it meant turning an entire recruiting class into football orphans.

"We can compete with anybody," Green said upon taking his leave of Evanston. "Northwestern has a real opportunity in 1986 to have a winning season. I'd planned on coaching this team."

Francis Peay, Green's defensive coordinator, was named the interim head coach, and managed to remove the first word of that title late in his first season.

The Cats went 4-7 under Peay in '86, the best record since Pont's 1975 club did the same. They could have been 5-6, but for Purdue's Jonathan Briggs kicking a game-winning 25-yard field-goal with four seconds left in the season's eighth game. Was there really light at the end of the tunnel?

Yes, and it was an oncoming train. The 1986 mark was misleading. Two of the wins were against Army and Princeton. The Cadets were missing Blanchard and Davis, and as for Princeton, well, the Ivy League isn't the Big Ten.

Northwestern was ridiculed for scheduling the Tigers, and at Princeton, no less, but scored a 37-0 shutout, the first for the Wildcats since that tie with the Illini in 1978. For NU, a win was a win was a win.

One taste of Big Ten football, though, was enough for Princeton, which attracted only 8,750 fans for their home game against the Wildcats. The second half of the home-and-home series was canceled.

In July, 1987, Single resigned after budget cuts resulted in the elimination of cross country and track. Bruce Corrie came in as his replacement that fall. On the football field, the Wildcats went back to sleep, with consecutive 2-8-1 seasons in 1987 and 1988 followed by an 0-11 year in 1989.

Once again, the opposition teed off when it could. The Wildcats were college football's equivalent of a miracle cure. Have an ailing program? Call 1-800-WILDCAT for fast, fast, fast relief.

Playing average teams was tough for NU. Powerhouses were merciless.

In '88, Michigan beat NU 52-7 at Dyche Stadium, the first visit of the Wolverines to Evanston in six years. In that previous stop by, a 49-14 wipeout, head coach Glenn "Bo" Schembechler didn't mince words.

"The only way to play is, when you get a team down, kick 'em," he said.

In '89, virtually everybody did. NU was within a touchdown of beating Minnesota and Wisconsin, and not even close to anyone else.

It was like '81 all over again, except the Cats were scoring. So, though, was the opposition. In the last four weeks, NU allowed an average of 59.25 points per game. It got so bad in East Lansing, Michigan State head coach George Perles was being kind when, after another Spartan touchdown gave MSU a 76-14 lead, he had the offense line up for a two-point conversion, then down the ball rather than run a play.

The game was such an embarrassment, NU alum Tim Weigel, calling the game on WGN Radio, suggested that Northwestern follow in the footsteps of the University of Chicago and drop out of the Big Ten.

Peay's 1990 squad went 2-9, and while a 3-8 record the next season included back-to-back wins over Illinois and Michigan State, Corrie wasn't impressed. On November 25, 1991, Corrie fired Peay, who had cobbled together a 13-51-2 record over six years.

One of those losses was a 34-3 whipping inflicted by Ohio State at a Northwestern home game. Sort of. It was played in Cleveland Stadium. Corrie, looking at a budget he didn't like, rented the Mistake on the Lake, moved the home game against the Buckeyes there, and drew 73,830 fans. Technically, it's NU's all-time high home attendance figure, but few were dressed in purple.

Corrie took heat for moving the game, and still more for firing Peay, who was 13-51-2 in six years. His rational for the move was simple.

"We improved, but not enough," said Corrie. "We can be a winner."

The search for a new head coach was on.

Randy Dean, one of many NU quarterbacks to take a beating, is run over by Notre Dame's Ken Dike (L) and Ross Browner at Dyche Stadium in 1976. (Ray Foli)

The Wildcat defense, led by Rodney Ray (r), gangs up on Notre Dame's Derrick Mayes in 1994. (Scott Strazzante/Daily Southtown)

Chapter 3
THE STRUGGLE

"Expect Victory!"
—Gary Barnett

AS HE PROMISED, Gary Barnett did not dally upon his arrival at Northwestern. Hired on December 18, 1991, he wasted no time in hiring a staff and in jumping into the always-competitive midwest recruiting wars.

"I will hit the floor moving," he said upon his introduction. "Grass does not grow under my feet. I'll be a relentless recruiter."

At Northwestern, being relentless in everything was absolutely necessary. The school, with the highest academic qualifying standards in the Big Ten, doesn't make exceptions for athletes. That's traditionally limited NU's prospects to the same high school seniors who also consider Notre Dame, Stanford, Duke, Vanderbilt, Rice, and a few non-Division I-A schools, notably the Ivy League.

Did Barnett consider the more restrictive standards a problem? If he did, he didn't say so.

"Just because you can run doesn't mean you can't write," Barnett said. "You can get some very good students who are football players to come to Northwestern, and we will do that, absolutely."

Then he went out and did it, even though the Wildcats were without the obligatory indoor football practice facility, even though seedy Dyche Stadium, while venerable, hardly had the charm of Notre Dame Stadium, to say nothing of the history, and even though the Wildcats' record of losing seasons was as old as the players he was trying to recruit.

"I've seen things that tell me in my heart that Northwestern can have great football teams," Barnett said that day. "My goal is to get student-athletes who play football with the same pride on the field as they show in the classroom.

"Competitors take great pride in seeking the highest level of competition. I want players who want to play against people like that. I'll meet with my players and ask if they want to tee it up against Notre Dame.

"If they don't, I'll bring in some people who do."

Barnett's first recruiting class was a beauty. It included quarterback Steve Schnur, fullback Mike McGrew (recruited as a quarterback), defensive backs William Bennett and Chris Martin, linebacker Danny Sutter, and the majority of the offensive line: Justin Chabot (Barnett's very first recruit), Ryan Padgett and Brian Kardos. Barnett, in one recruiting season, and with a late start, had landed a group of players who would become the foundation for the success enjoyed in 1995.

In great measure, Barnett was doing then what Northwestern coaches since Ara Parseghian had done. They sold the potential of the program, not the reality.

Sometimes, it paid off. Parseghian's 1962 club opened with six straight wins and was ranked No. 1 in the country in the Associated Press poll before dropping consecutive games to Wisconsin and Michigan State by lopsided scores and finishing 7-2.

It could be done, Barnett told prospects. Francis Peay had said the same thing. Dennis Green preached the gospel. Rick Venturi, a Wildcat player in the mid-1960s, professed belief. John Pont, who had taken an Indiana team from 1-8-1 in 1966 to 9-2 and Pasadena in the 1967 season, could point to his track record when he went calling on prospects.

Barnett could note the job a former fellow assistant at Colorado, Buffaloes offensive coordinator Jerry DiNardo, had just done at Louisiana State. The Tigers were 1-10 in 1990. DiNardo arrived and brought the 1991 edition of LSU to respectability at 5-6. Not great, not even .500, but better than NU had been since 1971.

For his assistants, Barnett first looked across the coaches' meeting room at Colorado and tabbed Ron Vanderlinden as his defensive coordinator. The previous five seasons, NU had allowed an average of 370 points, holding teams under two touchdowns only five times in 55 outings.

Vanderlinden, who would tutor the inside linebackers in addition to supervising the defense, was joined on the defensive side by line coach Vince Okruch, who had worked with Barnett and Vanderlinden in Colorado before going to Minnesota, outside linebacker coach Tim Kish, who joined NU from the U.S. Military Academy at West Point, and, in 1991, secondary coach Kevin Ramsey, the lone holdover from Francis Peay's last staff.

On the offensive side, Barnett brought in Greg Meyer from Toledo to coordinate and work with the tight ends, gave Colorado grad assistant John Wristen a full-time spot as the running backs coach, hired Craig Johnson out of VMI to coach the quarterbacks, convinced Gregg Brandon, who had played for Barnett at Air Academy High in Colorado Springs, to join NU from Utah State, and, in June of 1992, hired Tom Brattan to coach the offensive linemen.

The staff was complete, and, remarkably, there was only one change in the first four years. Ramsey left, and was replaced as secondary coach by former NU standout receiver Jerry Brown in 1993.

Barnett came up with a slogan: "Expect Victory." The NU marketing staff put it on the cover of the media guide, on schedules, on billboards, and used it as the tag line on a series of radio and television commercials.

Ads for the Wildcats? That was also new.

Expect Victory. Nay-sayers had a field day with it. But when? they retorted. Expect victory, but settle for a tie. Expect victory, but by who? And so it went.

Even before the slogan had been unveiled, Barnett received a taste of how tough turning the program around would be. Reality invaded quickly with the realization by Barnett that he may have been named the new coach by the administration, but that many of the players recruited by Francis Peay didn't want to see Peay leave, no matter who came in.

"One of the most difficult things a guy can do is take over for a coach who's been fired," Barnett said in the summer of 1995. "I thought they'd welcome new enthusiasm and new ideas.

"Try to walk in, as a white head coach, for a fired black head coach. I had to try to win over black players who were recruited by him and who came to Northwestern to play for a black head coach.

"I just assumed everybody wanted a change. They didn't want a change. Whoa! These guys didn't give you instant respect just because you were wearing a hat. You have to win over their trust, have to earn your respect."

It didn't come easily. To change the atmosphere and focus the players, Barnett moved preseason training camp from distraction-filled Evanston to the University of Wisconsin-Parkside in comparatively quiet Kenosha, Wisconsin. It was a first for NU, or for any Big Ten school.

Barnett promised NU's offense would "stretch the defense," even though quarterback Len Williams, in his third year as a starter, had

The Struggle 21

Notre Dame's Jeremy Sample drills NU back Dennis Lundy in the Wildcats' 42-15 loss in 1994. (Scott Strazzante/Daily Southtown)

three smallish receivers to throw to in 6-foot Michael Senters, 5-foot-9 Lee Gissendaner and 5-foot-3 Patrick Wright.

The camp was conducted in near-secrecy, not because Barnett feared spies, but because few were interested. One day, Barnett told the *Tribune's* Bill Jauss, the only reporter on hand for a practice session, "If there had been another name on our jerseys, you would have been one of 60 media people here today."

A name like Notre Dame, perhaps? Well, precisely what Barnett was doing in Kenosha would be on display for half the nation to see in Northwestern's first game. His arrival coincided with the resumption of the rivalry with the Fighting Irish.

A four-year deal engineered by former NU athletic director Doug Single and Fighting Irish brass called for games in 66,000-seat Soldier Field, about 17,000 seats larger than Dyche Stadium, in 1992 and 1994, and contests in 59,075-capacity Notre Dame Stadium in 1993 and 1995.

In the past, in a long series that ended in 1976, the Irish had played at Dyche, and, in latter years, there was more blue, gold and green in the stands than purple and white. But the economics of college football had changed, and the Irish wanted—demanded, really—a bigger slice of the action.

Playing home games at Soldier Field was the way to get Notre Dame on the schedule and get a measure of national TV attention for the Wildcat program, so Single, a tireless promoter who had coined his own slogan, "NU Direction," upon his arrival in Evanston, bought in.

Thus, on September 5, 1992, before a regional ABC television audience and 64,877 fans who fought their way through a massive traffic jam on the lakefront, the Gary Barnett years began at Northwestern.

It commenced with something of a thud. That final score once again: Notre Dame 42, Northwestern 7. The rushing totals: ND 391, NU 81. The rushing totals for the second half: Irish 261, Wildcats 1.

Expect Victory? The Wildcats did. They trailed by only 14-7 with 20 minutes to play, and, but for a missed field goal early and a missed scoring chance just before the half, NU could have led.

"It may sound crazy, but we thought we could win this game," said Wildcat defensive lineman and co-captain Frank Boudreaux in the bowels of Soldier Field. "I still think, if we play 'em again, we have a good chance to win. We could have been ahead at the half."

But they weren't, and when Notre Dame's defense arrived in the second half, the Wildcats went to the dance-hall attack: 1, 2, 3, kick. Reality set in, mostly on top of Cats quarterback Len Williams, who had time to throw early but was sacked thrice in the second half, including back-to-back drops courtesy of Irish defender Devon McDonald. Aside from the purple-on-purple uniforms NU was wearing, the whole scene looked very familiar.

Barnett, naturally, was displeased at the outcome, and could hardly take solace in the "close-for-a-half" theory.

"No," he said. "You don't stop in the heat of battle and say 'I'm proud of you guys.' "

Only the promising first half separated this Northwestern outfit from those of years past. And after the next two weeks, a 49-0 slapping by Boston College and a 35-24 loss to Stanford, there seemed to be no difference at all. A Barnett team at 0-3 looked little different from any other Northwestern team since 1971.

Then something happened. Then the Wildcats won. In the conference. On the road. And convincingly.

Purdue was favored by 14 points in West Lafayette. That was the margin of victory. Northwestern's victory, a 28-14 romp, the first win in a Big Ten opener for NU since 1983.

Did the Wildcats expect victory? What they wore the day before said they did. Barnett gave everyone black T-shirts with "Expect Victory Purdue '92" on them on Friday, a psychological ploy that paid off.

But the shirts didn't win the game. The players did. The Boilermakers were held to three plays and a punt on their first three possessions. The Wildcats, meanwhile, made big plays on offense.

No play was bigger than sophomore running back Dennis Lundy's 1-yard plunge early in the second quarter. This was something new for NU: a lead. It was 14-0 midway through the second quarter, when Williams, a poised se-

Notre Dame's Brian Magee (17) and Jeremy Nau (58) converge on Luther Morris in 1994. (Scott Strazzante/Daily Southtown)

Wildcats quarterback Tim Hughes is swamped by Notre Dame's defense in the 1994 opener. (Scott Strazzante/Daily Southtown)

nior who would end up starting 33 straight games in his career, hit the fleet Gissendaner on a 70-yard touchdown pass.

The same duo would hook up on a 21-yard pass with nine seconds left in the half, more than answering freshman Mike Alstott's 3-yard TD run. The pass was set up by a gamble moments earlier, when, on fourth-and-1 from the NU 29, Williams, the upback in punt formation, took the snap and found defensive back Willie Lindsey for a 29-yard gain.

When Gissendaner, who had 246 all-purpose yards and would be named the Big Ten's player of the week, collected 72 of them on a punt return to set up a 4-yard scoring run by Pat Wright, the Boilermakers were done.

Lundy would end up running for 154 yards, and Williams, the controlled passing game working to perfection, was 10-of-13 for 180 yards.

But Barnett was most pleased with his defense.

"Once we came out and stopped them three-and-out at the start of the game, we got reinforced and the adrenaline got flowing," he said.

Indeed, the game had in miniature all the earmarks of the season-long success that would be seen three years later, not that anyone knew it at the time. The defense stuffed the opposition, with a plus-3 turnover ratio. The offense ran well, and hung on to the ball. The special teams came through at the right time.

And there were two curious sidelights to the win, sidelights that would be seen time and again in the years to come. Northwestern spoiled Purdue's Homecoming, for one thing, and in doing so, snapped a 14-game losing streak in Ross-Ade Stadium. NU hadn't beaten Purdue in West Lafayette since 1950.

Losses to Indiana and Ohio State followed, and a third straight loss, to Illinois in Champaign, seemed likely, considering the Illini took a 26-6 lead into the fourth quarter.

There was no reason to think NU, which managed only a pair of Brian Leahy field goals in the first 45 minutes, would rally to win. But rally they did. And win they did.

Three touchdown passes from Williams, the last one into the hands of a diving Gissendaner in the back of the south end zone with 13 seconds left in the game, and three Leahy kicks, gave the Wildcats an astounding 27-26 victory. And, not incidentally, ruined another team's Homecoming.

"I was in a zone," Williams would say later.

So was Illinois in the second half, and that, along with a blocking scheme that gave Williams protection he wasn't getting earlier, made the difference. Williams, sacked four times in the first half, now was able to stay in the pocket.

Chris Gamble, who had never caught more than one pass in a game, became Williams' favorite receiver. With 13:35 left, he caught a 31-yard pass for a touchdown, cutting Illinois' lead to 26-13. He would be heard from again.

NU was at the Illinois 5 when Williams found Gissandaner open for a score with 4:53 left. Now, the Illini lead was 26-20, and the 52,332 fans in Memorial Stadium were nervous. Why wasn't Northwestern folding like a paper fan? Wasn't NU's win in Evanston the year before enough? What in the name of Red Grange was going on here?

The Illinois defense, the zone zonked, switched back to a man-to-man when it went back on the field, and that, thanks to a three-and-out performance by the Wildcat defense, was quickly. Gissandaner was guarded by Robert Crumpton, Gamble by Rod Boykin. There was 3:23 left.

That was more time than Williams needed. He found Gamble for 9 yards, then again for 21 more, then once again—Gamble's 10th reception of the day—for 15 more. That brought NU to the Illini 17.

The pocket broke down on the next snap, but Williams scrambled to the 9. He found Gissandaner with a toss that garnered four more yards, and, after an incomplete pass, found Gissandaner just free of Crumpton in the end zone for the tying score. Leahy's extra-point

Northwestern's Dennis Lundy gets away from Notre Dame's Jeremy Nau in the 1994 opener. (Scott Strazzante/Daily Southtown)

kick provided the margin of victory, in great measure because back in the first quarter, when it seemed meaningless, Wildcat linebacker Steve Shine had blocked an extra-point try by Chris Richardson.

This, then, was a sneak preview of another facet of NU's 1995 success: Superior halftime adjustments. Barnett and his staff made the right moves, and his players executed them to perfection. And suddenly, for the first time in 17 years, the Wildcats, while 2-5 overall, were 2-2 in the Big Ten.

Those who were in Dyche Stadium a week later will tell you Northwestern was 3-2 after playing Michigan State. The officials didn't see it that way. Specifically, they didn't see Leahy's 35-yard field-goal try as time expired as going through the uprights—even though viewers standing behind the goalposts, and even many in the press box, high above the action and at the 50-yard line, thought Leahy's kick was good. Even videotape taken from behind the posts seemed to confirm the kick as successful. Leahy celebrated. The game was won.

But it wasn't won. It was done. After an agonizing second, Leahy's kick was ruled wide right, and that allowed Michigan State to take away a 27-26 victory. For NU fans hoping the Cats would win on their own Homecoming, it was a Halloween horror story.

"I know in my heart it was good, yes," Leahy said minutes after the game. "A good kick for me is when I keep my head down. When I looked up, I saw it. From my angle, I thought it faded after it went through."

Even Michigan State linebacker Rob Fredrickson thought it went over the post, and was honest enough to say so. Barnett, aware that he could be fined and suspended by the Big Ten for criticizing the officials, kept his cool. Besides, he was steamed that his team had gone so far as to let Michigan State back into the game.

The Wildcats, paced by Williams' career-high 365 passing yards, led 17-10 after a 90-yard kickoff return score by Gissendaner. But a Wildcat offense that had only given the ball away six times in the first seven games lost it four times, three of the miscues leading to 17 Spartan points.

Even before Leahy's last-second try, NU had rallied. Williams hit Pat Wright with a 26-yard scoring strike with 5:14 to go. Then Barnett, eschewing a tie, went for two points and a 28-27 lead. Williams' pass to backup receiver Luther Morris was incomplete.

If NU didn't win the game, at least the Wildcats were winning their fans over. The crowd of 31,101 gave the players a standing ovation at game's end.

"I never saw that in my four years here," said Williams.

He'd see it one more time, in the season-ending win over Wisconsin, a victory assured only when Greg Gill forced a fumble in the Badger backfield with 49 seconds left. The 27-25 victory, which knocked the Badgers out of the bowl picture, gave the 1992 NU squad a 3-8 overall mark (one identical to 1991's), and a 3-5 record in the Big Ten. That was the best conference record for the Wildcats since 1973.

Gissendaner's 1,342 all-purpose yard season, which included the nation's best punt-return average, earned him the *Chicago Tribune's* Silver Football as the Big Ten's MVP. Northwestern hadn't had a league MVP since Mike Adamle, in 1970. What's more, Gissendaner was coming back for his senior year.

There was optimism in Evanston.

Barnett's second year began with another solid recruiting class. Among the new arrivals were linebackers Pat Fitzgerald and Casey Dailey, defensive backs Eric Collier and Hudhaifa Ismaeli, linemen Paul Janus and Matt Rice, and wideout Brian Musso, son of former Alabama and Bears standout Johnny Musso. Barnett could only hope the son of the "Italian Stallion" would earn his own nickname someday.

Additionally, by now, many of the holdover players recruited by Peay were paying attention to Barnett. But not all.

"A lot of 'em said, 'This isn't worth it,'" Barnett remembered.

Nevertheless, with fifth-year senior Williams back at quarterback, Gissendaner his No. 1 target, Lundy the top back, and the defense a year older, Northwestern figured to at least match the 3-8 record, if not better it.

After three weeks, that seemed a sure thing. An opening loss at Notre Dame saw the Wildcats leading 12-7 at halftime, only to watch the Irish rally to take a 27-12 decision.

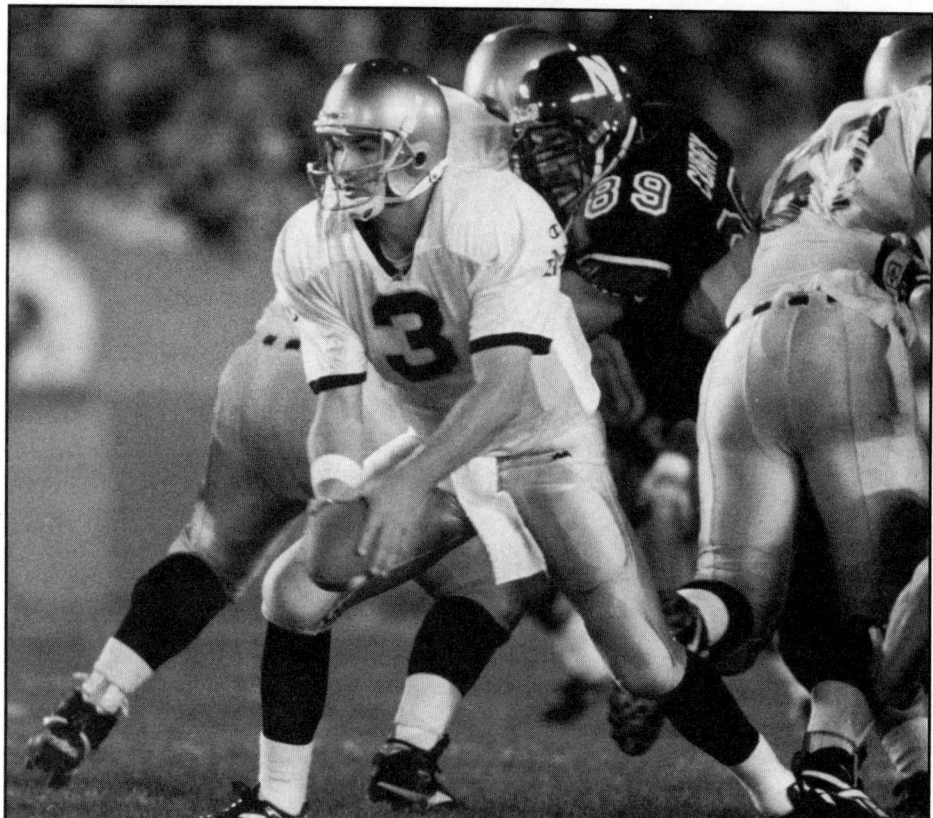

Notre Dame's Ron Powlus was unstoppable against NU in 1994. (Scott Strazzante/Daily Southtown)

"We made too many mistakes," said Barnett. "Where we have to improve is between the ears."

The improvement came quickly. The following week at Dyche Stadium, the Wildcats came from behind to defeat 22nd-ranked Boston College on a 9-yard pass from Williams to Gissendaner and a two-point conversion run by Lundy. The 22-21 win more than avenged a 49-0 loss to the Eagles in Chestnut Hill, Massachusetts a year earlier.

It also gave NU momentum. The following week, the Cats made it two straight at Dyche with a 26-14 whipping of Wake Forest.

"How many guys would have predicted we would have been 2-1?" said Barnett. "Only me."

And, probably, kicker Sam Valenzisi, who had been a walk-on the year before and had won the placekicking job from Leahy the week before the Boston College game. He kicked a pair of field-goals against Wake Forest in a driving rain.

The 2-1 record was the first for NU since 1986, Francis Peay's first season. With the offense clicking, the defense improving, and a deadeye walk-on kicker, the Wildcats seemed well-placed to make some noise in the Big Ten.

Then everything fell apart. They went winless in conference. Eight straight losses, beginning with a 51-3 debacle at Ohio State. That, on the heels of the win over Wake Forest, was a kick in the stomach. The 53-14 hammering by Wisconsin a week later wasn't any more pleasant.

The trouble started on the offensive line. Three sophomores, center Rob Johnson and guards Ryan Padgett and Todd Pawlowski, and junior Matt O'Dwyer, were injured to some degree. Against Ohio State, they were up against one of the great defensive lines in college history, one anchored by 305-pound Dan Wilkinson. It showed. With O'Dwyer's playing time limited, Wilkinson spent the afternoon hunting for Len Williams' head.

Loss piled upon loss. Gissendaner was double-teamed, but still managed 114 all-purpose yards per game. However, with the Wildcats trailing so often, the ball-control passing attack and the use of Lundy wasn't able to overcome the opposition.

Williams, a trouper, played the season finale with injured ribs, wearing a flak jacket when he could easily have sat out. And considering the opponent was Penn State, that would have been understandable. But he'd already missed the previous week's game against Iowa, so he played, throwing a pair of touchdown passes, one a 74-yarder to Dave Beazley, and completed 12 throws for 264 yards despite five sacks in a 43-21 loss.

Williams had bought into Barnett's plan. He was graduating now, though, as was Gissendaner, before either could see the payoff in the standings.

The good news for Barnett was that 19 starters would return in 1994. The better news was that another recruiting class would mean about three-quarters of the players would be his recruits. His third class of incoming freshmen included running back Darnell Autry, a pair of quarterbacks in D'Wayne Bates and Lloyd Abramson, kicker Brian Gowins and running back/defensive back Marcel Price.

All would become well-known in 1995, but it was Autry, a Tempe, Arizona product who considered hometown school Arizona State as well as UCLA, Colorado and Syracuse before settling on Northwestern because of its theater program, who would make an immediate impact on the program.

It would not be immediate enough, however. For the third straight year, the Wildcats opened with Notre Dame, and for the third straight year, Wildcat fans were teased early. It was scoreless after a quarter.

Then Irish quarterback Ron Powlus went to work. He riddled the Wildcat secondary with three touchdown passes in the second quarter and finished with four for the game in Notre Dame's 42-15 prime-time rout of the Cats before a sellout throng of 66,946 at Soldier Field. Lundy's 138-yard outing on the ground, the first of six 100-yard-plus games he'd have, wasn't enough.

"Everything that went wrong can be fixed," said Barnett. "We wanted to go into the game and make them throw the ball to beat us, and that's what they did. I'm not disappointed at all. If anything, I saw some bright spots."

So did O'Dwyer, the lineman who'd eventually go in the second round of the 1995 NFL Draft to the New York Jets.

"We were killing them," he said. "We were blowing them off the ball. Then we made them look better than they are."

The following week was an improvement, but not a win. The Wildcats and Stanford hooked up in a no-defense affair that featured five lead changes and a pair of ties, including the final score: 41-41.

It was the start of a stretch that saw NU go 3-2-1, with all three wins in Homecoming games, at Air Force, Indiana and Minnesota. Add in the loss to the Irish, and the Wildcats were 3-3-1 through seven games, 2-2 in the Big Ten, with one of the losses by just 17-15 to Ohio State.

That was followed by a 46-14 loss to Wisconsin. And that was followed by an extension of Barnett's contract by athletic director Rick Taylor, just as a few whispered that Iowa wouldn't mind hiring Barnett once Hayden Fry retired.

Taylor discounted that, saying, "A good idea's a good idea. Obviously, we wouldn't have done what we did unless we thought (the program) had progressed right on schedule.

"Normally, I think you throw out the first year (of a new coach). You've got to become familiar with the university, and that first year of recruiting is, generally speaking, a wash. So I really look at this as being Gary's second year.

"I look at the kids he's gotten into the program, I look at the way they're playing - young, but they're playing hard, doing things the right way. He, his staff and the kids have bought into the mission of the university.

"It's a given that there's a commitment to turning this thing around. Then you look at the leadership, and if the leadership's right, then you want to make sure there's a measure of continuity."

Two days after the contract extension was announced, Northwestern went to Minnesota and won 37-31 in the Metrodome, with Lundy gaining 213 yards and the freshman, Autry, picking up 100 in a backup role. The momentum carried over to the following week's assignment against Indiana. The Cats shut out the Hoosiers for the last three quarters in a 20-7 win.

So, as the leaves began to turn, the Wildcats had an outside chance at a bowl. Barnett knew it.

"It's an evolutionary process for our program," he said to a small group of reporters at his weekly Monday luncheon in McGaw Hall's "N" Club preceding the Illinois game. "Each success just buys you an admission ticket to a more difficult situation.

"We're at a point, at an opportunity, that our coaches have wanted to see, that our players have wanted to be at, our fans and our students have wanted us to get to. All this is is an opportunity. Now it's time to step up.

"I want to emphasize we're evolving. We're just taking the small steps you have to take to get to the level you want to participate at. We just want to continue taking steps forward. Every one is critical."

The Wildcats would take no further steps forward. Illinois would hand NU a 28-7 defeat, and that would be followed by lopsided losses to Michigan State, Iowa and Penn State to finish the season.

The finale was a study in contradictions. Northwestern controlled the ball 41 minutes, and for all but 19 seconds of the first quarter, yet lost 45-17. And NU held the ball without Dennis Lundy suspended for, it was later revealed, gambling on sports, though not on the Wildcats in particular.

Lundy's absence moved Autry into the starting tailback role, and he went to town, rushing for 171 yards in 39 attempts. It was another unbilled sneak preview of 1995, and, in this case, the coming-out party of the most exciting runner in Wildcat history.

Autry wouldn't score a touchdown, but his yards were the most ever registered in one game by an NU freshman, and the carries the most ever by anyone against the Nittany Lions.

With a 3-7-1 record and 2-6 league reading, the Wildcats had appeared to outsiders to be treading water. Statistically, they led only in punting, where Paul Burton's 43.0 average garnered him first-team All-Big Ten honors on both the media and coaches teams. They were last in the conference in turnover ratio, a minus-11, last in passing defense, eighth in rushing defense, and at the bottom of the league in offense as well.

In their last four games, they had been outscored 157-54. No game was close. If this was a foundation for the future, the basement was leaking, the pipes were cracked, and there was a short-circuit in the wiring. Some foundation.

There was nowhere to go but up. How far up, and how quickly, nobody could have predicted.

Northwestern's Jason Green chases Notre Dame's Jerome Bettis in vain during the 1992 season opener, Gary Barnett's first game as coach of the Wildcats. (Scott Strazzante/Daily Southtown)

Dedication in summer practice paid off for the Wildcats, including Darnell Autry (24), Kevin Peterson (72), and Farati Leary (37). (Scott Strazzante/Daily Southtown)

Chapter 4
HIGH HOPES IN KENOSHA

"I ain't gonna be a loser."
—Gary Barnett before Camp Kenosha

DID THE ROAD to the Rose Bowl begin on a heap of old garbage?

Many Northwestern players will tell you it did. Part of the team's voluntary summer training—voluntary in the sense that players can't be ordered to participate, but are expected to if they're on campus—involved running up and down a moderately picturesque man-made hill on Evanston's southern border.

Mt. Trashmore, it's called, because it's made of old garbage, sealed away under a deep clay base. It's tall enough to be everybody's favorite sledding area in the winter, and to be NU strength coach Larry Lilja's workout deluxe in the summer.

This year, with far more players participating in summer drills than in the past, Lilja was inspired. He made up a sign and stuck it on top of Mt. Trashmore. There were two words on it:

"Rose Bowl."

Seeing that, everybody worked a little harder.

Spring practice, a time dedicated to revamping systems and finding out who can replace graduating seniors, had been little different in 1995 than it had been the previous three seasons at NU, with one major exception.

Save for a half-dozen holdover seniors who had been redshirted and would be eligible to play in their fifth year at Northwestern in the fall, these were Gary Barnett's players. The holdovers had been recruited by Francis Peay. Everyone else had been brought in by Barnett.

They had heard his pitch, and bought in. They had come to Evanston, to Northwestern, planning to be a part of the team that snapped the school's string of losing seasons, a string that reached 23 straight in 1994. They did not know when it would happen, but they believed it would happen while they were there.

If the turnaround was to happen in 1995, changes would have to be made on defense, where nine starters returned. The Wildcats had allowed more points per game than any other Big Ten team, and more yards per game than any conference squad except Purdue. The 5-2 alignment NU employed was porous, and explained why free safety William Bennett was the team's No. 2 tackler, right behind linebacker Danny Sutter. It was because the defensive line wasn't stopping anyone.

In an effort to change things, Barnett and the defensive staff huddled with the Bears' defensive coaches and adopted the Bears' 4-3 defense. It came to be NU's bread-and-butter alignment, with Sutter and Tim Scharf flanking middle-linebacker Pat Fitzgerald.

"There are two areas we have to make significant improvements on," Barnett said. "That's

Camp Kenosha produced a hard-working Northwestern team that included D'Wayne Bates, shown here during a 72-yard touchdown reception in the second quarter of the Purdue game. (Scott Strazzante/Daily Southtown)

pass rush and pass efficiency defense. We have to rush the passer better and we have to stop the run.

"There's no question this is the best defensive team, and depth, we've had. There are four critical areas we're concentrating on: be better in sudden-change situations, which is after a turnover, be better on third-and-short yardage, be better on the goal line, and in two-minute situations."

Offensively, the Cats had gone back and forth between quarterbacks in 1994, with Tim Hughes starting the first eight games, but Steve Schnur seeing significant action in most of those, and starting the last three. It wasn't so much that Schnur won the job as it was Hughes lost it and Schnur was the next guy in line. Statistically, there was little to choose between them, Schnur completing 52 percent of his passes, Hughes 46 percent, but with fewer interceptions. Really, there was little reason to think both couldn't be beaten out.

By Lloyd Abramson, perhaps. Abramson had run the scout team in 1994 after injuring a shoulder at Camp Kenosha. It turned into a redshirt year for the freshman.

He was highly touted. Big at 6-foot-3 and 218 pounds, Abramson was 7-of-9 for 71 yards in the spring game. He'd been All-State in Michigan as a prep, and on All-America lists to boot. Penn State, Illinois and Miami (Florida) had been after him, but he chose Northwestern.

And if he didn't surpass Hughes and Schnur, junior Chris Hamdorf was waiting in the wings.

"We know that one of them will take it to the next level during preseason camp," said Barnett, calling the selection of a QB his "top priority."

"Lloyd Abramson is a very, very talented young man; I don't know if he's ready to play yet," said Barnett. "Chris Hamdorf has developed in the last year tremendously. He's just inexperienced. Steve Schnur is our leader in a lot of ways. He knows our offense, and kids really look up to him. Tim Hughes came in and showed the ability to make a lot of big plays, however, he did not know our offense very well, and made some critical mistakes. He made big errors that cost us the chance to win a couple ball games."

Given that assessment, it was no surprise Barnett was undecided. He knew, however, that whoever took snaps, a major part of their job would be handing off to Darnell Autry. With Lundy's departure, Autry, who had considered going home to Arizona because he was homesick, was the No. 1 back. There was no doubt of that.

Nor was there a doubt that D'Wayne Bates, shifted from the glut at quarterback to receiver, was perfect for the position. He'd caught eight passes for 145 yards in the spring game. Bates gave NU's mystery quarterback the deep threat that would otherwise have been missing with the departure of Mike Senters, Chris Gamble and Luther Morris, who had combined for 63 of NU's 125 receptions in 1994, including all but two of the nine touchdown catches.

Even coming off a 3-7-1 record, there seemed to be answers to most of the pressing questions as spring practice ended.

The larger participation in summer workouts—some 50 players compared to the usual 25—was pointed to time and again by players as the season wore on as the reason the Wildcats were succeeding. Barnett saw the full houses in the weight room and on Mt. Trashmore as a sort of parity with the rest of the Big Ten.

"The average Big Ten school has 55 players in summer school," said Barnett. "We had 21 we allowed to go to summer school, mostly because we don't have any more money allocated to summer school. They were trying to get a class ahead or caught up or whatever. The other 30 guys stayed in town and worked on their own. Now that's the commitment. We had not had that many in the past.

"It was the attitude they took into it. Part of that came out of spring ball, part of it just came from this group of kids."

What nobody knew was that the Wildcats would be a much different group when they regrouped in August. The world changed for NU's players on the night of July 16, when word came from Nashville, Tennessee that Marcel Price, a defensive back who would have been a sophomore, had been shot and killed in his home town. It was an accident, the reports said.

Ohmar Braden, 19, was charged with criminal homicide, and pleaded innocent. He was allegedly playing with a .357 handgun at a party when it went off, hitting Price in the chest. Price was taken to a nearby hospital, but died about two hours after the shooting.

It wasn't a drug deal or a gang war or any of society's great ills that killed Marcel Price, but a moment of foolishness that snuffed out one life and changed many others.

Price was 19 years old. He had been a member of the scout team in his freshman year, and was expected to back up Eric Collier at strong safety. An all-everything player at Whites Creek High School, he'd been a four-year member of the honor roll.

"Marcel had a plan," said Barnett at Price's funeral. "He knew what he was going to do, where he was going to go, and how he was going to do it."

Now, the Wildcats had to cope with Price's death.

"It really disrupted our younger kids and our players over summer workouts," said Barnett when camp began. "It brought things to a quick halt."

The team decided to honor Price by placing a patch on the left shoulder of every jersey. "Big Six," it read. That was Price's uniform number.

While Price's death was numbing, the departure of quarterback Lloyd Abramson was simply a surprise. He bolted from Evanston the day before the team left for Kenosha, as did center Adam Reed.

"I knew Adam Reed was thinking about it," said Barnett. "Lloyd, I wasn't sure about. He left practice and left school because of burnout."

Abramson's departure made the race for quarterback a three-horse affair, but Barnett still wasn't sure which one he'd saddle up.

What he knew was that the team had high hopes for the season. Literally, that is. Steve Musseau, Barnett's ancient motivator, talked to the team in Kenosha and introduced an old song to the players: "High Hopes," sung by Frank Sinatra and a chorus of kids with backing by Nelson Riddle's orchestra for the 1959 movie, "A Hole In The Head."

"So here were 100 kids singing along to Sinatra," Barnett remembered with a smile.

Sinatra sang of a little old ant trying to move a rubber tree plant. In football terms, Northwestern was used to playing the part of the ant. The Wildcats had been getting stepped on for decades.

At the Big Ten's annual football kickoff extravaganza in early August, where coaches are always optimistic, Barnett had labeled his team thusly: "A better defense and an inexperienced but talented offense. We're getting the program to the point that the guys that we recruited are old enough to play and old enough to compete in this conference the way we think we should be able to compete.

"I feel like we're at a point where we're ready to make a move in this league. We're probably a year away from maturity, being able to compete in the first division of this league, but we may be closer than that. We think it depends on how some young guys come through this fall."

These, then, were the key returnees as the Wildcats assembled in sweltering heat and humidity for Camp Kenosha IV:

On offense, it would start with Schnur or Hughes. Autry, with two 100-yard games and 556 yards as a true freshman, would be the tailback. He'd get blocking from sophomore Matt Hartl or senior Mike McGrew at fullback. For McGrew, it would be his second position in three years, and third of his career. He'd been a quarterback at Mount Carmel High School, leading the Caravan to back-to-back Class 5A titles, but moved to inside linebacker at NU, and became a force on special teams.

Up front, fifth-year senior Rob Johnson, one of the three captains, anchored a veteran line at center. He, as much as anyone on the team, had seen the Wildcats grow, even as the wins were far and few between.

Recruited by Francis Peay in 1991, Johnson had been an All-Catholic League first-teamer at offensive guard and a second-team linebacker playing for St. Francis de Sales. He was the best catch of what turned out to be Peay's last recruiting class, but never played for Peay.

The fall of 1991, Johnson red-shirted, ending up on the defensive line, actually trying to gain weight more than anything else. When NU went 3-8, Peay was fired, and Barnett hired.

By spring practice, Johnson was over on the offensive line, at, of course, guard. But he was a backup guard, so when No. 1 center Bill Koziel, like Johnson a sophomore, went down with a bum ankle, Barnett, short in the line, asked for volunteers.

Johnson, who had never once snapped the ball in high school, volunteered, telling Barnett he had experience. And won the job.

"I lied," said Johnson. "I saw the opportunity. I was gung-ho."

To start, that is. He grew into the job, literally, by going home each night for plenty of home cooking—so quickly, Johnson started every game in 1992. And 1993. And 1994. Johnson told Barnett the truth about his experience at center after his first season on the job.

He was impressive enough as a rookie to be named the offensive newcomer of the year by the NU Gridiron Network, the team's booster club.

What he did in 1993 was even more amazing. Johnson tore his medial collateral ligament, the tendon connecting the middle of the knee to the lower leg, against Boston College.

He was out — for one play.

Throughout the '95 season, Steve Schnur (12) and Darnell Autry (24) were key players in Northwestern's success. (Larry Ruehl/Daily Southtown)

One play!

"And a few days of practice," he recalled. "We had four offensive linemen get hurt that week."

Johnson, perhaps the ultimate risk-taker on the team of risk-takers, didn't miss any action the rest of the season, a bad one that concluded with eight straight losses in conference, starting with the 51-3 drubbing by Ohio State.

"That was a miserable year," Johnson remembered. "I probably kept playing because of the amount of belief in what coach Barnett was doing here. I didn't want to let him down."

With the first play of 1995, Johnson's consecutive-start streak would reach 34.

Senior Brian Kardos and junior Paul Janus would start at tackle, while seniors Chad Pugh and Ryan Padgett would flank Johnson as guards.

Bates, the surprise of spring ball, took one starting wide receiver spot, senior Dave Beazley the other. With Darren Drexler winning the starting job over Shane Graham at tight end, the offense was complete.

Well, almost complete. Fifth-year senior Sam Valenzisi couldn't be forgotten. A graduate student in journalism who, rather than do honest work after college, wanted to be a sportswriter instead, Valenzisi was born to communicate. Perfect on extra-points and 13-of-19 on field-goals in 1994 (with just one miss inside 40 yards), the human chatterbox was named one of the team's three captains.

"Rob (Johnson) put it best when he said they finally found a way to shut me up," said Valenzisi. "I was speechless."

The defense, now using the 4-3, would feature juniors Matt Rice and Ray Robey at tackle, fifth-year senior Mike Warren and junior Casey Dailey at end, and more kids at linebacker.

Fitzgerald, who started one game as a sophomore when Hugh Williams was injured, took over in the middle, with senior Sutter on one side and junior Scharf, the least experienced of the trio, on the other.

There was plenty of experience in the secondary, starting with cornerback Rodney Ray, a free-spirited fifth-year senior. Senior Chris Martin, who would have to stretch to reach his program height of 5-foot-9, would patrol the other corner, with senior tri-captain William Bennett and junior Eric Collier in the safety slots. Paul Burton, best in the conference the season before, would punt.

Like most coaches, Barnett was asked for his outlook on the league at the Big Ten's summer get-together.

"I think Northwestern will win it," he said. He was kidding. Sort of.

"I see this year a lot like it was the first year I was here, in 1992," Barnett went on. "Everybody was in it, and yet, everybody was out of it. It was really bunched up. I see the top five teams in this league — Ohio State, Penn State, Wisconsin, Illinois, Michigan—I don't see a lot of difference in those teams.

"I think the rest of us have crowded ourselves into a position where, if anybody slips up, we're going to slip into that upper division. I see tremendous improvement in Minnesota, Purdue and ourselves."

Why Northwestern? Because Barnett believed his defense would be the best in his four years in Evanston.

How strongly did he believe it? This strongly. As he said to a disbelieving reporter shortly before the season began, "I ain't gonna be a loser. We're going to win because the defense is going to play the way I think we can play."

It wouldn't take long to find out. The opener was against Notre Dame on the picturesque campus of the Fighting Irish, and it was just days away.

AP PRESEASON TOP 25

Rank	Team	94 Record	Points	Previous
1.	Florida State (31)	10-1-1	1,498	4
2.	Nebraska (15)	13-0-0	1,439	1
3.	Texas A&M (6)	10-0-1	1,366	8
4.	Penn State (1)	12-0-0	1,308	2
5.	Florida (6)	10-2-1	1,299	7
6.	Auburn (2)	9-1-1	1,238	9
7.	Southern California	8-3-1	1,151	13
8.	Tennessee (1)	8-4-0	1,024	22
9.	Notre Dame	6-5-1	1,011	–
10.	Alabama	12-1-0	974	5
11.	Miami (Fla.)	10-2-0	893	6
12.	Ohio State	9-4-0	863	14
13.	Colorado	11-1-0	689	3
14.	Michigan	8-4-0	642	12
15.	Oklahoma	6-6-0	527	–
16.	UCLA	5-6-0	517	–
17.	Virginia	9-3-0	516	15
18.	Texas	8-4-0	368	25
19.	Arizona	8-4-0	337	20
20.	North Carolina	8-4-0	290	–
21.	Wisconsin	7-4-1	270	–
22.	Boston College	7-4-1	263	23
23.	West Virginia	7-6-0	215	–
24.	Virginia Tech	8-4-0	196	–
tie	Washington	7-4-0	196	–

First place votes in parentheses. Previous ranking is final 1994 rank.

NORTHWESTERN'S 1995 SCHEDULE

Sept. 2	at Notre Dame
Sept. 16	MIAMI (OHIO)
Sept. 23	AIR FORCE
Sept. 30	INDIANA
Oct. 7	at Michigan
Oct. 14	at Minnesota
Oct. 21	WISCONSIN
Oct. 28	at Illinois
Nov. 4	PENN STATE
Nov. 11	IOWA
Nov. 18	at Purdue

Guard Ryan Padgett ignores the toehold Notre Dame's Corey Bennett has on his face mask to clear the way for the Wildcat attack. (Athlon Sports Communications)

Chapter 5
THE UPSET OF THE CENTURY

"This is a marathon and not a sprint."
—Gary Barnett after Northwestern's 17-15 win over Notre Dame

ON AUGUST 23, a warm summer night on Chicago's South Side, Notre Dame head coach Lou Holtz arrived at Reilly's Daughter, a popular Oak Lawn pub just across the street from Chicago proper.

Located in the Ranch Manor Shopping Center, and famed for both its support of local sports and its atmosphere—it isn't hard to find a picture of either Mayor Daley on the wall near posters promoting a fan bus to the Marist-Brother Rice high school game, and, up near the ceiling, a autographed photo of President Reagan —Reilly's is a place where Wildcats fans, if they venture there at all, go in disguise.

Holtz was at Reilly's for more than a beer. He was on hand for the taping of his television show's preseason edition, right there in the bar. Proprietor Boz O'Brien had lured Holtz to South Side Irish country for the Fiesta Bowl preview show the previous year, and Holtz loved it so much, he wanted to come back.

So here was Holtz, wearing a bright green jacket, with 300 of his closest friends, wearing Holtz masks, shouting "Go Irish!" and waving beer bottles for the SportsChannel cameras, taping his show, answering questions from the audience and moderator Steve Kashul. All was going well until the time came to discuss the opener against the Wildcats.

And Holtz couldn't remember Gary Barnett's name.

"Gary Burtnett," said Holtz, stumbling. "Who?" went some observers.

"Can we go back?" Holtz then said. "I meant Gary Barnett. I mixed him up with the coach at Purdue."

Actually, Holtz mixed him up with the former coach of the Boilermakers, Leon Burtnett. Holtz got Barnett's name right and professed worry about the Wildcats when the taping resumed.

Just a slip, meant without malice, and hardly out of the ordinary coming from a brilliant coach who can X-and-O with the best of 'em but has, on occasion, referred to one of Notre Dame's opponents as "the University of Navy."

Small wonder, then, that Holtz didn't go all the way and call NU "the University of Northwestern."

However confused Holtz was as to Barnett's name in the summer, there was no reason for anyone not connected with the Wildcat program to think Notre Dame would lose to Northwestern at Notre Dame Stadium on the second day of September, the first full Saturday of college football's 126th season.

There was no reason to think the Wildcats, 28-point underdogs to some bookies, would even come close. Sure, NU had come close in

1992 and 1993 against Notre Dame, and sure, the Cats had something —that intangible called pride—to play for, but it wasn't as if the Fighting Irish were coming into the game as also-rans.

They also had something to play for. For one thing, the Irish had been hammered in their last outing, losing 41-24 to Colorado in a Fiesta Bowl many said Notre Dame shouldn't have been invited to in the first place. They were brought in, despite a 6-4-1 record, for the television ratings, critics said.

(If that was the case, they delivered as poorly in the living room as they did on the field. The Fiesta drew only a 6.0 rating, the fourth-best of the games played on New Year's Day, and trailed the Rose, which featured powerhouse Penn State against surprise Oregon, in the late-afternoon time-slot.)

To get the Irish off on the right track, Holtz arranged to have the team train away from Notre Dame's storybook campus, which is always crawling with fans, even in the dead of summer.

Just as NU worked out at Wisconsin-Parkside, ND would toil at the Culver Academies in Culver, Indiana, about 45 miles south of South Bend. To Holtz, going to "Camp Culver" was the perfect way to focus his players.

"It's about 15 miles from Plymouth, Indiana, by telephone," he quipped.

Quarterback Ron Powlus' continuing development was considered critical to Irish hopes. He'd looked sensational against NU in his first action as a collegian, throwing for a school-record tying four touchdowns. Brent Musburger, calling that game at Soldier Field on ABC, was ready to crown Powlus king. The rest of the season wasn't as easy for the kid, but here was that Wildcats defense again, the one that ranked last in most key Big Ten stats in '94. Powlus would tee off, right?

Wrong. This game wouldn't end 42-15 in Notre Dame's favor. This game wouldn't be over at the half.

This game would be Northwestern's. The Wildcats beat Notre Dame at Notre Dame, beat the Irish 17-15, beat them in the line of scrim-

William Bennett, NU's "Secretary of Defense," wraps up an Irish ball carrier. (Athlon Sports Communications)

mage and at the skill positions. It was a most convincing two-point victory over the ninth-ranked team in the country. Ask anyone who was there in the sun-kissed crowd of 59,075. Ask the millions watching coast-to-coast on NBC.

Ask Holtz.

"I'm very disappointed," he said.

He should have been. This was supposed to be a lay-up for the Irish and a milestone victory for him. Instead, it was Notre Dame's fifth loss in eight games, to go with two wins (over Navy and Air Force) and a tie with Southern California. And Holtz was at 199 career wins—and, for the moment, holding.

Ask Powlus.

"This is awful," he said. "We looked sick."

Irish fans were shocked at losing to Northwestern, but Wildcat fans, used to losing and losing big, were absolutely stunned by the outcome.

Beat Notre Dame? And do it at Notre Dame, under the shadow of the Golden Dome? Without a fluky play? Sure, Barnett said he'd have a good team, but, Notre Dame? Wow!

For Northwestern, it was an achievement of almost incomparable magnitude, certainly the biggest win for the Wildcats since a famed 1971 victory at Ohio State, on a par with back-to-back wins over Bud Wilkinson's Oklahoma juggernauts in 1959 and '60, perhaps the biggest since the top triumph in Northwestern history: the Cats' 20-14 come-from-behind win over California in the 1949 Rose Bowl.

No question, it was big, the lead story on Chicago newscasts that night, taking precedence over the ills of the world.

The next day, the *Sun-Times* headlined the outcome "The Upset of the Century," and, save little Notre Dame's win over Army in 1913 or even smaller Carlisle's win over the Cadets the season before, even the oldest old-timers couldn't come up with evidence to dispute the notion.

It was not, though, celebrated in like fashion. That was Barnett's doing.

In the early morning, when the Wildcat players and staff gathered for breakfast in the Michigan City Holiday Inn, Barnett told his charges that when the game was over and Northwest-

Steve Schnur eludes an Irish defender on the way to a short gain. (Athlon Sports Communications.

ern had won, that he didn't want to be carried off the field.

"I wanted them to act like we knew how to win," he said.

So, when the final seconds ticked off, when the gun sounded, his players may have been floating as they hugged each other, their helmets held sky-high, but Barnett's feet were firmly planted on the ground.

"We're 1-0," he said of his 17th career victory. "But we've got a long way to go. This is a marathon and not a sprint."

It was obvious from the first play from scrimmage that strange things were going to happen. Two footballs ended up on the field. The first one, the real one, was being carried by Darnell Autry, and not far. He ranged to the right side, near the Notre Dame sideline, and was dropped for a two-yard loss.

As he went down, another football appeared nearby. Irish linebacker Renaldo Wynn pounced on it, and thought he'd come up with a loose

Brian Musso hauls in one of his two receptions from Steve Schnur. (Athlon Sports Communications)

ball. He had, but not the one Autry was carrying. It was a football that freshman Irish punter Hunter Smith had mis-punted on the sidelines. The ball caromed off the net used to catch warm-up kicks, went over the heads of everyone on the sideline, and landed behind Autry, who still had the game ball in his hands. It was a fitting start to a contest that would have people across the country shaking their heads at the finish.

Northwestern led all the way, right from the moment quarterback Steve Schnur's 6-yard touchdown pass was grabbed by senior wide receiver Dave Beazley, who beat Allen Rossum to the ball in the left corner of the end zone 6 minutes 15 seconds into the game before crashing into a set of drums.

This was the first indication of the Wildcats' season-long inclination to take advantage of opposing teams' mistakes. The scoring drive was set up by Irish tailback Randy Kinder, who simply dropped the football at midfield. NU linebacker Danny Sutter pounced on it, and seven plays later, the Wildcats were on the board.

This was also the first notice given that Autry and the NU offensive line would be a season-long force. Autry gained 42 of the 50 yards on the drive, including runs of 16 and 14 yards. It was instantly apparent that the 1994 games against Minnesota and Penn State were not aberrations. Autry could run. On this day, he'd run for 160 yards on 33 carries.

One of the stalwarts on the offensive line, senior Ryan Padgett, once thought he'd be playing for the Irish, not against them. A star lineman for Newport High School in Bellevue, Washington, just outside Seattle, Padgett was recruited by some 70 schools, including Notre Dame.

Padgett, the fifth-ranked offensive guard in the country his senior year in high school, wanted to go to Notre Dame. Wanted to go so much, he traveled there on his own money — in NCAA parlance, an "unofficial" visit. While on campus, linebacker coach Jay Hayes and he talked. Padgett believed he was offered a scholarship, and said he was told as much again when he called ND near Thanksgiving in 1991.

"They said, 'When you come back on your visit, coach Holtz will offer you a scholarship,'" Padgett recalled. He canceled "official," school-paid-for visits to Stanford and Washington, and made his official trip to Notre Dame in mid-January 1992. Then came bad news.

"We were sitting in coach Holtz' den, and he said they didn't have a scholarship for me. He explained that they had more people accept than usual, percentage-wise, and basically, tough luck."

Padgett was in a bind. The signing season was well underway.

"I flew back (to Seattle) completely distraught, because I was really worried about what people would think. Would they think this kid's a liar? Was he just hoping? It really bothered me, because I consider myself a man of my word."

So Padgett pulled out his box of 70 letters and got on the phone.

"The only teams that had (scholarships) left were Northwestern, Cal and Washington. I had a visit mid-week at Cal-Berkeley, then came here, and flew back to Seattle.

"When I landed in Seattle, my mom said, 'Washington's coming over with the (signing) papers.' I told her I'd made my decision, and to tell them not to come.

"I was really bitter (at Notre Dame) for a while. I thought I was misled, but looking back, I don't know how intentionally I was misled. You do this once as a 17-year-old, or 16-year-old. You don't know the intricacies, that an oral commitment is really not set in stone like you would hope. These guys have been doing this for 30-40 years. They know what they can and can't do.

"I feel I was taken advantage of a little bit, just from ignorance."

The whole episode served to spur Padgett on once he took a look at Northwestern's schedule. Every year, there was Notre Dame, at the top of the list.

"My biggest motivation was for Lou Holtz to think, 'We screwed up. We shoulda taken this guy.' But, looking back, I think everything worked out for the best. I don't regret one thing about Northwestern. This is the perfect place for me.

"I've exacted my revenge," Padgett said after the season was over.

Revenge wasn't on Padgett's mind during the game, just executing.

An exchange of field goals, Sam Valenzisi's 37-yarder matching the 35-yarder kicked by Notre Dame's Kevin Kopka, kept the Wildcat lead a touchdown strong at 10-3. The 5,000 or so Wildcat fans in the end zone and to the south of the NU bench were gleeful. They arrived hopeful, and now were starting to believe.

They had also made noise in 1992, when NU had led at the half, before a Holtz stemwinder triggered a second half Irish comeback. This time, the comeback appeared to begin earlier. Notre Dame took the ensuing kickoff and, with Powlus looking sharp, marched the ball down the field.

Facing third-and-8 on the NU 27, he found Derrick Mayes, his favorite target, in traffic for a 17-yard gain. Soon after, Robert Farmer plowed in from the 5, and the Irish were within an extra-point kick of tying the game.

There would be no tie. Ryan Leahy's snap was off-target, forcing holder Charlie Stafford to lunge for the ball. That was enough to upset Kopka's rhythm. The conversion try was missed, going wide right. Northwestern would carry a 10-9 lead, and a faint pulse of momentum, into the intermission.

The Wildcats would also get the ball to start the third quarter. If the Irish were going to send a message to Schnur, Autry and the rest of NU's offense, now was the time to send it.

Placekicker Sam Valenzisi hammers a 37-yard field goal, the first of his string of 13 straight. (Athlon Sports Communications.)

44   PURPLE ROSES

Darnell Autry just keeps his balance on the way to some of his 160 yards rushing. (Athlon Sports Communications)

There was no message. Instead, there was a 10-yard punt return by Brian Musso, to the Wildcat 45, and a pair of big plays. First, Autry, on second-and-10, took advantage of a gaping hole created by Brian Kardos and Chad Pugh on the right side, and streaked down the sideline to the Irish 26. Then, Schnur found wideout D'Wayne Bates breaking open at the Irish 5. Bates grabbed the pass and, while being tackled by the all-but-beaten Shawn Wooden, managed to get the ball into the end zone.

As first receptions of college careers go, Bates' was pretty good. It jumped the Wildcats' lead to 17-9.

The Wildcats had moved 55 yards in 54 seconds. A team that had scored touchdowns in the third quarter of only three games in 1994 had already rolled a seven. Nearly 27 minutes remained, and it was now clear to the Irish that Northwestern wasn't just going to go away this time.

The Wildcat offense was getting the job done. So was the defense. The new 4-3 alignment allowed it to attack more.

"We zone-blitzed 'em," Barnett explained. "Before, we'd been blitzing 'em in man coverage, and really got ourselves burned. We'd made some critical mistakes.

"We played zone behind, and still brought five-man pressure. We brought Hudhaifa Ismaeli, and twice he went around their left tackle like the guy didn't even know he was there.

"That was our plan. We felt by keeping the ball in front of us and making them go 80 yards in 14-15 plays, rather than playing man, we liked our percentages.

"Notre Dame has a great system. They've used it for years. Part of a system is that it's predictable. The problem was, we've known where they're going. We just haven't been able to stop 'em. We physically couldn't get there. This time, we had guys there who could make the play. And they did."

Ismaeli sacked Powlus twice after zipping around end. Another leader on defense was Pat Fitzgerald, like Padgett, another Notre Dame reject. Not quite as highly regarded as Padgett nationally, Fitzgerald was nonetheless one of the best players in the Chicago area, helping Sandburg High School in Orland Park to a 9-2 record in 1992 while playing linebacker and tight end.

He looked at Notre Dame. Notre Dame looked at him. Then Notre Dame looked elsewhere, canceling his official visit to the campus the day before it was to take place.

"The reason I came to Northwestern was to beat Notre Dame," Fitzgerald would say later. "Sweet victory."

Fitzgerald would make them pay, leading the Wildcat defense with 11 tackles.

Confronted by something they hadn't seen before, the Irish offense stalled until midway through the fourth quarter. It was then that Powlus, harassed all day and sacked on four occasions (NU had managed 14 sacks in all of 1994), received enough protection to make the big plays he was recruited for. Notre Dame's defense had itself stiffened, Paul Grasmanis' sack of Schnur forcing Paul Burton to punt from the Wildcat end zone. The punt gave the Irish the ball on the NU 45, and Powlus found Marc Edwards for a 14-yard gain. Soon after, Kinder, making up for his early miscue, ran for 15 yards. Finally, he scored from the 2.

The gap had been closed to 17-15. There was 6:16 to play. Holtz decided to go for two points, a logical decision, because one point wouldn't tie the game, and missing a two-point conversion meant at least a field-goal would be needed anyway. Going for two was the thing to do.

What would Powlus do? Hit Mayes, who caught eight of the 13 balls thrown to him in the course of the day, in the corner? Find Kinder coming out of the backfield? Hand off to Kinder or Edwards? Try some kind of option rollout maneuver, the kind of play Holtz loves?

What Powlus would do was get his right foot stepped on by center Dusty Ziegler and hit the turf before he could do anything at all.

It was not yet time for the Wildcats to *not* carry Barnett off the field. Notre Dame would get the ball one more time. The Irish moved the ball, but only to their 44. On fourth-and-2 with 4:02 remaining, Holtz, with two timeouts left, refused to burn one. He sent Kinder up the middle, smack into the middle of a covey of white-clad Wildcat defenders led by Matt Rice, playing on and ignoring a bad ankle. Kinder, who believed there was an opening, went nowhere, and the ball went over to Northwestern.

Touchdown Jesus blinked.

"Matt Rice played an outstanding game, and really, his stop on the last fourth-down play was an amazing football play," Barnett said upon reflection. "He played the whole game that way. He had as fine a performance by a defensive lineman as I've seen."

"Hindsight is always 20-20," said Holtz. "Maybe we should have punted. Maybe everybody on the sideline talks too much, saying, 'We can do it.' We had two timeouts left. We could have held them and gotten the ball back. We probably should have punted."

Now, in some ways, came the tough job. Running out the clock while not letting the imagination run wild is a vital part of winning, and the Wildcats had very little experience at it. Schnur did the logical thing, handing off to Autry more often than not. Autry did the dirty work, including scampering 26 yards to the Irish 41 smack in front of one of the two large sections of NU fans. After he went out of bounds, he celebrated.

Into the clear blue sky flew a yellow flag, an official enforcing the new "good behavior" rules in the college game. The unsportsmanlike conduct call pushed NU back, but it really didn't matter. The clock ran out, and Northwestern, ranked at or near the bottom of the conference by every preseason prognosticator from Playboy to Street & Smith's, had beaten the most famous team in college football on its hallowed home turf.

Of which Sam Valenzisi, the kicker who began his career as a walk-on, took home a chunk.

"We started believing we could win this game as soon as last year's game was over," said Schnur, the QB with the near crew-cut whose stats (14-of-28, 166 yards, two touchdown) were more than the equal of Powlus' numbers (17-of-26, 175 yards). "In that game, we had a lot of mental breakdowns that ended up costing us the victory. For me, personally, this is something I've dreamed about all my life."

Dreams turned to belief during the game, if not before. The kids from Camp Kenosha had bought into what they were taught more than the kids from Camp Culver.

Darnell Autry turns the corner and goes upfield against the Irish. (Athlon Sports Communications)

Cornerback Hudhaifa Ismaeli takes off on a 29-yard kickoff return. (Athlon Sports Communications)

"We knew we were going to win from the first quarter," said tight end Shane Graham. "We just had a feeling. The change from this year to last year is unbelievable. I was so impressed with the defense that I kissed almost everyone."

Padgett, too, called it "unbelievable." Then the guard, who had believed the Wildcats would beat NU in 1994, only to see Powlus and Co. go crazy, said something that would be said again and again during the season:

"We established we could play with the big guys."

"History's history," said Fitzgerald, the spurned linebacker. "You read it in books. This was business."

Big business, the kind of business most people didn't think NU had a chance to conduct. It was, for the first time to start a season since 1975, a win. Incredibly, twenty years had passed since the Wildcats got out of the box with a 'W.' John Pont's 1975 club beat Purdue in its opener. Since then, only the 0-0 tie with Illinois to open the 1978 campaign had brought relief to a string of season-opening defeats.

It had also been 15 meetings, dating to 1962, when Ara Parseghian was the head coach in Evanston, since the Wildcats had beaten the Irish.

"For a defense that has been much-maligned over the last three years, and given up a lot of yards, to go in there and hold that team with big-play potential to 15 points and the yardage we did, it's Ron Vanderlinden and our defensive coaches, and our players, making plays," Barnett said later. "It was the finest defensive effort since we've been here."

Notre Dame gained only 331 yards, 165 on the ground, but the most amazing number was ND's punt return yardage: minus-3. That's unheard of.

Actually, the most amazing number was on the scoreboard: 17-15.

"The only way we're going to get respect is through victories," Fitzgerald said outside the Wildcat locker room. "Wins talk. That's all that matters. You don't gain respect from one victory. It's a season-long thing."

The four-year series between the Irish and Wildcats, agreed upon when Doug Single was NU's athletic director, had run its course. Did Barnett want to keep it going?

"I'd just as soon it'd be over," he said. "Maybe we'll catch them in a bowl game."

Northwestern? In a bowl game? What a dreamer.

NORTHWESTERN VS. NOTRE DAME

Saturday, September 2, 1995 at Notre Dame Stadium, Notre Dame, IN
Weather: 77° Wind SW 5 Sunny
Attendance: 59,075

SCORE BY QUARTERS	1	2	3	4	SCORE
Northwestern (1-0-0)	7	3	7	0	17
Notre Dame (0-1-0)	0	9	0	6	15

First Quarter
		NU	ND
NU 8:45 Dave Beazley 6-yard pass from Steve Schnur, (Sam Valenzisi kick) (7 plays, 51 yards, 3:02 TOP)		7	0

Second Quarter
ND 11:12 Kevin Kopka 35-yard field goal (13 plays, 63 yards, 6:30 TOP)	7	3
NU 7:05 Sam Valenzisi 37-yard field goal (11 plays, 44 yards, 4:07 TOP)	10	3
ND 2:35 Robert Farmer 5-yard run (Kevin Kopka failed kick) (10 plays, 74 yards, 4:30 TOP)	10	9

Third Quarter
| NU 12:02 D'Wayne Bates 26-yard pass from Steve Schnur (Sam Valenzisi kick) (3 plays, 55 yards, 0:54 TOP) | 17 | 9 |

Fourth Quarter
| ND 6:16 Randy Kinder 2-yard run (2-pt conversion rush failed) (6 plays, 45 yards, 2:03 TOP) | 17 | 15 |

TEAM STATISTICS	NU	ND
First Downs	14	20
Rushing	6	10
Passing	8	9
Penalty	0	1
Rushing Attempts	39	47
Yards Gained Rushing	181	224
Yards Lost Rushing	16	28
Net Yards Rushing	165	196
Net Yards Passing	166	175
Passes Attempted	28	26
Passes Completed	14	17
Had Intercepted	0	0
Total Offensive Plays	67	73
Total Net Yards	331	371
Average Gain per Play	4.9	5.1
Fumbles: Number-Lost	1-1	3-2
Penalties: Number-Yards	8-64	1-6
Number of Punts-Yards	9-330	7-312
Average Per Punt	36.6	44.6
Punt Returns: Number-Yards	6-67	2-3
Kickoff Returns: Number-Yards	3-68	2-53
Interceptions: Number-Yards	0-0	0-0
Fumble Returns: Number-Yards	1-0	1-0
Possession Time	28:17	31:43
Third-Down Conversions	6 of 18	3 of 13
Fourth-Down Conversions	0 of 0	0 of 2
Sacks By: Number-Yards	4-26	2-11

Big Ten Standings
1. Michigan (1-0-0)
2. Northwestern (0-0-0)
3. Ohio State (0-0-0)
4. Purdue (0-0-0)
5. Michigan State (0-0-0)
6. Indiana (0-0-0)
7. Minnesota (0-0-0)
8. Iowa (0-0-0)
9. Penn State (0-0-0)
10. Wisconsin (0-0-0)
11. Illinois (0-1-0)

AP Top 25
1. Florida St.
2. Nebraska
3. Texas A&M
4. Penn State
5. Florida
6. Auburn
7. Southern Cal
8. Tennessee
9. Ohio St.
10. Colorado
11. Michigan
12. UCLA
13. Alabama
14. Oklahoma
15. Texas
16. Virginia
17. Arizona
18. Washington
19. Miami
20. Virginia Tech.
21. Kansas St.
22. Syracuse
23. N. Carolina St.
24. Oregon
25. Notre Dame

Scores of interest
Michigan 38, Illinois 14
Purdue 26, West Virginia 24
Colorado 43, Wisconsin 7
Florida State 70, Duke 26
Nebraska 64, Oklahoma St. 21
Texas A&M 33, LSU 17
Florida 45, Houston 21
Auburn 46, Mississippi 13
Tennessee 27, E. Carolina 7
UCLA 31, Miami 8
Virginia 40, William & Mary 16
Arizona 41, Pacific 9
Syracuse 20, N. Carolina 9
Washington 23, Arizona St. 20

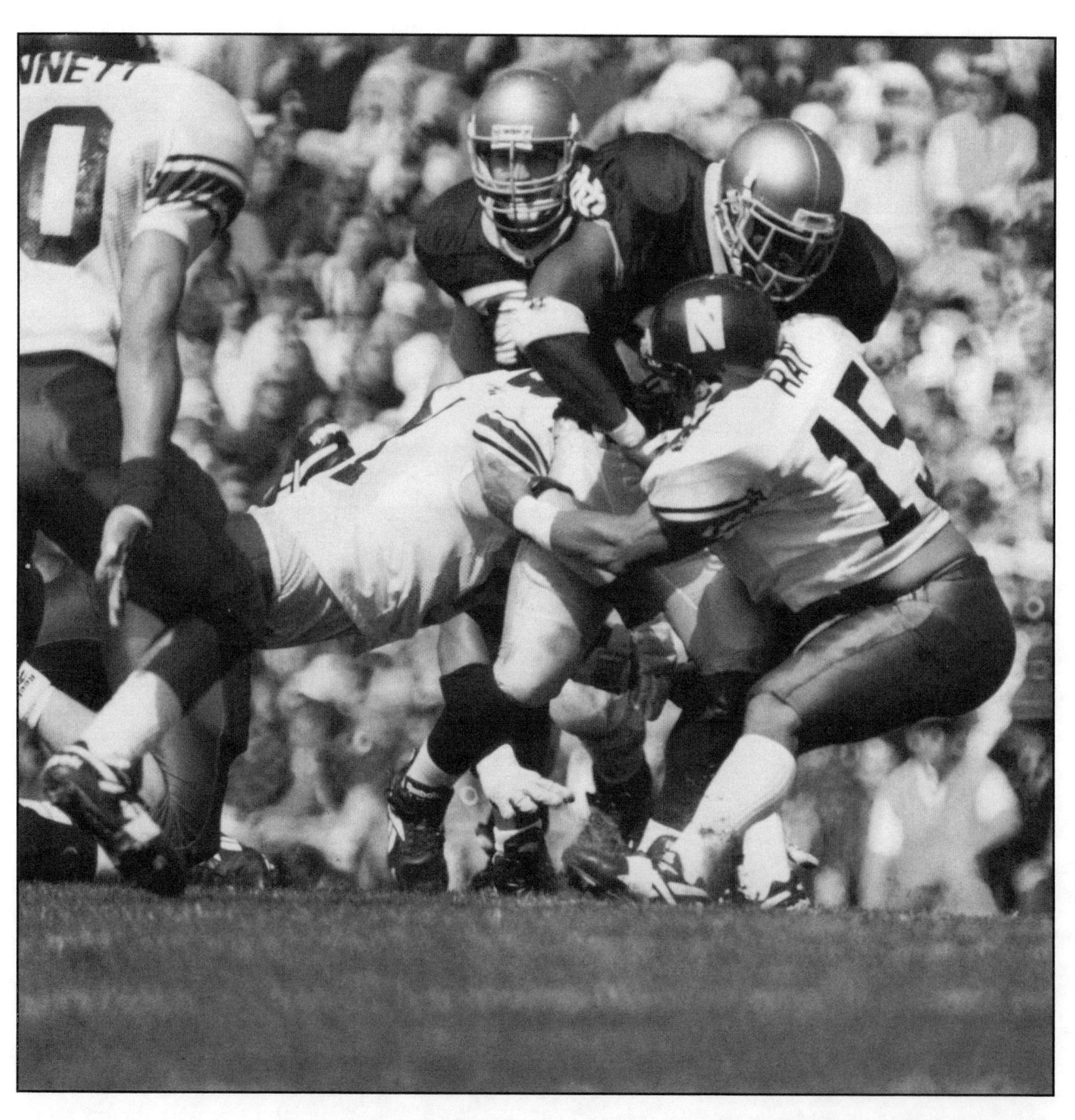

The Northwestern Bandwagon picked up hundreds of new members after the September 2 defeat of Notre Dame. (Hans Scott)

Chapter 6
RECOGNITION WITHOUT RESPECT

"It's an upset in everybody else's eyes."
—Steve Schnur on beating Notre Dame

THE FINAL SCORE from that private school on the Hollywood-set campus in St. Joseph County—Northwestern 17, Notre Dame 15—drew gasps and roars from fans at stadia across the country.

In Champaign, Illinois, where many of the midwest's leading sportswriters gathered at Memorial Stadium for the season-opening Big Ten showdown between Michigan and Illinois, the game on the field became secondary to the game on the television screen in the back of the press box.

At the start, when NU had taken a 7-0 lead, Andrew Bagnato of the *Chicago Tribune,* a Northwestern grad, eyed the board where the score was posted, then eyed a buddy from another Chicago broadsheet.

"Naaah. It's early," they said in unison. "They did that two years ago. Right? Right."

A couple of hours later, with Michigan pounding the Fighting Illini, Bagnato and the other guy were in the crowd watching the lone TV screen in the press box tuned to NBC. Someone else in that crowd was Big Ten commissioner Jim Delany. With Michigan-Illinois, he had to be neutral. Here, though, was a game he could watch with rooting interest, albeit silently.

"Hey," said *Peoria Journal Star* columnist Phil Theobald. "Isn't the commissioner of the Big Ten supposed to watch the game he's at?"

Delany craned his neck back toward Zuppke Field for a second, said, "I'm watching it," then turned back to the Wildcats and the Irish, and stayed, eyes glued to the screen, until the score was final.

If the outcome spread like a shock wave across college football, the wave was rather weak in Evanston. Since classes at NU wouldn't start until September 18, there were few students on hand to do much celebrating.

As a result, there was no wild scene on Sheridan Road. Only a smattering of the faithful chomped on hot dogs at Mustard's Last Stand, the place on Central Street a half-block from Dyche Stadium where the Wildcat elite meet to eat before home games.

But enough folks to pass for a crowd were waiting for the Wildcats when their busses rolled in from what the players termed a mostly quiet ride around the edge of Lake Michigan on Saturday night.

One of the faithful was Northwestern band director John Paynter. When Gary Barnett stepped off the bus, Paynter told him, "This may be the greatest day of my life."

Barnett was amazed.

"John's not a spring chicken," said Barnett the following Monday, which happened to be Labor Day. "Greatest day of my life? I mean, that's pretty significant. I think a lot of John

With 8:27 to go, the Wildcats led Notre Dame 17-9, leaving Northwestern fans to wonder if the Cats could hold on to win. (Hans Scott)

Paynter, and he's got a nice family, and I know there's the birth of children and marriages, and things like that should be pretty significant.

"To think this is more significant than that, I don't know. And John's just one indication of people who've called or given us faxes or left messages. And Todd Martin said 'Cat blood' is flowing through him, and he kicked butt in two matches in the U.S. Open.

"That's pretty strong. I don't know if it was the greatest day of *my* life, but it was a good day."

It also meant the Northwestern bandwagon, long in storage, was now out and ready to be boarded. It had been long held around Chicago sports departments that if Northwestern's football team ever did anything significant, anything at all—say, win three in a row or beat just one someone like Notre Dame—that the coverage accorded them would be at least equal to what Notre Dame received week-in and week-out.

That was true on Labor Day. The previous Monday, the first media briefing of the season drew seven reporters and one television camera crew. The post-Notre Dame briefing, which wasn't even going to be held if the Irish had won, had 11 writers on hand and six TV crews.

Nothing like a little upset to get attention, right?

"It's an upset in everybody else's eyes," said quarterback Steve Schnur. "We played the game we thought we were gonna play."

That the rest of the country expected something else was why Schnur was up before dawn to appear on Good Morning America. It was why lunch was being served in Nicolet Center on Labor Day. It was why Barnett was trying to measure, if not temper, the magnitude of what had occurred 48 hours earlier.

"I don't mean to at all not have the same sense of what this game means to Northwestern that many of the people who've been around here a long time have," Barnett said. "I think it's just a case of our coaches and our players have chosen to look at where we are and where we're going, rather than dwell so much on where we've been and what hasn't been done here.

"We've sort of been a little ignorant of the things that have gone on in the past and why this victory is so important to so many people around here. I don't want to demean that or play it down at all. I just want you to understand that we really, literally, have thought and known this was going to happen and it was just a matter of time.

"We could see this building and coming. You don't ever know when it's going to happen, and when it does, it is something you expect to have happen, rather than something you're totally surprised at. If we could step back and look at it, we'd probably have a much greater understanding of the significance of it.

"Right now, it seems to be what we've all come here to do."

At the same time, he understood why the win was already regarded by outsiders as a one-in-a-hundred occurrence.

"To (the players), it's just what they expected to have happen," he said. "It's those who have heard us talk about these things, and turned their heads and have gone, 'Hah, hah, hah, right,' who are so surprised. I think if you talk to anybody who's jumped in and has been with us in the last 3½ years and is close to the program, they will tell you they are not that surprised this has happened.

"It's just everybody that felt this was probably some crazy group of coaches talking, which is what we probably were. All of a sudden, something does happen, and, 'Hey, they got lucky.'

"I think it's more than that."

Northwestern earned plenty of attention, including a spread in *Sports Illustrated,* which had ranked the Wildcats 79th in their preview issue (Southern California, ironically, was No. 1 to *SI*), but didn't crack the polls. The writers and broadcasters who vote in the Associated Press poll dropped Notre Dame from No. 9 to No. 25, but didn't rank NU. The Wildcats received 99 votes compared to Notre Dame's 157. Those 99 votes were good for the mythic 29th position.

"Polls don't mean anything," said kicker Sam Valenzisi. "It's just numbers."

Nor, to him, did the historic nature of the victory, the first over Notre Dame since 1962, when Ara Parseghian coached the Wildcats, mean much.

"Ara Parseghian was 30 years ago," Valenzisi said. "What we hear about every day is the losing streak in the '80s. We don't hear about that. Nobody talks about that. There are very few people who remember that who we come in contact with. The history we see every day is the losing. I don't know much about that at all. I don't see this as a historic win. This is something we've expected of ourselves.

"Rather than being historic, this is sort of the culmination of the work we've put in over four years."

To Barnett, the most satisfying aspect of the victory was the quality of it. A pair of Irish turnovers were converted into Northwestern touchdowns. Even better, and an indicator of what was to come, the Wildcats dominated the line of scrimmage on both sides of the ball. For over 75 years, Notre Dame's strength has

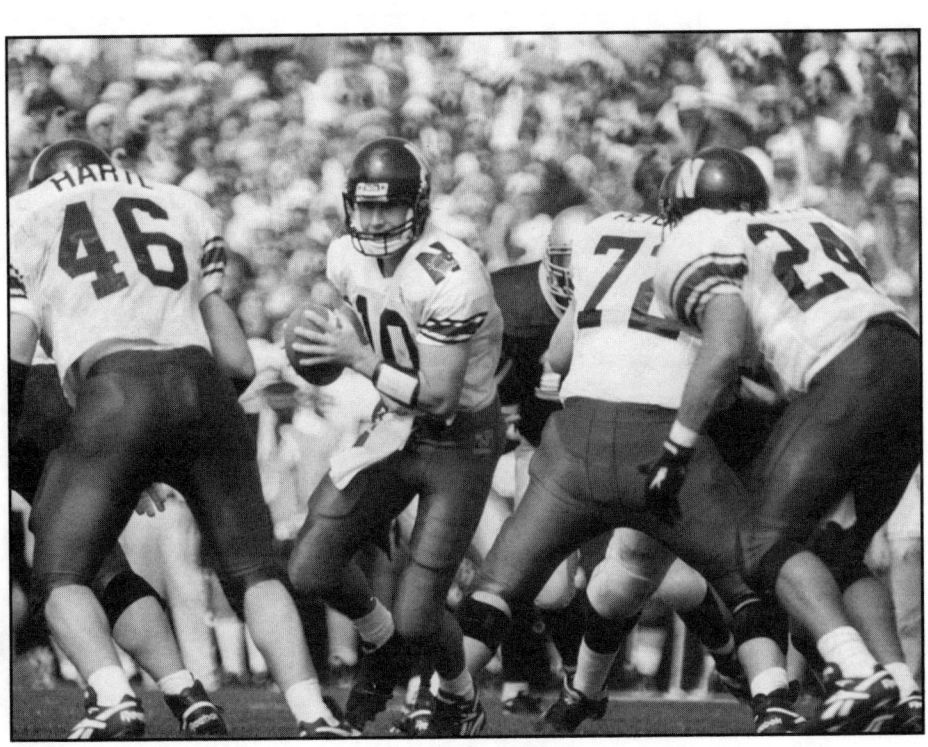

Quarterback Steve Schnur (10) discussed Northwestern's "upset" of Notre Dame the morning after on Good Morning America. *(Hans Scott)*

been in the interior lines, where winning football begins. Now, here was NU, blowing the Irish off the ball.

Likewise, the game didn't turn on a bizarre play. This victory was not only expected, it was earned.

"I don't think anybody can say this was a fluke win," said Barnett. "Our offense, our defense, our special teams won the game. That's the way we wanted it to happen. We deserved it, and we earned it, and we have it."

What would happen next? For the Wildcats, having a week off— their next game, against Miami of Ohio, wasn't until September 16 — was a mixed blessing.

"The week off is good because we can deal with all the attention we're getting," said Valenzisi. "I can't say we'd have an easy week of preparation. We'll be better able to concentrate next week."

Schnur, the early-morning TV star, agreed.

"If we approach the next few weeks with this in the back of our minds rather than out front, we'll be all right," Schnur figured.

"In some ways, I'd like to go out and capitalize on this emotion," Barnett said. "Maybe it would sell a few more tickets right away. I hope they don't forget about us in two weeks."

There was no line for tickets outside Dyche Stadium for the Miami game. Since it was a holiday, the ticket office was closed.

"On the other side, there's been so much publicity and so many distractions that it's probably good for us to have a couple days for the distractions to take place," Barnett went on. "This will allow them to get their feet back on the ground and let us get down to business."

Once before, similar attention had gotten to Barnett's team.

"When we were 2-1 (in 1993) and had just beaten Wake Forest and Boston College, we had a lot of publicity, and I don't think this program handled it very well. We went right into Ohio State and ended up getting our fannies kicked."

Having learned from that, Barnett saw a way to build on the win. Namely, through sweat equity.

Said Barnett, "It will certainly give our kids a lot of confidence, but it also creates some expectations for 'em—by me. If you think we're gonna let 'em play on a lesser level than that — that's just the first game. We have to be better in the 11th game than we were in the first game.

"They have now created a license for us to work their butts off, soon. But I think they're expecting it. We'll have to be better in the 11th game that we were in this one. And we'll have to be better in the second game than this one."

The Wildcats gained confidence and solidarity from the win over Lou Holtz's team. (Hans Scott)

Recognition Without Respect   53

Northwestern's win over Notre Dame was considered a "fluke" by many observers. The Wildcats would have 10 more games to prove them wrong. (Hans Scott)

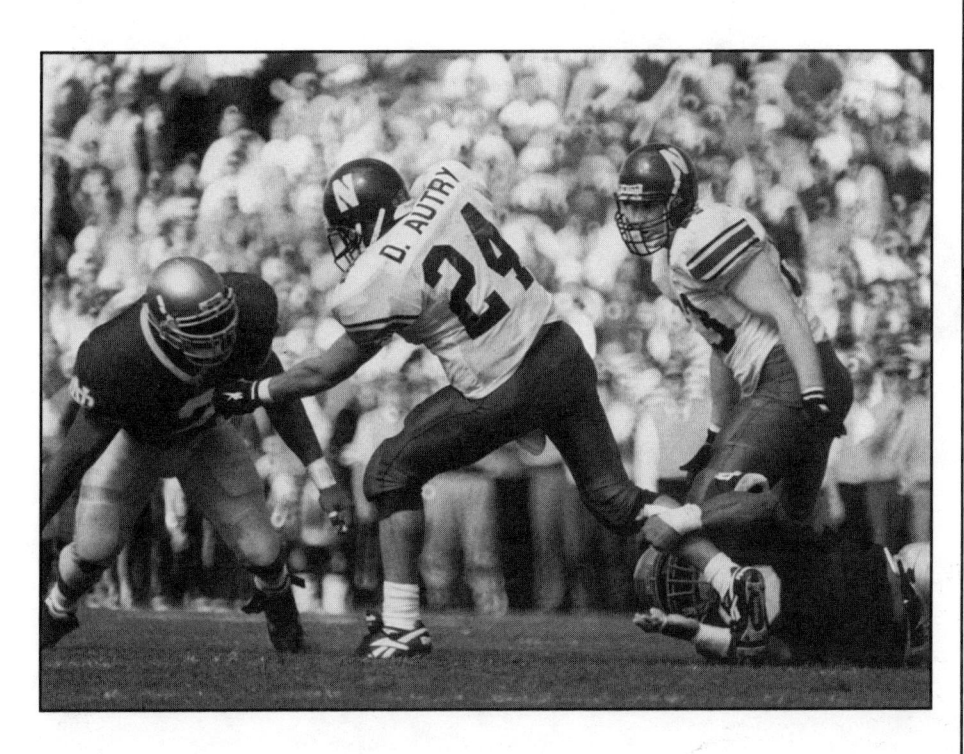

Big Ten Standings

1. Michigan (1-0-0)
2. Iowa (0-0-0)
3. Northwestern (0-0-0)
4. Ohio State (0-0-0)
5. Penn State (0-0-0)
6. Indiana (0-0-0)
7. Purdue (0-0-0
8. Minnesota (0-0-0)
9. Michigan State (0-0-0)
10. Wisconsin (0-0-0)
11. Illinois (0-1-0)

AP Top 25

1. Florida St.
2. Nebraska
3. Texas A&M
4. Florida
5. Auburn
6. Southern Cal
7. Penn St.
8. Tennessee
9. Colorado
10. Ohio St.
11. Michigan
12. UCLA
13. Alabama
14. Oklahoma
15. Texas
16. Virginia
17. Arizona
18. Washington
19. Miami
20. Oregon
21. Air Force
22. Kansas St.
23. Georgia
24. Notre Dame
25. **Northwestern**

Scores of interest

Nebraska 50, Michigan St. 10
Penn St. 24, Texas Tech 23
Michigan 24, Memphis 7
Iowa 34, N. Iowa 13
Notre Dame 35, Purdue 28
Indiana 24, W. Michigan 10
Florida St. 45, Clemson 26
Florida 42, Kentucky 7
Auburn 76, Tenn.-Chatt. 10
UCLA 23, BYU 9
Alabama 24, S. Miss. 20
Oklahoma 38, S.D. St. 22
Virginia 29, NC State 24
Arizona 20, Ga. Tech 19
Miami 49, Florida A&M 3
Va. Tech 14, Boston College 14

D'Wayne Bates heads to the end zone after hauling in one of his two touchdown receptions from Steve Schnur. (Peter Pawinski/The Daily Northwestern)

Chapter 7
THE TEFLON BANDWAGON

"There's 95 guys on this team, and every single one of them played a part in this loss."

—center Rob Johnson

THE 13 DAYS between the Notre Dame game and the home opener with Miami of Ohio saw little change in Evanston.

The front-page headlines about the win had receded into memory. The students were still on vacation. Tickets for the Wildcats-Redskins contest in Dyche Stadium were selling slowly.

One thing changed. Thanks to upsets on September 9, the Wildcats were now ranked among the nation's college football elite.

There were just enough surprises around the country for Northwestern to draw the votes necessary to grab the No. 25 ranking in the Associated Press poll, up from the phantom 29th spot the week before. It wasn't much, not even a traditional Top 20 ranking (the AP had expanded its ranking from 20 to 25 teams in 1989, to answer the challenge of *USA Today's* inflated poll), but it was recognition that, hey, that win over Notre Dame was real.

The kicker was, Notre Dame, 1-1 after a sloppy win at Purdue, was ranked 24th. So the Wildcats were real, but not as real as the team they'd beaten. And to the coaches, the Wildcats weren't real at all. The *USA Today*/CNN ranking had them 28th.

"I don't think that means anything," said defensive lineman Matt Rice of the ranking a few days before the game. "I saw it on TV and thought, 'Wow!,' but it's more important to be ranked at the end of the year."

But a ranking is a ranking, and that made the game that much more attractive for ESPN2 to come in and televise it.

"Coming off a 3-7-1 season, it's good to get some national attention," said D'Wayne Bates. "The ranking's something to build on."

"The downside is we got ranked by not playing," said Gary Barnett. "I don't put a lot of credence in it. I'd feel better if we got in last week. I guess we've got to creep in sometime.

"Do we deserve it? I don't know. I know if they'd seen our practice last Friday, they wouldn't have voted us."

That practice was eight days before the Redskins came into town.

"The ranking and the publicity and that sort of thing makes Miami a huge game for us, because everybody warns you about letdowns," said Barnett. "I don't think it's in the makeup of our team to do that.

"We hold the Miami program in high regard. When you talk about Miami football, you talk about a program that's like USC and Notre Dame. You talk about their coaching legends and the upsets they've provided."

Miami, with 15 Mid-Continent Conference titles to its credit, hasn't been called the Cradle of Coaches" for decades for nothing. For one

The Wildcat team, including Casey Dailey, Geoff Schein, Gerald Conoway, Tim Scharf, and Mike Giometti, during a moment of silence for Marcel Price, killed in an accidental summertime shooting. (Peter Pawinski/The Daily Northwestern)

thing, Woody Hayes and Bo Schembechler coached there before moving to Ohio State and Michigan, respectively. Red Blaik, architect of Army's greatest teams, was a Redskin, as was Paul Brown, who created a pro dynasty in Cleveland. Weeb Ewbank cut his football teeth at Miami. Ara Parseghian was in charge in Oxford, Ohio before coming to Northwestern in 1956. One of his successors, John Pont, also coached at both Miami and Northwestern. Bill Mallory and John Mackovic started there. As coaching legacies go, Miami's is unparalleled.

Upsets? Well, the Redskins upset Northwestern, and considerably so, in 1955. Miami's 25-14 win did plenty to convince the NU hierarchy that this Parseghian guy was worth hiring. In fact, the Redskins had compiled a 3-1 record against NU, always playing in Evanston, going into this year's game.

As it turned out, Barnett was partially prophetic. The Wildcats were warned about a letdown. Then they went out and let down.

Injuries, errors and poor fortune conspired to allow Miami, a 17-point underdog that hadn't beaten a ranked team in nine years, to come from 21 points behind at the start of the fourth quarter and post a 30-28 victory over NU. Aside from a few thousand red-clad Redskin backers, the 26,352 fans who turned out at Dyche Stadium expecting to see the team that beat Notre Dame, and saw it for 45 minutes, saw the old Wildcats in the final 15 minutes.

In that final quarter, everything that could go wrong did.

Everything. It was an ugly turn of events, one that could be detailed, but not really explained to the satisfaction of anyone on the team or the coaching staff.

How, for instance, can the team that who knocked the opposing team's quarterback and halfback out of the game lose?

How, for instance, can a three-touchdown lead disappear?

How, for instance, can an injury to one player—and the long snapper, at that—have such a critical effect on the game?

Northwestern led 28-7 when the fourth quarter began. The Wildcats seemed sure of winning at Dyche for the first time in two seasons. Since then, they had gone 0-9-1 at home, the tie coming against Stanford in 1994. Surely, this win was in the bag.

The bag broke. Actually, it exploded.

It came down to the final play, when Chad Seitz kicked a 20-yard field goal to win the game as time expired. But Northwestern started to lose long before that.

The first thing that went wrong was the loss of offensive tackle Paul Janus, who doubles as NU's long snapper. It didn't seem like a big deal at the time, when Janus, just a few plays into the game, left the action with a strained right shoulder. Jason Wendland took over at tackle, but it became a big deal.

Larry Curry, Janus' replacement as the long snapper to the punter and placekick holder, picked the worst possible day to have a series of bad snaps.

The first one came late in the first half. To this point, NU had breezed to a 21-0 lead. Steve Schnur had looked even better than he did against Notre Dame, throwing three touchdown passes in the first 21 minutes, two to Bates and one to Darnell Autry. It was impressive stuff.

Then the trouble began. The Redskins stopped NU at the Wildcat 24, and Paul Burton came in to punt. Curry snapped the ball low, and by the time Burton was dropping it to kick it, here was Dee Osborne, the son of former Bear Jim Osborne, storming in, as unblocked as a dust storm on the open prairie.

Burton, who didn't see Osborne coming since he had to look down for the ball, couldn't get out of the way, and his kick was blocked at the NU 10. Osborne picked the ball up and ran into the end-zone, cutting NU's lead to 21-7 with 1:55 left in the half.

That was troubling enough, but there was more to come. Much more. Too much more.

Halfway through the third quarter, a low snap by Curry on a field-goal attempt had Burton, the holder, scrambling to tee the ball up. That allowed Miami's Jamie Taylor to rumble in and block Sam Valenzisi's 52-yard attempt.

On the second play of the final quarter, with Valenzisi lined up to try a 46-yard attempt, a Curry snap sailed past Burton. He covered the ball on the Miami 45 for a 16-yard loss.

And still, the Wildcats led 28-7. It appeared they'd be able to weather the storm. After all, Miami had lost starting quarterback Neil Dougherty late in the first half with a torn plan-

Darnell Autry is aided in celebrating his 12-yard touchdown reception against the Redskins. (Peter Pawinski/The Daily Northwestern)

Miami wide receiver Tremayne Banks jumps on top of the pile after one of the Redskins' fourth-quarter touchdowns. (Peter Pawinski/The Daily Northwestern)

tar fascia in his foot. Earlier, starting halfback Damian Vaughn had gone down with a possible broken right leg. The Redskins were reeling.

Then, they reeled the Wildcats in. Dougherty, a classic drop-back quarterback, was replaced by Sam Ricketts, for whom the term "scrambler" was coined. Where Dougherty would wait in the pocket, Ricketts was everywhere but there. He presented a new challenge to a Wildcat defense that had drilled for weeks preparing for the slow-footed Ron Powlus and had been facing a similar customer in Dougherty.

Even against Ricketts, NU was doing the job. The first pass he threw in the second half, Rodney Ray picked off and ran in for a touchdown, expanding the lead to 28-7. For most teams, that would have been a killer play. Not for the Redskins.

Miami's comeback commenced immediately after Burton covered Curry's wild snap. Ricketts hit Ned Washington for 11 yards, and three plays later, on third-and-11, found diving receiver Jay Hall for a 10-yard pickup. With fourth-and-1 on the NU 35, Miami head coach Randy Walker, who had been the running backs coach on Francis Peay's NU staff in 1988 and '89, decided to go for it. Down 21 points with under 13 minutes left, he had to go for it.

The ball went to tailback Ty King, who went up the middle, as Notre Dame's Randy Kinder did a fortnight before. Kinder was stopped. King got the yard he needed, and Miami's drive was alive.

King used Hall's great trap block to gain 24 yards on the next play, and picked up seven more on the subsequent snap. One incompletion later, Ricketts moved left and found Hall behind Ray in the left-hand corner of the end zone. Now Miami trailed 28-14. With 11:14 left, Northwestern was still in command.

Or was it? The Wildcat offense couldn't get anything going, and Miami took over at its 32. In two plays, passes moved the Redskins to the NU 37. There, they stayed until fourth-and-10, when Ricketts hit King over the middle for 28 yards and first-and-goal on the 9.

Now things were getting serious. In the press box, wary reporters stopped typing their early leads. It was clear the NU defense wasn't able to go after Ricketts the way they jumped on Powlus. And the cornerbacks were backpedaling. When Ricketts hit halfback Jeremy Adkins in the same corner of the end zone he'd found Hall, with Ray beaten again, the Redskins had moved to within seven. It was 28-21 with 8:16 left.

What the Wildcats needed was a solid drive, something to chew up yardage and the clock simultaneously. They got one.

There was Darnell Autry up the middle for seven yards, then Autry for eight more, then, after an incompletion, off left tackle for 12 more.

With 6:37 left, Autry flew around the left side for 18 yards. The ball was on the Miami 35. It didn't get much further. NU moved to the Redskin 32 before Burton was forced to punt. His kick found the end zone, giving Miami the ball on its 20.

There was 5:38 remaining. If the Wildcats defense could hold, NU would win.

The defense couldn't hold. Ricketts was looking at a third-and-3 at the Redskin 27 when he hit Adkins on a 32-yard completion to the NU 41. Then he found Hall, who made the catch despite interference by Eric Collier, for 27 more.

Now the ball was on the Wildcat 14. A touchdown would tie it. Two plays gained four yards, forcing a third-and-6 from the 10. Ricketts wasted little time in hitting Washington, who got to the 2. That meant a handoff to King was in order and he crashed through for the score.

Walker boldly went for the win via a two-point conversion. And here, it appeared Northwestern's luck had turned. Ricketts went looking for wide receiver Eric Henderson in the right corner of the end zone, but with corner Hudhaifa Ismaeli blanketing Henderson, Ricketts' thread-the-needle pass floated too high, eventually hitting the turf.

With 2:22 left, NU had a 28-27 lead. All the Wildcat offense had to do was run out the clock, and for a time, the plan was working. Autry, who finished with 152 yards, gained a critical pair on a third-and-2 from the NU 28 with 2:10 left. However, even as the Redskins burned their last time-out, the drive bogged down. With fourth-and-3 on the NU 37, Burton was called in to punt.

He called for the snap. Curry snapped it, and snapped it low. The ball skidded along the smooth AstroTurf, skidded between Burton's legs, and the chase was on. It was Burton versus a crew of Redskins, all in pursuit of the ball, which was rolling deep into Wildcat territory.

Burton eventually smothered the ball, but on the 1-foot line. The Redskins would take over there, a point behind and with 43 seconds left in the game.

What was inconceivable at the beginning of the quarter was now next to inevitable Miami was going to win.

On first down, Ricketts took the snap and tried to sneak it by hopping over his center, but ran into Ismaeli.

He may have wanted to do the same thing on second down, but fumbled the snap and had to cover it. The clock was ticking down, under 10 seconds now. Officials stopped it briefly because the Northwestern players were taking their time getting back to their side of the line, then restarted it.

Ricketts promptly spiked the ball on third down. Three seconds remained, and placekicker Chad Seitz trotted onto the field. Northwestern took time, trying to freeze the senior. The ploy didn't work. Seitz lined up at the right hashmark, watched holder Scott Trostel tee up the low snap of Matt Barnes, and tore into the ball. It split the uprights at the north end of Dyche Stadium, and Miami, as time ran out, had an astonishing victory.

Northwestern had an unforgettable loss. People left Dyche shaking their heads. Notre Dame, the upset of the century, was a long way away. This was just upsetting.

"They outhustled, outplayed, outhit and outcoached us," said Barnett. "We were never in control of the game. Even when Rodney Ray made the interception (for a 28-7 lead), we weren't in control.

"This is about as low as it gets."

Barnett, who said this, his 25th loss as a coach at NU, was his toughest, went out of his way not to pin the blame on Curry.

"I feel bad for Larry," he said. "We put him in a bad position. Larry's good. He was our snapper two years ago. Larry had a bad day. Special teams, which had been our strength, let us down tremendously."

Not to mention the offense and defense. Barnett, then and in retrospect, believed his players did what he didn't expect them to. They eased up.

"We'd seen Miami on film, and they play hard. We didn't continue to play hard. We lost our focus. There were problems we didn't solve.

"I'd say this hurts quite a bit."

For one thing, it erased all the good feeling that beating Notre Dame had generated.

Redskins Quarterback Neil Dougherty feels the sting of a Pat Fitzgerald hit. (Peter Pawinski/The Daily Northwestern)

"We created a bandwagon, and everybody jumped on," said Barnett. "But it's Teflon-coated, and now they're going to slide off."

There wasn't much doubt of that. What there was was doubt that the Wildcats, who had last lost on a game's final play to Syracuse in 1984, could bounce back. Here, after all, was a team that lost to an outfit using its backup quarterback. But the different styles of Dougherty and Ricketts did, finally, take a toll.

"That's a new game plan when you have to stop a mobile quarterback," said Barnett.

Walker admitted calling a different set of plays, "a little bit," when he was forced to insert Ricketts.

"Sam gives it a different flavor, but we made a decision a long time ago not to develop two packages. He runs more."

"We knew 16 was a scrambling quarterback," said NU safety William Bennett, who, with fellow captains Valenzisi and Rob Johnson, were the only players to talk with reporters. "We had to readjust. Scrambling takes a toll on a defense, because receivers break routes and get open.

"Now we'll watch films, learn about our mistakes, and get ready for Air Force."

Valenzisi could only say, "Everyone else had the season decided for us already. We can't really put it into words."

Johnson could, to some extent.

"We just didn't execute, period," he said. "We shoulda had the game won. We just didn't execute in all phases of the game."

Then Larry Watts of *Pioneer Press,* who has covered the Wildcats for over a decade, asked what could be said to Curry, and Johnson, peeved, nearly bit Watts' head off.

"That's a ridiculous question," said Johnson, bristling. "If anyone else wants to ask any other questions about any particular person about this loss, we're done (talking).

"There's 95 guys on this team, and every single one of them played a part in this loss. It's not Larry Curry, not Paul Burton. We look at ourselves, not anybody else."

So Johnson was asked why it all happened.

"I think we put ourselves into a bad position," he said, calming down. "We were up 21 points and we let everything go."

That summed it up as well as it could be summed up in the minutes after the game. By Monday, tape had been reviewed and souls had been searched. And the answers didn't change much. Or so Barnett had it pegged.

"At the end of the game, in the locker room, I said to the players, 'Everyone in this room could have done something that would have won that game.' After looking at the film, that's just what I saw.

"There was just an incredible set of circumstances, little things like Darnell ran out of bounds in the last two minutes. Had he stayed in bounds, the clock would have ran out. We'd have run an additional 25 seconds off the clock.

"If we'd have called one more running play instead of one more passing play. We would all have been disappointed in the way we played, we would have disappointed in the fact we let it get so close, but we would have had a victory, not a loss.

"Larry had two successful snaps before the last one. The chances of the snap going through Paul Burton's legs. What are those chances?

"The only way you could lose this game was if absolutely everything went wrong, and that's just about what happened."

It was a lesson of enormous proportions.

"We found ourselves in uncomfortable surroundings," Barnett said. "That was a large lead, and not knowing how to put somebody away. We haven't been in that position since, I don't know how long it's been.

"Since I've been here, my gut's ached at the end of every game."

With that, it was time to look forward. Barnett found it difficult to do.

"Probably the most difficult coaching job now is what I have in front of me, and what our coaches have in front of us. You come out of these games wounded. The players' hearts are wounded. We've got a challenge on our hands.

"Somebody said, this too shall pass, but it's like a half-inch kidney stone."

And one on film, or at least videotape.

"It was pretty hard watching the films," said Bennett. "It came to the fourth quarter and you could see our intensity go down. Those mistakes can't happen again. If they do, we'll lose.

"We'd been stuffing them all game. All of a sudden, we're fighting to hold on. They kick a field-goal and we lose."

Bennett admitted that before the game was lost, drive, momentum, spirit, call it what you will, was lost, because the Wildcats were watching the scoreboard.

"If you lose it, it's hard to get back, especially against a team that still has it and is pounding at you."

Miami was that team.

For his part, Walker was still impressed with Northwestern. It didn't seem, he believed, to be the same place he coached at under Peay.

"They're obviously made a commitment, as a university, to have a better football team with better players," he said after the game. "They'll have to be reckoned with in the Big Ten. There's people with better players, but I don't know if there are people who'll be better prepared."

His words fell on deaf ears. Northwestern was done, cooked by the Redskins and flipped out of the frying pan. A teflon frying pan.

Quarterback Steve Schnur, head hanging, leaves the field with his teammates after Miami's shocking win. (Peter Pawinski/The Daily Northwestern)

MIAMI-OHIO VS. NORTHWESTERN

Saturday, September 16, 1995 at Dyche Stadium, Evanston, IL
Weather: 75° Wind SW 13 Sunny
Attendance: 26,352

SCORE BY QUARTERS	1	2	3	4	SCORE
Miami-Ohio (2-1-0)	0	7	0	23	30
Northwestern (1-1-0)	14	7	7	7	28

First Quarter
		MU	NU
NU 10:50 D'Wayne Bates 27-yard pass from Steve Schnur (Sam Valenzisi kick) (9 plays, 69 yards, 4:10 TOP)		0	7
NU 3:49 Darnell Autry 12-yard pass from Steve Schnur (Sam Valenzisi kick) (11 plays, 64 yards, 4:58 TOP)		0	14

Second Quarter
| NU 4:06 D'Wayne Bates 36-yard pass from Steve Schnur (Sam Valenzisi kick) 5 plays, 53 yards, 2:28 TOP) | | 0 | 21 |
| MU 1:55 Dee Osborne 10-yard punt block return (Chad Seitz kick) | | 7 | 21 |

Third Quarter
| NU 14:09 Rodney Ray 20-yard interception return (Sam Valenzisi kick) | | 7 | 28 |

Fourth Quarter
MU 11:14 Jay Hall 3-yard pass from Sam Ricketts (Chad Seitz kick) (9 plays, 55 yards, 3:00 TOP)		14	28
MU 8:16 Jeremy Adkins 9-yard pass from Sam Ricketts (Chad Seitz kick) (8 plays, 68 yards, 2:02 TOP)		21	28
MU 2:22 Ty King 2-yard run (2-pt conversion pass failed) (8 plays, 80 yards, 3:16 TOP)		27	28
MU 0:00 Chad Sietz 20-yard field goal (4 plays, 2 yards, :43)		30	28

TEAM STATISTICS	NU	MU
First Downs	20	14
Rushing	12	8
Passing	8	6
Penalty	0	0
Rushing Attempts	51	35
Yards Gained Rushing	207	136
Yards Lost Rushing	65	23
Net Yards Rushing	142	113
Net Yards Passing	187	249
Passes Attempted	26	39
Passes Completed	13	20
Had Intercepted	1	1
Total Offensive Plays	77	74
Total Net Yards	329	362
Average Gain per Play	4.3	4.9
Fumbles: Number-Lost	0-0	2-0
Penalties: Number- Yards	4-32	6-40
Interceptions: Number-Yards	1-20	1-3
Number of Punts-Yards	6-218	4-157
Average Per Punt	36.3	39.3
Punt Returns: Number-Yards	2-31	2-32
Kickoff Returns: Number-Yards	1-20	3-49
Possession Time	31:54	28:06
Third-Down Conversions	7 of 16	6 of 18
Sacks By: Number-Yards	0-0	0-0

Big Ten Standings
1. Michigan (1-0-0)
2. Iowa (0-0-0)
3. Ohio St. (0-0-0)
4. Penn St. (0-0-0)
5. Minnesota (0-0-0)
6. Indiana (0-0-0)
7. Northwestern (0-0-0)
8. Michigan St. (0-0-0)
9. Purdue (0-0-0)
10. Illinois (0-1-0)
11. Wisconsin (0-0-0)

AP Top 25
1. Florida St.
2. Nebraska
3. Texas A&M
4. Florida
5. Southern Cal
6. Penn St.
7. Colorado
8. Ohio St.
9. Michigan
10. Oklahoma
11. Virginia
12. Oregon
13. Texas
14. Auburn
15. Tennessee
16. UCLA
17. Miami
18. LSU
19. Kansas St.
20. Georgia
21. Notre Dame
22. Washington
23. Alabama
24. Maryland
25. Arizona

Scores of interest
Penn St. 66, Temple 14
Illinois 9, Arizona 7
Kentucky 17, Indiana 10
Iowa 27, Iowa St. 10
Ohio St. 30, Washington 20
Michigan St. 30, Louisville 7
Michigan 23, Boston College 13
Wisconsin 24, Stanford 24
Minnesota 31, Ball St. 7
Florida St. 77, NC State 17
Nebraska 77, Arizona St. 28
Texas A&M 52, Tulsa 9
Florida 62, Tennessee 37
Auburn 6, LSU 12
USC 45, Houston 10
Colorado 66, NE Louisiana 14
UCLA 31, Oregon 38

Wildcat students, celebrating the first home win in two years, go for the goalposts. (Peter Pawinski/The Daily Northwestern)

Chapter 8
BACK ON THE FLIGHT PATH

"There were a bunch of guys flying around."
—linebacker Pat Fitzgerald after playing Air Force

TWO DAYS AFTER losing to Miami, the scene around the Northwestern program seemed to be back to normal. The normal number of reporters. The normal number of camera crews. No ranking in the AP's Top 25. Not a single, solitary vote, in fact. That, too, was normal.

One thing was different from years past: a sense of urgency. Here, just two games into a season Gary Barnett believed could be a good season, was a critical juncture.

Would the Wildcats, after a summer of hard work and a glorious upset of Notre Dame, fold up? Could the fatal fourth quarter against Miami breed pessimism among the players?

Barnett remembered all too well the 1993 season, when an overconfident club strolled into Ohio Stadium with a 2-1 record, got hammered 51-3 by Ohio State, and went winless in the Big Ten.

Barnett walked into the Nicolet Center auditorium, began to talk about the loss, and held up the post-Notre Dame injury report from trainer Steve Willard. It was blank. Then he held up the post-Miami report. It spilled onto a second page.

"It's significant," said Barnett. "If we had to play today, we couldn't play with (William) Bennett, with Casey Dailey, with (Pat) Fitzgerald, with Rob Johnson, with Ray Robey. We can't play with (Paul) Janus, regardless. And we couldn't play with Mike Warren.

"Yet, after Notre Dame, just as tough an opponent, obviously, the hurts don't hurt as much."

It was reminiscent of John Kennedy's famed statement that victory had a thousand fathers and defeat was an orphan.

"After Notre Dame I said that one game, a season doesn't make. And after two, I have to say the same thing. It has to hurt, or you don't learn from it.

"Our coaches, and me, specifically, I have to lead by example here, so I can't stay any longer in this fetal position than I did. I've got to get out of it and go into this week with a great deal of confidence in our plan, and a great deal of confidence that our kids are going to execute it.

"I have to believe that they want to do the right thing, that they want to come back and make amends for the last week. Every player deserves a coach who believes in him, and that's just what you're gonna find here."

In a way, it was a blessing that the Air Force Academy was next up on the schedule. For one thing, the Wildcats had beaten the Falcons last year in Colorado Springs, winning 14-10 on

Darnell Autry scoops by grounded Falcon Kelvin King (11) and LeRon Hudgins on the way to a chunk of his then career-high 190 yards. (Peter Pawinski/The Daily Northwestern)

Chris Martin's 96-yard fumble recovery touchdown run after a hit by Joe Reiff. For another, and more important, the Falcons, with a 2-1 record, were the only team Northwestern would play that used the wishbone offense. That, at least, would give the defense a reason to look forward, rather than reflect back on the horror story they had just authored.

"This game is going to be more of a game of character than anything because we're playing a consummate team," said Barnett. "We're playing a team that is always underdogs. Their offense is the consummate team offense, as boring as it's been called. They do the best job anybody ever has done running this thing.

"We not only have to regroup and regenerate ourselves, we have to learn something and prepare for something absolutely new and different."

The year before, the Falcons had run for 246 yards to Northwestern's paltry 66, but had fallen largely on the strength of Martin's long fumble return. Thus, the Falcons had experienced what the Wildcats were going through: dealing with an inexplicable loss.

"This is the time when all those things that you talk to your team about, you've got to go back and read 'em yourself and make sure you're believing what you've been saying," said Barnett. "That you're not just talking the talk, but walking the walk as well, as coaches. The senior leaders have to do the same thing.

"If you've got a team that's used to winning, and they experience something like this, they don't stand for it the next week. If you've got a team that isn't used to winning, they don't have that sort of character to draw upon.

"You're hoping to build that character. This team doesn't have the tradition to draw upon. It's really going to come down to whether this is a new breed, the effects of a new program or not. This could be a pretty clear picture as to whether or not it's taken effect.

"I don't want to put too much pressure on 'em myself, but I guess I sorta have by saying that."

Barnett would, in his words, "create some tough times in practice," not as punishment for Miami, but to drive home the point that the game must be played to the end. Besides, getting ready for the Falcon offense, which had rushed for 1,130 yards in three games, wouldn't be easy.

The practices healed the wounded players, except for Janus, out for the week. They also honed the Wildcats, on defense and offense.

By Saturday, September 23, Northwestern was sharp again. The Wildcats played for 60 minutes the way they had for 45 against Miami, and scored a decisive 30-6 victory over the Falcons, who came into half-empty Dyche Stadium three-point favorites.

"It was a lot harder for us to beat Air Force under the circumstances than it was for us to beat Notre Dame under the circumstances," Barnett said. "It wasn't just that we won, but the kind of performance, the way our kids played, from the start of the game to the end of the game, was a true indicator of the kind of character this team has.

"You've got to take your hat off to those kids playing that way. There aren't a lot of people who could be as low as we were, traumatized as much as we were. To come out and totally dominate a team the way they did, especially on the one side."

The defensive side. It led the way. With the Cats leading 3-0 on the first of Sam Valenzisi's three field-goals, end Casey Dailey clobbered Falcon halfback Jake Campbell. He fumbled, and William Bennett corralled it.

That was the cue for Darnell Autry to go to work. He took it in from the 1 five plays later, and NU led 10-0. Autry would score again, this time from 7 yards out, three seconds into the fourth quarter. And, carrying the ball 37 times, he would finish with a career-high 190 yards, his fourth straight game over the 100-yard mark, the streak going back to the Penn State finale a year earlier.

"We were angry and we came out to win," said Autry.

The most impressive part of his game was revealed after close examination of the tapes by NU's coaches. Autry, with great leg drive for a sophomore, gained 101 of his 190 yards after the first hit.

There was more to Northwestern's attack than Autry. To help shift the momentum, the Wildcats used a pass by punter Paul Burton off a fake punt to gain a critical first down, recovered an onside kick (which led to Valenzisi's game-opening field goal), and also tried to advance the ball on a fake field-goal. The latter play failed, but the first two succeeded, wowing the smallish crowd of 26,037 at Dyche, not to mention those watching on ESPN.

"We always look for a way to beat a team with special teams," said Barnett. "We saw some weaknesses and took advantage of them."

Quarterback Steve Schnur also had a good day, with a career-high 204-yard day on 16-of-22 accuracy. It was somewhat overshadowed, as was the remarkable performance of D'Wayne Bates. All seven of Bates' receptions were for first downs, and worth a career-high 110 yards.

Before the game, safety and co-captain William Bennett had said of the Falcon attack, "To beat it, we have to be very disciplined. We

Pat Fitzgerald, always happy to roam in the opposition's backfield, sacks Falcon quarterback Tom Brown. (Peter Pawinski/The Daily Northwestern)

have to focus on the little things. We have to take the right steps, be in the right position. We have to know what coverage we're in."

They knew so well, they held the vaunted Air Force option, the third-best rushing offense in the country, to 53 fewer yards on the ground than Autry had gained. It had few options and was held to 137 ground yards.

So, yes, the Air Force was forced to go to the air, and quarterback Beau Morgan didn't fare particularly well in the Wild Blue Yonder, going 11-for-25, worth 120 yards, and throwing an interception. The NU defense held Air Force to a pair of field-goals by Randy Roberts, and to absolutely nothing at all in the second half.

Keeping Air Force out of the end zone was the first time the Wildcats had done that to anyone in 100 games. The last time, NU had scored a shutout over Princeton. This wasn't a shutout, but nobody wearing purple was complaining.

"Northwestern beat us at our own game," said Falcons head coach Fisher DeBerry. "They did a better job controlling the ball. We didn't execute our offense. Their defense had a lot to do with that."

Overall, NU allowed Air Force just 271 yards of total offense, the best performance by the defense in two years.

"There were a bunch of guys flying around," said middle linebacker Pat Fitzgerald, who wasn't really speaking about the Falcons. "The whole team on defense was making plays."

Fitzgerald, a junior, made more than anyone else, with 11 tackles, including a half-sack, garnering the lone interception of Morgan, and recovering a Falcon fumble. That line score caused him to be named the Big Ten's co-defensive player of the week, along with Penn State's Kim Herring.

"That was probably as fine a game as we've had here by a linebacker," said Barnett.

"It was a consummate team effort, not just one guy," said Fitzgerald, whose pickoff set up Darnell Autry's second touchdown. "I might have had a lot of tackles, but I wouldn't have been able to do it without the guys up front. My name was called, but they did all the work."

Much work was being done. All three Air Force turnovers were turned into touchdowns by the Wildcats, with Darnell Autry scoring twice and Adrian Autry, his unrelated backup, scoring the other TD.

Only three games into the season, five of the turnovers the Wildcats had forced had been turned into scores, all of them touchdowns. Impressive, yes, and all the more impressive considering the minus-11 turnover ratio the Wildcats had compiled in 1994.

With Gary Barnett watching from the sidelines, safety Eric Collier breaks up a pass to Danta Johnson. (Peter Pawinski/The Daily Northwestern)

Back on the Flight Path   69

Adrian Autry ignores the tackle of Air Force linebacker LeRon Hudgins as he goes over the goal line. Matt Hartl (46) cheers him on. (Peter Pawinski/The Daily Northwestern)

Two of those scores came in the fourth quarter, the first final-frame points of the season for NU.

"They were well aware we needed to be a better fourth-quarter team," said Barnett. "To me, it indicated we were going to play four quarters. That's the kind of team we want to be."

Barnett had wanted to see his seniors step up. They did.

"Coming out of Miami, a lot of the younger players and the backups were looking to see what was going to happen," said senior offensive tackle Ryan Padgett. "It was a sense that we know we can be good, and we know we can be bad. Who's going to come out?

"The seniors talked about being the examples. It's going to be like Notre Dame, not like Miami. Let's come out early, let's show these guys who's boss. Everybody really followed that. If we hadn't come out strong at first, there might have been a little doubt.

"We're still thinking about it. It would be nice to be 3-0. By the same token, I think we might gain some extra wins later in the season by losing to Miami. We realize we are mortal, and if we don't watch the little things, we're going to get beat."

Fitzgerald couldn't help but recall the headlines of a week before.

"I remember, 'Same old Northwestern, here we go again,' blah, blah, blah," he said. "For us to be able to change that attitude toward our team, we have to win. We have to keep progressing every week."

Fitzgerald also noted that Notre Dame had gone 3-0 since losing the opener to the Wildcats, including a 55-27 blistering of Texas at the same time the Wildcats were whipping the Falcons, and said he believed that made NU's season-opening triumph all the more important.

"I'd love to see 'em go to a nice bowl game and win, and we finish about two rankings ahead of 'em when the final polls come out," he said of Notre Dame. Then, only a seer could have predicted that Northwestern would eventually climb to third in the both polls prior to the Rose Bowl, while Notre Dame, hindered by a late-September loss to Ohio State, would go into the Orange Bowl ranked No. 6 in the AP writer/broadcaster poll and No. 9 in the CNN/USA Today coaches poll.

Padgett wasn't predicting a final record, but he thought after Air Force that the season could be better than average.

"The future is a lot of wins," he said. "We've got a hell of a defensive unit. This year, the offense has so much respect for our defense now. We realize we're going to have to go back on the field quick, because these guys are stopping 'em three-and-out."

The win at Dyche was the first for NU on the AstroTurf installed prior to the 1994 sea-

Darnell Autry looks for running room against Air Force. (Peter Pawinski/The Daily Northwestern)

son, and the first in the ancient arena in 11 games. It snapped an 0-9-1 string (0-10-1 adding in the 1994 loss to Notre Dame at Soldier Field).

Even better, NU moved to 2-1 for the second time in three years. Only twice in the 16 years prior to Barnett's arrival had the Wildcats opened with a 2-1 mark. That had to be worth something. Barnett looked at the alternative, and winced.

"Launching into the Big Ten with two losses would have been very difficult for us," he said. "We went through a grieving session after Miami, but by Wednesday I knew we had bounced out of it. The kids were ready to go."

The 2-1 record was worth something in the polls. Northwestern was knocking on the Top 25 door again. The writers and broadcasters in the AP poll had NU 26th, with 60 votes, behind the 118 votes of No. 25 Kansas.

There was even an oh-so-mild case of Wildcat fever on the campus. After the game, some NU students ran onto the field and tried to tear down a goalpost. Valenzisi, named the Big Ten's special teams player of the week for his three-field-goal effort, for extending his consecutive point-after kick string to 44, and his expertise in laying down the onside kick, didn't like the reaction.

"After last week (against Miami), I would have thought they would have patted us on the back instead of doing what they did," Valenzisi explained. "To me, that doesn't show they have very much respect for us."

The enthusiasm was understandable. Here was NU, finally winning a home game. The Wildcats had been 0-4-1 at Dyche the season before, and had blown the Miami game. Besides, students, after years of getting into games on a pass — not that anything close to a majority of the student body had shown up — were now being charged $5 for admission. A little celebrating wasn't a bad thing.

And Northwestern, for 11 of 12 quarters, had resembled a really good football team. DeBerry, his Falcons humbled for the second straight week, had nothing but praise.

"Northwestern did a much better job recovering and bouncing back from disappointment than we did," he said. "They have enough weapons to make a rumble in the Big Ten. Everybody they play had better be ready."

The rumble was about to commence.

AIR FORCE VS. NORTHWESTERN

Saturday, September 23, 1995 at Dyche Stadium, Evanston, IL
Weather: 53° Wind SW 7 Sunny
Attendance: 26,037

SCORE BY QUARTERS	1	2	3	4	SCORE
Air Force (2-2-0)	0	6	0	0	6
Northwestern (2-1-0)	10	6	0	14	30

First Quarter
			MU	NU
NU	7:21	Sam Valenzisi 46-yard field goal (13 plays, 58 yards, 6:03 TOP)	3	0
NU	4:20	Darnell Autry 1-yard run (Sam Valenzisi kick) (5 plays, 20 yards, 2:48 TOP)	10	0

Second Quarter
AF	13:09	Randy Roberts 26-yard field goal (15 plays, 68 yards, 6:11 TOP)	10	3
NU	9:36	Sam Valenzisi 26-yard field goal (9 plays, 60 yards, 3:33 TOP)	13	3
NU	7:16	Sam Valenzisi 35-yard field goal (5 plays, 28 yards, 2:20 TOP)	16	3
AF	0:31	Randy Roberts 39-yard field goal (7 plays, 47 yards, 2:41 TOP)	16	6

Third Quarter
no scoring

Fourth Quarter
| NU | 14:57 | Darnell Autry 7-yard run (Sam Valenzisi kick) (9 plays, 62 yards 3:54 TOP) | 23 | 6 |
| NU | 8:37 | Adrian Autry 5-yard run (Sam Valenzisi kick) (5 plays, 80 yards, 1:30 TOP) | 30 | 6 |

TEAM STATISTICS	AF	NU
First Downs	17	22
Rushing	7	10
Passing	8	9
Penalty	2	3
Rushing Attempts	39	49
Yards Gained Rushing	156	266
Yards Lost Rushing	19	17
Net Yards Rushing	137	249
Net Yards Passing	134	219
Passes Attempted	27	23
Passes Completed	13	17
Had Intercepted	1	0
Total Offensive Plays	66	72
Total Net Yards	271	468
Average Gain per Play	4.1	6.5
Fumbles: Number-Lost	4-2	2-1
Penalties: Number-Yards	4-27	13-112
Interceptions: Number-Yards	0-0	1-7
Number of Punts-Yards	4-136	2-62
Average Per Punt	34.0	31.0
Punt Returns: Number-Yards	1-0	2-3
Kickoff Returns: Number-Yards	5-83	3-64
Possession Time	27:40	32:20
Third-Down Conversions	5 of 15	3 of 12
Fourth-Down Conversions	1 of 2	2 of 4
Sacks By: Number-Yards	0-0	2-9

Big Ten Standings
1. Michigan (1-0-0)
2. Ohio St. (0-0-0)
3. Penn St. (0-0-0)
4. Iowa (0-0-0)
5. Indiana (0-0-0)
6. Northwestern (0-0-0)
7. Illinois (0-1-0)
8. Minnesota (0-0-0)
9. Michigan St. (0-0-1)
10. Purdue (0-0-1)
11. Wisconsin (0-0-0)

AP Top 25
1. Florida St.
2. Nebraska
3. Florida
4. Colorado
5. Southern Cal
6. Penn St.
7. Ohio St.
8. Michigan
9. Texas A&M
10. Oklahoma
11. Virginia
12. Tennessee
13. Auburn
14. LSU
15. Notre Dame
16. Kansas St.
17. Maryland
18. Washington
19. Oregon
20. Alabama
21. Texas
22. Stanford
23. Arkansas
24. Texas Tech.
25. Kansas

Scores of interest
Penn St. 59, Rutgers 34
Ohio St. 54, Pittsburgh 14
Florida St. 46, Cen. Fla. 14
Nebraska 49, Pacific 7
Texas A&M 29, Colorado 21
USC 31, Arizona 10
Oklahoma 51, N. Texas 10
Virginia 22, Clemson 3
Oregon 28, Stanford 21
Texas 55, Notre Dame 27
Tennessee 52, Miss. St. 14

Matt Hartl's block of IU's Nathan Davis allows Darnell Autry to hop to it. (Peter Pawinski/The Daily Northwestern)

Chapter 9
A SUCCESSFUL CONFERENCE CALL

> *"We're trying to turn the corner with winning the games we should win and winning the games we shouldn't win."*
> —Darnell Autry after the 30-7 win over favored Indiana

BEATING AIR FORCE renewed the faith of the Wildcat players in themselves, but there was little time to enjoy the return to winning form. After three nonconference outings, it was time to play a Big Ten opponent.

Northwestern's success in conference play has been, to be polite, limited. In 99 previous conference seasons, the Wildcats had finished over .500 only 22 times, and at .500 seven more times. On 68 other occasions, NU's teams were under .500. And in two years, 1906 and 1907, when the violence of what was then a brutish, unsophisticated game was under attack from President Teddy Roosevelt on down, Northwestern didn't even field a football team.

The Wildcats had won five Big Ten football championships, the first coming in 1903, a curious year where NU went 1-0-2 in the league. With ties discarded from figuring in the standings, the one win, over Illinois, was enough to snare a share of the title with Michigan and Minnesota, each of which were 3-0-1 in the league and 11-0-1 overall.

Northwestern, 9-2-3 overall, was clearly the weakest of the trio. Two of its wins were over high schools and another came against the soldiers of Fort Sheridan. The Cats also beat the NU Alumni team. It was obviously a far different era.

The Cats' greatest era came during the so-called "Golden Age" of sports. NU earned co-championships in 1926, 1930 and 1931, and collected its only outright title in 1936, going 6-0 in the league. The only loss in a 7-1 season came at Notre Dame in the season finale, a 26-6 surprise. The success of the Wildcats coincided with the decline and fall of the University of Chicago, a football powerhouse for most of the four decades Amos Alonzo Stagg, the great innovator, was head coach.

When the UC board, prodded by school president Robert Maynard Hutchins, opted for tougher academic standards for athletes, the Maroons began to lose and lose big. Their last hurrah was the selection in 1935 of back Jay Berwanger as the first winner of what a year later would be known as the Heisman Memorial Trophy.

Northwestern's salad days were not long-lasting. The overwhelming majority of in-league success came before the end of World War II.

Since V-J Day, the Wildcats had fallen on hard times. Only five times, in 1948 when a second-place finish earned a Rose Bowl berth because Michigan had repeated as Big Ten champion, twice under Ara Parseghian and twice under Alex Agase, did Northwestern finish over .500 in conference play. There were three other .500 records.

Eric Collier and Danny Sutter combining to make it tough on Indiana's Sean Glover. (Peter Pawinski/The Daily Northwestern)

And there were plenty of losses, 273 of them in Big Ten play, beginning with the 1945 season. The 1995 Wildcats, at 2-1, didn't exactly have those losses charged to their account, but the history was always there, hidden away, deep in the record book. Indeed, Northwestern hadn't won a conference game at home since 1992, when the Wildcats vanquished Wisconsin 27-25.

Quite visible in the week leading up to the conference opener against 2-1 Indiana, the one school in the league NU has a winning record against (35-31-1 coming into the game), was the concern about the Hoosiers' running game.

It was shaping up as a great year for runners in the Big Ten, perhaps the best since 1988, when three backs finished in the top seven rushers nationally. That year featured Indiana's Anthony Thompson in third place, Michigan's Tony Boles fourth, and Michigan State's Blake Ezor seventh.

This time around, there were five Big Ten running backs in the top 10 in Division I-A. NU's Darnell Autry, averaging 167.3 yards-per-game, was second, behind another sophomore, Iowa State's Troy Davis, who had gained 912 yards to Autry's 502. Carl McCullough of Wisconsin was fourth, Eddie George of Ohio State seventh, Sedrick Shaw of Iowa ninth and Chris Darkins of Minnesota 10th.

Not on that list was the guy the Wildcats were concerned with: Indiana's Alex Smith. The year before, Smith had gained 1,475 yards, the sixth-best mark in Division I-A and third highest in college history by a freshman, redshirt, as Smith was, or otherwise. Only Herschel Walker and Tony Dorsett were ahead of him in the latter category.

The week before facing NU in 1994, Smith had gained 232 yards on 43 carries against Iowa. The Wildcats, clamping down, held Smith to 87 yards, and used that as a springboard to a 20-7 win that snapped a nine-game losing streak to the Hoosiers.

"He'll be the best back we've faced so far," said Wildcat linebacker Pat Fitzgerald. "Those two guys from Notre Dame (Randy Kinder and Robert Farmer) are tremendous, but all in all, he'll be the best so far. It'll be really hard for us to shut him down. This is how the whole season will be. It'll be a new challenge week-to-week."

In Indiana, the Wildcat defense would be looking at an offense that was similar to NU's. And the Hoosier defense would have the same benefit. IU ran Smith plenty, witness his 161.5 yards-per-game average. NU ran Autry plenty, as the aforementioned 167.3 yard average attested. Anyone watching tapes of either team on a black-and-white TV would have trouble telling one from the other.

"I'm glad to be back to playing against a 'normal' offense," said Fitzgerald. "We can work on the isolation and toss sweep and play-action instead of the triple-option."

"This is a completely different animal," said NU head coach Gary Barnett.

But it was an animal Barnett had seen before. Indeed, these were mirror-image teams, perhaps the only difference on offense the tendency for Steve Schnur to throw to Autry more often than IU quarterback Chris Dittoe would look for Smith.

Northwestern, likely because it was home, was established as a three-point favorite. Since they were favored by 17 going into Miami, the Wildcats tried to ignore the honor.

In some ways, the game was ignored. Despite the marquee matchup of running backs, none of the Big Ten's television outlets chose to cover the game. Even though the September 30 weather was spectacular, only 29,223 fans ventured out to Dyche Stadium for the second NU home game in as many weeks.

They saw the matchup they expected. Autry gained 162 yards, Smith 136, including 61 on one carry midway through the first quarter. They also saw Northwestern struggle early, gain the lead for good on a 42-yard Autry touchdown run, his first of two, late in the second quarter, then pull away in the second half.

Northwestern's 31-7 victory didn't seem that dominant until the late stages of the game. Only by then had the Wildcats, outgained by 142 yards in the first half, scored 28 straight points. The Hoosiers had entered the game having committed nine turnovers in their first three games, and three more against the Wildcats helped lead to their downfall.

"The second half, that tells the story," said IU head coach Bill Mallory. "They outplayed us. They did what they were supposed to do, and we didn't. We just got outplayed in the second half.

"They got a wake-up call (from Miami), and they woke up better than we did. Everybody pooh-poohs the MAC, but I grew up in the Mid-American Conference, and if you're not ready, they'll smack you right in the kisser. That's what happened to them."

The Wildcats didn't have a great day on offense. Autry's 136 yards comprised 55.7 percent of NU's offense. Schnur was 7-of-14 passing for just 45 yards, misfiring on several deep throws that were designed to loosen up the Hoosier defense. But a win was a win, and it was NU's second win in a row for the first time in two years.

"I think it says a lot about the mettle of our team," said Barnett. "This team wanted to win this game badly. It's a different team (from before). Two years ago, we'd go into the Big Ten 2-1 and we were happy to be there. Now we were 2-1 and mad we were 2-1 going into it." Autry agreed.

"We've got a history of win one, lose one, win one, lose one," he said. "We've got to end that, or else we're going to be nowhere. We came in as a favorite and pulled it out, whereas we were the favorite against Miami, and you saw what happened there."

Darnell Autry runs away from Indiana end Roger Murray. (Peter Pawinski/The Daily Northwestern)

"We're trying to turn the corner with winning the games we should win and winning the games we shouldn't win."

Indiana had led 7-3 on the strength of Dittoe's 2-yard touchdown run, a dash to the left where only his right arm, ball in his outstretched hand, crossed the goal-line. That score, in the game's 21st minute, would not only be Indiana's only visit to the end zone, it would be the only time the Hoosiers got near it with the game in doubt.

Aside from their final drive, where a fourth-down pass from the NU 5 would fall incomplete, Indiana's deepest penetration was to the NU 29, two possessions before Dittoe's score. After it, except for the final surge, Indiana couldn't get past midfield.

Two plays, coming back-to-back, exemplified Northwestern's swarming defense.

The Wildcats led 21-7 early in the fourth quarter when the teams lined up at the Hoosier 41. Smith ran off right tackle, and gained eight yards before he was sandwiched by safeties Eric Collier and William Bennett. Smith didn't get up, hit so hard he had to be taken off the field on a cart. He was held overnight at Evanston Hospital, where X-rays revealed three broken ribs. He'd miss most of the rest of the season.

The next snap came at the Indiana 49. Dittoe dropped back to pass. The Wildcats called a corner blitz, and cornerback Hudhaifa Ismaeli slammed into Dittoe at the Indiana 43. The ball popped loose, and end Casey Dailey, who was also lining up Dittoe, picked it up and raced into the end zone. In two plays, Northwestern had inflicted injury and insult.

"We were very conscious of stripping the ball this week," said Dailey. "Dittoe's a big kid, 6-foot-6, and he holds the ball so low. He's fumbled a lot. He throws the ball low and he holds the ball low. He had, what, 10 knocked-down passes against Kentucky and the kid's 6-6."

Dailey was also playing hurt at that juncture. Ill late in the week, he'd left the game in the first half because of dehydration. After an IV at halftime, he was ready to go again.

"He was throwing up all last night and this morning," said Barnett. "He was really sick, so we hydrated him at halftime. It sounds sorta cruel, but it worked. Then he made a great play."

"I started to get kinda dizzy on the field, didn't know what was going on," said Dailey, a junior from Covina, California. "I wasn't really sweaty and was kinda hot inside. I came off and had a resting heart rate of 160."

Darnell Autry breaks away from Hoosier end Luis Pinnock for a 42-yard touchdown run in the second quarter. (Peter Pawinski/The Daily Northwestern)

Darnell Autry and Indiana cornerback Joey Eloms go one-on-one at midfield. (Peter Pawinski/The Daily Northwestern)

The recovery was quick and complete, enough so that Dailey was able to get to the end zone when Ismaeli knocked the ball loose from Dittoe.

Ismaeli had a big day, beginning in the last minute of the first quarter, when his interception of Dittoe had set up the first of Sam Valenzisi's three field-goals. A pickoff of backup quarterback Adam Greenlee set up Valenzisi's last field-goal. Thus, the Wildcats converted on all three turnovers, turning them into 13 points.

The Wildcat special teams were even better, and not just because Valenzisi's three field-goal day was the fifth of his career.

Punter Paul Burton boomed three of his kicks over 50 yards, including a multiple-hop 90-yarder that skittered all the way to the Hoosier 3 before going out of bounds. That kept Indiana from threatening early.

"I was just blessed to get the wind behind me," said Burton, son of Ron Burton, an All-American at running back for the Wildcats in the 1959 season. "Then you ride it out as far as you can go. I hit it pretty good. You practice that sometimes. You can't really plan those things out there."

The punt matched a Northwestern standard, and helped Burton, who averaged 56.6 yards on five punts, to the second-best average in Big Ten conference action since records have been kept. In 1949, Ohio State's Fred Morrison averaged 57.3 yards per-punt against Wisconsin. The 90-yarder equaled the record punt NU's Steve Toth had nailed against the Badgers in 1934, and was Burton's longest since a 70-yarder against the Buckeyes in 1994.

The punt-return team also came through, with Brian Musso's 86-yard punt return, the second-longest in NU history, setting up Autry's second touchdown run. The Hoosiers should have been keying on Musso, who had scored the year before on a 56-yard punt return.

Autry's score gave NU a 21-7 lead with 4:24 left in the third quarter, and effectively sealed IU's fate.

"It was very irking for that to happen," said Mallory of Musso's jaunt, the longest punt return against Indiana in Hoosier history, and exceeded in NU annals only by Otto Graham's 93-yard return against Kansas State in 1941. "Our gunners, our wide guys, were down there, but Musso got past, and I don't know where our wings were, or what happened. He made a juke on 'em and got by."

Where they were was sprawled on the Dyche Stadium turf, looking at Musso after being blocked by Josh Barnes and Fred Wilkerson. Musso had grabbed the punt, a 55-yard bomb by Alan Sutkowski, at the NU 7, deeper than most punt returners will dare attempt a catch, and was

Indiana's Aaron Warnecke gets help to bring down Adrian Autry. (Peter Pawinski/The Daily Northwestern)

already scooting up the right side of the field.

"We work hard on our punt coverage, but that really hurt us," Mallory went on. "It was a tight ball game before that."

"The coverage spreads out so much on a big punt, there are gaps in the defense," said Musso. "If there was somebody faster (on the return), we might have scored."

Autry took care of that, zipping around the left side from the 6. Earlier, his 42-yard run through heavy traffic, a run that displayed his ability to improvise, had given NU a 10-7 lead.

"I saw everyone was pretty much flowing (right)," said Autry. "I figured if there was that many people flowing, there's gotta be a cutback somewhere. When I cut back, it was huge, and I just took it. I was gassed (at the end)."

Autry's 162-yard game wasn't just his fifth straight 100-yard game. It was his fifth game in a row, which is to say all of his career starts, in which he gained at least 152 yards. Stunning numbers, but he wasn't about to crow.

"It's our offensive line and our defense," he said. "That's what those yards are a result of."

"He's got great vision," said Mallory. "He catches those creases. If there's a seam, he'll take it."

The dividend paid by the victory was obvious. NU was 3-1, its best start since 1963, when Ara Parseghian's last Wildcat team opened 4-1. And the Cats had copped a conference opener for the first time in three years.

What was less obvious was the degree of dominance NU established in the course of the game. The Wildcat defense scored another second-half shutout, its second in as many weeks. And the 24-point margin of victory was

Northwestern's largest in a conference game since 1975 in a 30-0 win over the Hoosiers.

"At halftime, we were really fortunate to be where we were, because we'd shot ourselves in the foot on offense, but we felt we had some answers and were sorta in control, and just had to come out and play the second half," Barnett figured.

He further believed that controlling the ball against the 21-mile-per-hour south wind in the third quarter was vital. The Wildcats opened the second half with a 17-play drive, and while it finished with only a field-goal for a 13-7 lead, it chewed up 7 minutes 56 seconds.

The Hoosiers were defeated, but not discouraged. Coming into the season, Mallory said he believed this would be one of his best teams since coming to Indiana in 1984. That attitude had rubbed off on his players.

"No one goes to the Rose Bowl undefeated," said linebacker Matt Surface.

In three victories, Northwestern's defense had stopped a passing/rollout attack (Notre Dame), the best wishbone offense in the country (Air Force), and, in Indiana, their own bread-and-butter rushing offense.

They had allowed, in 15 quarters of play, only 35 points. The other 23 of the 58 they'd allowed overall were scored by Miami in the final quarter of that fiasco. NU was on a pace to have its best defensive unit since 1970, when the 6-4 squad of Alex Agase allowed only 161 points.

The Wildcats, even with the offense having something of an off-day, had scored 30 points or more two games in a row, which hadn't happened since 1989. And they'd won those two games, which hadn't happened in 30-point-plus scoring efforts since 1962, when the Cats trampled South Carolina, Illinois and Minnesota in succession, scoring no less than 34 points in those three games.

That NU could win big on a day the offense wasn't great boded well for the future. Three wins in four games meant the Wildcats were halfway to the six triumphs needed for bowl-eligibility. Any of the Big Ten's five bowl hook-ups were within reach, if everything broke right, and there was always the chance for an at-large bid from the Liberty or Independence bowls if NU finished lower than fifth in the league.

In other words, it was time to dream a little bit. The dreams were enhanced by the result from the only other conference game on this day. At State College, Pennsylvania, Wisconsin surprised Penn State, handing the Nittany Lions a 17-9 loss. The Badgers snapped Penn State's 20-game winning streak, which meant the Badgers, Michigan and Northwestern were alone at the top of the Big Ten. The records were just 1-0, but a tie for first was something else Northwestern hadn't experienced in ages.

Indiana flanker Dorian Wilkerson tries to figure out what happened after Chris Martin, Eric Collier and associates assure an incomplete pass. (Peter Pawinski/ The Daily Northwestern)

INDIANA VS. NORTHWESTERN

Saturday, September 30, 1995 at Dyche Stadium, Evanston, IL
Weather: 79° Wind S 21 Partly sunny
Attendance: 29,223

SCORE BY QUARTERS	1	2	3	4	SCORE
Indiana (2-2-0)	0	7	0	0	7
Northwestern (3-1-0)	3	7	11	10	31

First Quarter
NU 0:01 Sam Valenzisi 40-yard field goal (6 plays, 12 yards, :57 TOP) — NU 3 IU 0

Second Quarter
IU 9:26 Chris Dittoe 2-yard run (Bill Manolopoulos kick)
(13 plays, 80 yards, 5:35 TOP) — NU 3 IU 7
NU 5:27 Darnell Autry 42-yard run (Sam Valenzisi kick)
(7 plays, 80 yards, 3:59 TOP) — NU 10 IU 7

Third Quarter
NU 7:04 Sam Valenzisi 34-yard field goal (17 plays, 64 yards, 7:56 TOP) — NU 13 IU 7
NU 4:24 Darnell Autry 6-yard run (Steve Schnur pass to Dave Beazley)
(1 play, 6 yards, :04 TOP) — NU 21 IU 1

Fourth Quarter
NU 9:06 Casey Dailey 43-yard fumble return (Sam Valenzisi kick) — NU 28 IU 7
NU 6:30 Sam Valenzisi 32-yard field goal (6 plays, 17 yards, 2:28 TOP) — NU 31 IU 7

TEAM STATISTICS	IU	NU
First Downs	20	14
Rushing	10	11
Passing	9	2
Penalty	1	1
Rushing Attempts	42	44
Yards Gained Rushing	207	213
Yards Lost Rushing	26	14
Net Yards Rushing	181	199
Net Yards Passing	194	45
Passes Attempted	37	14
Passes Completed	19	7
Had Intercepted	2	0
Total Offensive Plays	79	58
Total Net Yards	375	244
Average Gain per Play	4.7	4.2
Fumbles: Number-Lost	1-1	1-0
Penalties: Number-Yards	7-70	6-57
Interceptions: Number-Yards	0-0	2-12
Number of Punts-Yards	6-256	5-283
Average Per Punt	42.7	56.6
Punt Returns: Number-Yards	2-17	3-112
Kickoff Returns: Number-Yards	2-42	0-0
Possession Time	33:59	26:01
Third-Down Conversions	9-18	4-12
Fourth-Down Conversions	0-2	0-0
Sacks By: Number-Yards	1-10	3-24

Big Ten Standings

1. Michigan (1-0-0)
2. Northwestern (1-0-0)
3. Wisconsin (1-0-0)
4. Michigan State (0-0-1)
5. Purdue (0-0-1)
6. Ohio State (0-0-0)
7. Iowa (0-0-0)
8. Minnesota (0-0-0)
9. Penn State (0-0-0)
10. Indiana (0-0-1)
11. Illinois (0-0-1)

AP Top 25

1. Florida St.
2. Nebraska
3. Florida
4. Colorado
5. Ohio State
5. Southern Cal
7. Michigan
8. Texas A&M
9. Virginia
10. Tennessee
11. Auburn
12. Penn St.
13. Kansas St.
14. Oklahoma
15. Washington
16. Alabama
17. Oregon
18. Arkansas
19. Stanford
20. Texas
21. LSU
22. Wisconsin
23. Notre Dame
24. Kansas
25. **Northwestern**

Scores of interest

Iowa 59, New Mexico St. 21
Michigan 38, Miami-Ohio 19
Michigan St. 25, Boston Col. 21
Minnesota 55, Arkansas St. 7
Ohio St. 45, Notre Dame 26
Purdue 35, Ball St. 13
Wisconsin 17, Penn St. 9
Nebraska 35, Wash. St. 21
Florida 28, Mississippi 10
Oklahoma 17, Colorado 38
Virginia 35, Wake Forest 17
Tennessee 31, Oklahoma St. 0
Auburn 42, Kentucky 21
LSU 20, S. Carolina, 20
Kansas St. 44, N. Illinois 0
Maryland 3, Ga. Tech. 31

Darnell Autry gains some key yards before being tackled by a Wolverine. (Bob Kalmbach/The Wolverine)

Chapter 10
THE DEFENSE NEVER RESTED

> *"We plan on winning this football game."*
> —Gary Barnett to ESPN the night before playing Michigan

BEATING INDIANA not only moved Northwestern back into the No. 25 position in the Associated Press' weekly survey, it also set up the closest thing to a showdown the Wildcats had experienced in years. Nay, in decades.

On Saturday, October 7, the Wildcats would travel to Ann Arbor to take on No. 7 Michigan. Both teams were 1-0 in the Big Ten, along with Wisconsin. By the end of the day, barring a tie, either NU or U-M would still be on top of the league, with or without the Badgers.

This kind of thing hadn't happened at Northwestern in, well, nobody knew quite how long. In 1994, NU, at 3-3-1, had a big game against Illinois, was drilled, and then proceeded to lose its final three games as well.

That, though, didn't have first-place riding on it. This one did. In 1971, NU chased Ohio State, but never played in a game for the lead. It might not have happened since the 1962 Wildcat squad opened 6-0, with a 4-0 league mark. That team lost 37-6 to Wisconsin in the season's seventh week.

At the very least, this was new to the players. They hadn't been in this position before at NU.

And the game would be played not in cozy Dyche Stadium, where crowds had averaged 27,204 for the first three home games, but mammoth Michigan Stadium, a 102,501-seat edifice which ABC's Keith Jackson always liked to call the "biggest house in college football."

The Wildcats had already won a big game in one of the sport's grand venues, beating the Fighting Irish in Notre Dame Stadium on the first Saturday in September. Now, on the first Saturday in October, they'd be in another packed arena, taking on a heavily-favored foe. By game day, Michigan would be a 16-point favorite.

Small wonder. The Wolverines had owned the Wildcats, and in more ways than one, since the mid-1960s. In 1965, the Wildcats had snapped a three-game losing streak against the Wolverines with a 34-22 win at Ann Arbor. Since then, Michigan had won 18 in a row, extending its lead in the overall series to 44-11-1. Six of those 18 wins were shutouts. Four times, the Wolverines had scored at least 59 points against NU, a statistic legendary coach Fielding "Hurry Up" Yost, whose "point-a-minute" teams put U-M football into the forefront, would have loved. Yost's ghost may have been on the sideline next to Glenn "Bo" Schembechler in 1975, when the Wolverines teed off to the tune of 69-0, a day Michigan rushed for 573 yards to NU's 91. Three Wolverine backs, Harlan Huckleby, Rob

Lytle and Gordon Bell, all had 100 or more yards and two touchdowns apiece.

That was the game, it seemed, that was the grid equivalent of pulling the lever on the trap door. Northwestern had come into the game with a 3-2 record, but from that point forward, Wildcat football was in a free-fall. Loss piled upon loss, home crowds dwindled, and NU sold one home game back to Michigan, where the Wolverines were attracting over 100,000 to each home game. That allowed the Wildcats to take home nearly $300,000, rather than struggle to break even hosting Michigan before thousands of empty seats at Dyche.

It was longtime Michigan athletic director Don Canham, a promotional wizard on a collegiate par with Bill Veeck, who built Wolverines home games into a happening. Michigan Stadium's capacity was then 101,701, the team averaging about 85,000 in the early 1970s. Canham saw the 16,000 empty seats as an opportunity. He stepped up advertising, and, on November 8, 1975, was rewarded when the Purdue game drew 102,415 spectators. It was the first six-figure crowd in a string that would reach 126 when the Wildcats came calling.

Far from being intimidated by the throng, it was what NU's players wanted to see. Dyche Stadium, as a football field, was fine since the resurfacing prior to the 1994 season. The locker room was good enough for game day. What it didn't have was atmosphere, something that could only be created by a full house. The Cats wanted that, wanted attention paid to what they had accomplished so far.

"There'll be a lot of fans there, so we won't have to worry about that," figured defensive end Casey Dailey.

"It's a big stadium and the kids like to play in front of big crowds," said head coach Gary Barnett. "And that's about as big as it gets. There are three or four places that are revered in college football, and you get the chance to play in one."

The other side of the bargain was having to play the Wolverines. Michigan was 5-0, including the conference-opening whipping of Illinois by a 38-14 score. Under interim head coach Lloyd Carr, the Wolverines had managed to quickly establish themselves as a typical Michigan team.

The turmoil of the summer brought on by the fast, almost hasty, firing of Gary Moeller, who had been arrested for public drunkenness at an area bar, had passed. The elevation of Carr, who had been an assistant for 15 years, most recently as defensive coordinator, calmed the waters. So, of course, did the unbeaten start.

The Wolverines had narrowly escaped Virginia in their opener, taking the on-campus "Pigskin Classic" with a last-second 18-17 win. The rout of Illinois followed, and since then, Michigan had hardly been challenged.

Two of the reasons were at wide receiver. Seniors Mercury Hayes and Amani Toomer each had the gift of speed and the ability to hang on to the ball. Having to defend against one of them was trouble enough. With both of them out there, zone coverage became a difficult task. Man-to-man coverage could get the job done, if the defenders were good enough. If they weren't, well, ask Virginia. For Northwestern, the task fell into the hands of Rodney Ray and Chris Martin.

Then there was tight end Jay Riemersma. He, too, was a legitimate target.

That's why the Wolverines, even with junior tailback Tshimanga Biakabutuka in their backfield, were gaining more yards through the air than on the ground.

Barnett knew what he was in for.

"This week is, without question, one of my greatest challenges in coaching," he said the Monday before the game. "This is probably the best defense I've seen in the Big Ten. They're very physical. The nose guard (Jason Horn) has eight sacks. The turnovers they've produced have created a very short field for the offense."

Horn, clearly, was Michigan's bell cow. As he went, so went the Wolverines. And, usually, he went after the ball. Thirteen of his 33 tackles were in the opposing backfield. He'd also broken up a pair of passes.

In Northwestern, Horn and Co. would be facing a one-back offense with a passing game that was sub-par against Indiana, but still managed to put 30 points on the scoreboard. Carr knew who he had to worry about.

"You have to stop (Darnell) Autry if you're going to stop Northwestern," he said.

That wasn't far off. Through four games, Autry had scored five of NU's 10 touchdowns, four on the ground and one on a reception of a

Darnell Autry continues his string of 100-yard games, gaining 103 against a tough Michigan defense. (Bob Kalmbach/ The Wolverine)

Steve Schnur pass, and had rushed for 664 yards. His worst game, against Miami, still was a 152-yard day, and even including that game, he'd dashed for 504 yards in the last three outings. He'd broken that obscure school mark, 491 by Mike Adamle in 1970, over the course of the first three games (502 yards), and had expanded it by rushing for 162 yards against Indiana, as opposed to 160 against Notre Dame.

All Carr knew was that he had to stop Autry somehow, someway.

At the same time, Michigan had come down with a very mild case of Redskinitis the week before. The Wolverines led Miami of Ohio 31-0 at the half, then dozed off for a time, only to awaken to post a 38-19 win.

"We turned the ball over too much," said Carr. "Our defense started missing tackles. Was it fatigue? Was it concentration? We've got to find out.

"(Northwestern) should be 4-0 instead of 3-1. Their loss to Miami is similar to what happened to us last Saturday."

Not that similar. A win doesn't resemble a loss in any way, shape or form.

Carr would find out with certainty by midafternoon. It was by then that the Wildcats had beaten the Wolverines 19-13, using four field-goals from Sam Valenzisi and a touchdown pass from Schnur to fullback Matt Hartl to get the job done on offense, and a bundle of big plays to get the job done on defense.

It was Northwestern's first win in Michigan Stadium since 1959, but more than that, it gave legitimacy to the argument, heard with deaf ears by many, that the Wildcats were a real football team, not an outfit which benefited from a fluke outcome against Notre Dame.

Here was a team that was now 4-1 overall, 2-0 in the Big Ten, and with wins over both the Wolverines and the Fighting Irish in the span of a month, and both of them coming on the road, at that.

Here was a team that also barely escaped in Ann Arbor. The six-point margin of victory was three times that of the 17-15 win at Notre Dame, but things could have been much, much different.

Consider the effort of Biakabutuka. He ran for a career-high 205 yards, including a 47-yard scoot on the final play of the first quarter, but never got into the end zone.

Actually, he did get there. Biakabutuka crossed the goal-line once, doing so after breaking two tackles midway through the second quarter. His 23-yard blast two plays after U-

M's Thomas Mondry recovered Dave Beazley's muffed kickoff return appeared to give Michigan a two-touchdown lead.

It didn't, because while Biakabutuka was slamming off left tackle, Riemersma was making it possible by holding NU linebacker Danny Sutter. The hold was detected, a flag flew, and the touchdown that could have put the game out of reach was instead called back.

That was break No. 1, coming as it did about a minute after Michigan quarterback Brian Griese scored on a 3-yard bootleg to the right, capping a 10-play drive. Replays on ESPN showed Griese's knee was down before he tumbled into the end zone, but the call was touchdown, and that was that. The score snapped a 6-all tie.

A follow-up score by Biakabutuka two plays after Beazley failed to grab the kickoff and hold on might have drowned the Wildcats' hopes. Instead, Riemersma's penalty started to turn the tide. Two plays later, Remy Hamilton lined up a 37-yard field-goal attempts from the left hashmark, and kicked it left.

The miss was break No. 2. Northwestern, whose offense had gone three plays and out on four on its seven drive, still trailed by just a touchdown, rather than 10 or 14 points.

To this point, most of the offense had been Valenzisi, who had kicked two 29-yard field goals in the second quarter, the first set up by a trio of completions by backup quarterback Chris Hamdorf, who came in when Schnur was popped by the firm of Jason Horn, Trent Zenkewicz and Rasheed Simmons.

"To come in out of the bullpen like that, hit 3-for-4, and run our club down there like he did under the circumstances is a real tribute to (quarterbacks coach) Craig Johnson and Chris' awareness and preparation," Barnett said.

Valenzisi's second 29-yarder came about when Toomer muffed a punt return with 31 seconds left in the half. Chris Martin, a stalwart all day, glommed onto the football, and after Schnur, back to health, hit Darnell Autry over the middle on an 11-yard completion to the Wolverine 11, the stage was set for Valenzisi's second kick. It tied the game at 6-all with a second to go in the half.

A third Valenzisi field-goal (and his NU-record 10th straight over five games), from 32 yards to cap a 65-yard drive, brought Northwestern within 13-9.

The defense, though, would have to come up big for the hang-tough Wildcats to go ahead. After an exchange of punts, that's precisely what happened.

The momentum began to swing on the second play of the fourth quarter. An overcast day that had featured a spot of sunshine at times

The Wildcat defense, including Rodney Ray (15), Danny Sutter (50), Don Holmes (53), and Mike Warren (68), gets fired up. (Scott Strazzante/Daily Southtown)

had turned gloomy. It had started to rain. Michigan had the ball at its 27.

Griese, in his second career start with Scott Dreisbach injured, dropped back and looked to his right. He spotted Toomer, open in the right flat. But as he threw, he slipped a bit. The ball sailed. Toomer, trying to adjust, slipped and fell on the wet grass. And Eric Collier, reading the play all the way, intercepted the pass at the Michigan 35.

Ranging to his right, he found enough running room to advance his pickoff to the Wolverine 31 before running out of bounds.

For the second time, Northwestern would start a drive deep in Michigan territory. The first occasion resulted in Valenzisi's end-of-half field goal. They needed more than field goals to beat Michigan.

They needed something fancy, and offensive coordinator Greg Meyer called for something fancy. Schnur took the snap and lateraled back to the left, where wide receiver D'Wayne Bates was waiting. The Michigan secondary was about to learn that Bates was a quarterback in high school. He threw a perfect strike to tight end Darren Drexler, ignored by the defense, a 26-yard gain that put the ball on the Wolverine 5. After two runs by Autry netted three yards against the stout Michigan defensive line, Schnur looked for a receiver, and found Hartl, the fullback who had looped out of the backfield. Three yards deep in the right side of the end zone, he caught Schnur's 2-yard pass as he fell.

After Valenzisi's extra-point kick, Northwestern led 16-13 with 12:42 to play.

Michigan began to drive again. A run by Biakabutuka brought the ball into Wildcat territory. It was third-and-6 at the NU 46 with just under 11 minutes left when Griese looked for his receivers and saw, instead, the large and angry form of Pat Fitzgerald coming his way. Fitzgerald sacked Griese and forced the football loose. Hudhaifa Ismaeli, right behind Fitzgerald, grabbed the ball on the Wolverine 48. The Wildcats had another turnover.

Six plays later, they had another three points. A 46-yard completion from Schnur to Bates on a post route moved the ball to the U-M 6, but, with the going heavy, Valenzisi was called on to connect on a 22-yard field-goal. That was automatic, and, with 8:42 left, the Wildcats led by six.

The score would stay that way, even though Michigan had the ball for 5:50 down the stretch. The Wolverines' first sortie ended with a punt after three plays lost two yards, but their second series was extremely effective.

For one thing, Biakabutuka was on the loose again. He gamboled for 17 yards on a draw play that moved the ball near midfield. After a penalty, a pair of handoffs to freshman Clarence Williams, spelling the tired Biakabutuka, garnered 13 more. The big guy came back in, picked up nine more yards on two plays, after Griese snuck for a yard on third-and-1, Michigan was sitting pretty, on the NU 34 with well over two minutes left.

In its opener, Michigan had trailed Virginia by 17 points with 12:55 left and came back to win as tie expired. Even though it was Dreisbach who had found Mercury Hayes from 15 yards out on that occasion, rather than Griese, surely the Wolverines could draw on that experience now.

Aside from the Northwestern players, coaches and fans, there were 104,642 people in Michigan Stadium—the largest crowd to ever see the Wildcats in person—who figured as much. Most of those watching on ESPN probably thought so too.

Instead, things went haywire for Michigan. NU defensive coordinator Ron Vanderlinden, knowing that his secondary had corralled Hayes and Toomer all day, ordered a series of blitzes to put the heat on Griese.

On first down from the Wildcat 34, Griese looked for Toomer in the right side of the end zone. Only a perfect throw would have dropped into Toomer's hands, so well was 5-foot-8 Chris Martin shadowing his 6-foot-4 adversary.

On second down, Biakabutuka got the call, and lost the ball. Tackle Jon Runyan fell on it to keep Michigan's hopes alive. There was 1:40 left, and Michigan called time.

Griese would go back to the air on third-and-15 from the NU 39. Thanks to Fitzgerald, who came up the gut almost unchallenged, he couldn't find anybody, and had to throw the ball away.

Now it was fourth down. Griese needed a completion at or deeper than the Wildcat 24 to keep the drive alive. NU blitzed again, Fitzgerald, who had 14 tackles and too many hurries for Griese's tastes, once more coming to visit like a madman. Griese saw Hayes, and fired. William Bennett stepped in front of Hayes, intercepting the ball as he hit the turf.

There were 90 seconds left. Northwestern was a series of snaps away from an even bigger upset, in many ways, than the win at Notre Dame.

To this point, Autry only had 75 yards rushing. Michigan had done the job on him. But the string of 100-yard games wouldn't die. Rather than just kneel down on second down, Schnur handed off to Autry, and, using his blockers, he'd rumble around left end for 28 yards and a total of 103 on the day.

Only then did Schnur run out the clock on Northwestern's first win in Michigan Stadium since the Eisenhower Administration.

Once again, as at Notre Dame, the Wildcats celebrated stylishly. They didn't raise Barnett up on their shoulders. They didn't douse him with Gatorade. They just danced around, helmets held high, accepting the plaudits of what few NU fans were on hand, and a warm hand from the Michigan faithful, who know a fine effort when they see one.

"That was a very classy group of people in the stands, and everybody we ran into with the Michigan program," Barnett would say upon reflection.

"As we left on the busses, their fans were tipping their hats to our players."

It was a long way to the bus, however. At midfield, Barnett was grabbed by ESPN sideline reporter Adrian Karsten, who played for Northwestern from 1979-81. Barnett was a little emotional in the seconds after beating Notre Dame when NBC's John Dockery interviewed him, but this time, Barnett's voice was on the verge of breaking.

"Our kids, all week, they just practiced like I thought we were gonna win the game," said Barnett. "What an effort by our defense and our secondary to play those receivers the way we did."

Griese aimed 20 of his 34 passes at Toomer and Hayes. They caught six of them.

Hayes caught four, worth 43 yards, dropped two, and saw the six other passes directed his way go otherwise incomplete, with one of them tipped and another intercepted.

Toomer grabbed two of the eight balls aimed his way. Two of the six incompletions were batted away, another picked off.

"Early in the game, Chris (Martin) and I discussed pressing their receivers," said Ray, a fifth-year senior. "We wanted to find out the type of speed they had and what type of release they'd use to get off the press. After the first time, we came back to each other and said, 'We think we can handle them.'

"See, we've got great receivers. We face them every day (in practice), so we're prepared for any receivers we face."

Martin had been starting at cornerback since his sophomore season, after switching from wide receiver during spring practice. Now a senior, there wasn't anything he hadn't seen in the secondary.

Ray had also started the previous two seasons, though his road was rougher. He'd been suspended for the 1993 game against Iowa, thanks to getting into a scrap the previous week at Michigan State. And that was triggered, to some degree, by the many losses.

"Things just got out of control," Ray remembered two years later. "It was a good learning experience. I learned a lot from it."

Ray was a running back at Florissant McCluer High School in Ferguson, Missouri, and played the same position his freshman year at NU, Francis Peay's last as head coach. When Gary Barnett opened his first training camp, Ray was penned in as the starting tailback.

Alas, a dislocated shoulder suffered in camp did more than knock him out for the season. It threatened his career. Nerve damage left his arm paralyzed for a week.

"They told me I would never play again, but God brought me through that," he said. "So I came back and they asked me to play defensive back. I'd never played defense. I always thought I was a running back."

Saying he "still had the heart of a runner," Ray tried the position in the spring of 1993, and even though he dislocated the shoulder again in the fall, played through the season wearing a shoulder harness.

"It was more competitive to me, because I was out there on my island, by myself. If I get beat, then it's a touchdown. I started liking that. I felt I could show my ability out there. I loved one-on-one."

Adrian Autry (32), Chad Pugh (77), and Steve Schnur celebrate a good play. (Scott Strazzante/ Daily Southtown)

It was defensive backs coach Jerry Brown who molded Ray into a corner who would be able to match up against a Toomer or a Hayes and hold his own.

Griese's most effective receiver all day was Riemersma, who caught five of the six passes directed toward him. Overall, Griese's 14-of-34, 96-yard performance was not what the Wolverines needed.

"They came with some blitzes and got some pressure on us, and that resulted in some turnovers," Griese said softly. "They didn't do anything that confused us. We just didn't get the job done."

Schnur, who outplayed Griese and also outstatted him (11-of-23, 126 yards, with the touchdown pass to Hartl), was delighted.

"This win is huge for our program," he said. "We believe in ourselves more every win we get. We have a confidence about us."

Somebody brought up the "M" word. And he didn't mean Michigan. He meant Miami.

"We all learned our lesson from that," said Schnur. "It's a shame it had to happen."

Then somebody mentioned the "R" word. Rose Bowl.

"We've been thinking about that all year," he said.

Then, perhaps worried about jinxing himself, he backed up a bit. After all, there were six conference games remaining, and a myriad of possibilities.

"You've got to take them one at a time," Schnur said, pulling out sports' most worn cliche. "That (the Rose Bowl) is one of our goals."

Obviously, Northwestern already had established a team chemistry (goal No. 1) and had proved itself relentless (goal No. 2). Goal No. 3 was a winning season. At 4-1, they were two-thirds of the way to that one.

"This is a special group of kids," said Barnett. "It was just a great team win. It's a heck of a way to get to 4-1, beating Michigan and Notre Dame, both away.

"I dream about those things, but it's hard to pull those things off."

Because it was a conference win, because Barnett had worked for Bill McCartney, who had worked for Schembechler as an assistant, Barnett ranked beating Michigan ahead of beating Notre Dame. The Wildcats hadn't beaten both schools in the same year since 1959.

What it did was move Northwestern to 2-0 in the league, a half-game ahead of Iowa, Minnesota, Wisconsin and Ohio State, which saddled Penn State with its second straight loss. That quartet was 1-0. Eventually, the off-weeks would all balance out, but for the moment, Northwestern's long-suffering fans could point to the newspaper and say the Wildcats were on top of the Big Ten.

By Sunday, they could also say the Wildcats were the No. 14 team in college football. Just as 5-0 Kansas jumped from 24th to 10th in the Associated Press poll on the strength of its 40-24 whipping of previously undefeated Colorado at Boulder, Northwestern moved up 11 places by beating the Wolverines.

For NU, this was relatively uncharted water. The Wildcats, a regular tenant of the Bottom Ten for ages, hadn't been ranked this high in the AP rankings since, ah, er, well, nobody knew.

"I think anybody could look at the first game and say, 'Anybody could upset anybody on any given Saturday,' but I don't know about two," said Barnett. "We've got to be fairly legitimate. As long as we keep playing hard, playing every play and playing together with the kind of chemistry we've got right now, we're going to have a chance to be in every game.

"As someone said to me the other day, 'You're playing with the big boys,' and I said, No, we are the big boys, and now we're playing like the big boys.'

"I think that's what it is. We're in the Big Ten conference, arguably the best conference. We're one of the 11 teams, and now, we're playing very representative of that conference."

The legitimacy of the win at Michigan, of course, was derived from the effort expended.

"I don't think I've seen a secondary play better than the five guys that played in our secondary on Saturday," said Barnett, referring to Ismaeli, Collier, Martin, Bennett and Ray. The longest pass Griese completed was a 13-yarder to Hayes. So much for deep threats.

At the same time, the Big Ten picked Fitzgerald as the defensive player of the week for the second time in three weeks, and tabbed Valenzisi as the special teams star for the second week in succession.

"I'd been waiting to play against Michigan all my life," said Valenzisi, who grew up in Westlake, Ohio as a die-hard Ohio State fan. "I'd been waiting so long to play there. It was hard for me the whole week to keep my enthusiasm in check. I didn't want to get too pumped up for the game.

"When you play a good team like Michigan, somebody's got to be the difference. A lot of guys who said they we're gonna step up, so I figured I should throw my hat in the ring too. And this is the Big Ten. There's a certain aura about playing Michigan. Anybody who plays football in the Big Ten will tell you that. Everybody's big game is against the Wolverines.

"If we were going to have people take us seriously, we needed to play well against them."

Obviously, Valenzisi did. His four field-goals tied the school mark he had established two years earlier in a 28-26 loss to Minnesota.

Barnett went way back to the second quarter, when Michigan held a 3-0 lead, in remembering a critical juncture. It came on the Wolverines' third possession, one that featured Biakabutuka's 47-yard run, one that would have been a touchdown had not Ray dragged him down at the NU 14.

The Wildcat defense stiffened near the goal-line. Biakabatuka was stopped for no gain on first-and-goal at the 2 when Danny Sutter led a defensive charge, then lost a yard when a run to the left was met by Fitzgerald and Collier. Griese's third-and-goal pass to Toomer in the left side of the end zone was batted down by Martin, forcing the Wolverines to accept a 21-yard field goal by Hamilton. It gave Michigan a 6-0 lead, but kept four more points off the board.

"The goal-line stand was a terrific display of teamwork and coaching at a critical time," Barnett said. "We were really able to tighten things up once they got in the red zone."

Actually, the Wildcats stopped the Wolverines further out. Michigan drove to Northwestern's 20 or deeper on just three of the 12 occasions it had the ball, collecting a field-goal and touchdown. The other field-goal, Hamilton's first, came when Michigan's drive stalled at the NU 24.

Barnett said in his Monday briefing that he wouldn't hesitate to put Hamdorf in at quarterback again, if an injury to Schnur made it necessary, but that junior Tim Hughes, who had been expected to back up, would not see action this year.

"During the Indiana game, I went to Tim Hughes, and said, 'I'm going to play another quarterback here, and you would be the quarterback to play,'" Barnett explained. "'If you redshirt this year, you'll have two years to play. If it were my decision, that's what I'd do with you, but I want you to make this decision.'

"He said, 'I appreciate it. Let me think about it.' So we put Chris in (against Indiana) and Tim came to me Sunday (before Michigan) and said, 'I agree, I want to be redshirted.'"

Five games into the 1995 season, it was obvious Northwestern had come quite a distance under Barnett. A football team than once struggled to find depth at any position now could afford to redshirt quarterbacks in midseason.

The Cats hadn't come far enough for Barnett to follow in Schnur's footsteps and begin to talk about bowl possibilities, though.

"We don't talk about it," Barnett said. "I think, because of what we learned in the Miami game. You just can't do that. It's like letting water into a crack in a rock. If it freezes, it'll break that rock up. We're going to seal their brains somehow, hermetically seal 'em from that kind of stuff. Put earmuffs on the guys."

Good luck.

"When you're in the middle of it, you don't want to screw it up," Barnett explained. "And we're in the middle of it. I don't want to screw it up. So pardon me if I'm sort of narrow-minded right now."

The Wildcat defense sacks Michigan quarterback, Brian Griese, in the 19-13 win over the Wolverines. (Bob Kalmbach/The Wolverine)

NORTHWESTERN VS. MICHIGAN

Saturday, October 7, 1995 at Michigan Stadium, Ann Arbor, MI
Weather: 57° Wind: WNW 15-25 Cloudy with occasional rain
Attendance: 104,642

SCORE BY QUARTERS	1	2	3	4	SCORE
Michigan (4-1-0)	3	3	7	0	13
Northwestern (3-1-0)	0	6	3	10	19

First Quarter
UM 9:33 Remy Hamilton 40-yard field goal (14 plays, 52 yards, 5:27 TOP) UM 3 NU 0

Second Quarter
UM 12:43 Remy Hamilton 21-yard field goal (8 plays, 58 yards, 2:47 TOP) 6 0
NU 4:15 Sam Valenzisi 29-yard field goal (11 plays, 68 yards, 3:58 TOP) 6 3
NU 0:01 Sam Valenzisi 28-yard field goal (18 plays, 4 yards, 0:30 TOP) 6 6

Third Quarter
UM 8:02 Brian Griese 3-yard run (Remy Hamilton kick)
          (10 plays, 80 yards, 4:50 TOP) 13 6
NU 3:48 Sam Valenzisi 32-yard field goal (11 plays, 65 yards, 3:17 TOP) 13 9

Fourth Quarter
NU 12:42 Matt Hartl 2-yard pass from Steve Schnur (Sam Valenzisi kick)
           (4 plays, 31 yards, 1:54 TOP) 13 16
NU 8:42 Sam Valenzisi 22-yard field goal (6 plays, 44 yards, 2:02 TOP) 13 19

TEAM STATISTICS	UM	NU
First Downs	19	13
Rushing	13	4
Passing	6	9
Penalty	0	0
Rushing Attempts	46	32
Yards Gained Rushing	270	118
Yards Lost Rushing	20	18
Net Yards Rushing	250	100
Net Yards Passing	96	210
Passes Attempted	34	28
Passes Completed	14	15
Had Intercepted	2	0
Total Offensive Plays	80	60
Total Net Yards	375	244
Average Gain per Play	4.7	4.2
Fumbles: Number-Lost	4-2	2-1
Penalties: Number-Yards	6-41	5-35
Interceptions: Number-Yards	0-0	2-4
Number of Punts-Yards	4-164	7-288
Average Per Punt	41.0	41.1
Punt Returns: Number-Yards	2-9	2-11
Kickoff Returns: Number-Yards	5-103	4-65
Possession Time	33:38	26:22
Third-Down Conversions	7	3
Sacks By: Number-Yards	1-6	0-0

Big Ten Standings

1. Northwestern (2-0-0)
2. Ohio State (1-0-0)
3. Iowa (1-0-0)
4. Minnesota (1-0-0)
5. Wisconsin (1-0-0)
6. Michigan (1-1-0)
7. Illinois (1-1-0)
8. Purdue (0-1-1)
9. Michigan State (0-1-1)
10. Penn State (0-2-0)
11. Indiana (0-2-0)

AP Top 25

1. Florida St.
2. Nebraska
3. Florida
4. Ohio State
5. Southern Cal
6. Tennessee
7. Auburn
8. Kansas St.
9. Colorado
10. Kansas
11. Michigan
12. Alabama
13. Oklahoma
14. Northwestern
15. Oregon
16. Stanford
17. Notre Dame
18. Texas
19. Virginia
20. Penn St.
21. Wisconsin
22. Texas A&M
23. Iowa
24. Washington
25. Texas Tech

Scores of interest

Ohio State 28, Penn State 25
Florida State 41, Miami 17
Florida 28, LSU 10
Colorado 40, Kansas 24
USC 26, California 16
Texas A&M 7, Texas Tech. 14
Virginia 17, N. Carolina 22
Tennessee 49, Arkansas 31
Kansas St. 30, Missouri 0
Oklahoma 39, Iowa St. 26
Notre Dame 29, Washington 21
Stanford 20, Arizona St. 28
Texas 37, Rice 13

Northwestern's first 3-game winning streak in over 20 years was largely due to the talents of #24 Darnell Autry. (Scott Strazzante/Daily Southtown)

Chapter 11
FOOTSTEPS IN THE NIGHT

"We may not be real pretty, but we're sort of alley cats."

—Gary Barnett

WITH A THREE-GAME winning streak for the first time since 1971, with a 4-1 record for the first time since 1963, Northwestern should have felt confident about its September 14 game at Minnesota.

Yes, the Golden Gophers were 3-1, their best start in a season since 1989, and had opened Big Ten play with a madcap 39-38 win over Purdue.

Yes, they had a fine runner in Chris Darkins, a senior who ran for a school-record 294 yards on 38 carries against the Boilermakers, scoring three touchdowns along the way.

Yes, Minnesota was 3-0 in the Hubert H. Humphrey Metrodome, site of the game.

However, Minnesota wasn't ranked 14th in the country, like Northwestern. It wasn't 2-0 in the Big Ten, like Northwestern. Most of all, as the Purdue game proved, it didn't have a defense like Northwestern's.

So was NU head coach Gary Barnett worried? Of course he was worried. Coaches worry when they lose, and worry more when they win, because more is on the line.

He worried about Darkins, the 6-foot-1, 215-pounder from Houston whose big night against Purdue moved him into seventh in the Division I-A rushing stats, two places below Darnell Autry.

"Darkins is a great player," Barnett would say in previewing the game. "He's really learned patience. A year ago, he would just run. Now, he uses his blocker, makes the appropriate cuts. He's turned himself into a very, very fine football player.

"Their offensive scheme is very similar to Michigan's. Against Minnesota, you've got to have two different defensive plans, because they can run with Darkins, but they can also pass, and when the do, they empty their backfield, giving them five receivers. It creates some problems trying to prepare for it, and they know that. That's why they do it."

In 1994, Darkins ran for 110 yards on 37 carries, but Northwestern posted a 37-31 victory.

Barnett was worried about the numbers Minnesota had posted.

"I looked at the national stats, and Minnesota was in the top 25 in 11 categories," he said. "Michigan was in the top 25 in only six categories."

So?

"So this is a very, very hot football team we're facing," Barnett said.

And he was worried about the game time. Minnesota, since moving into the Metrodome a decade earlier, had played most of its home games at 6 p.m. This was no exception. It provided Minnesota with television exposure (and the Wildcats' surge prompted SportsChannel to pick up the game locally, for live pickup on its Plus channel and a taped showing on the regular outlet), and upset the routine of the opposition. Teams used to playing at 1 p.m., as Big Ten teams did before TV networks juggled game times to suit their fancy, had to wait five more hours for the kickoff. Rather than getting up, having breakfast and a team meeting before hopping a bus for the game, teams would loll around the hotel for hours, trying to kill time. Often, that would dampen the fervor to play at a high level.

Most of all, given the magnitude of the win at Michigan, he was worried about a letdown. And the Gophers, if Darkins kept running wild, were a team that could spring a surprise.

Darnell Autry (#24) on his way to his seventh consecutive 100-yard plus game against Minnesota. (Scott Strazzante/Daily Southtown)

Minnesota head coach Jim Wacker had some numbers of his own to furrow his brow. Northwestern's numbers.

"They're leading the Big Ten in the most important statistics there are, and that's pass defense and scoring defense," said Wacker.

And in one more: turnover margin. The Wildcats, minus-11 the season before, went into the game plus-9 in turnovers, with 13 takeaways and four giveaways, and had turned 11 of the 13 takeaways into points.

One of the reasons NU had been so successful in converting the turnovers into scores was Autry. Through five games, he'd gained 767 yards, and was seriously threatening the NU single-season rushing record of 1,291 yards, set by Bob Christian in 1989. While the 103-yard output against Michigan was Autry's lowest total of the year, it extended his 100-yard game string to six games, starting with the finale against Penn State in 1994.

That was Autry's first start, and it came about because Dennis Lundy, who had started the previous 14 games at tailback, and had 26 starts over three seasons, was suspended before the game. It wasn't for weeks that the nature of the suspension—gambling—was announced. All Autry knew was that he'd be opening against Penn State in Happy Valley.

"I had some mixed emotions," he said. "I was happy I was going to get my opportunity to start, but I was obviously upset. He was a good player. He taught me a lot. You hate to feel good about someone else's misfortunes. But it happened, and I had to step up and do the job."

He'd gained 385 yards in spot duty before that, including a 100-yard effort in mop-up duty against the Gophers at midseason, and had also excelled at kickoff returns. But the 171-yard day against the Nittany Lions opened eyes around the Big Ten.

It wasn't long after the Penn State game that Autry, tired of the freshman grind, told Barnett that he was going to leave Northwestern. Not that he was thinking of transferring. That he was going to bolt and go to Arizona State, back in his hometown of Tempe, Arizona, never mind that ASU coach Bruce Snyder told him when Autry called that first he had to get a release from Barnett.

And the reason behind Autry's decision?

"I was homesick, that's all. Nothing to do with anything here," Autry explained. "I'd like to think it was, 'Oh, the weather's horrible' or 'My roommate's a jerk,' and it wasn't any of that.

"During my freshman year, I was really not thinking too straight. I wanted all the old (high school) stuff back. But you've just got to grow up sometimes, be a man about it."

Barnett, naturally refusing to grant the release, said he took Autry's decision "with a bottle of Maalox." Then he set about trying to explain that he wasn't the first freshman to feel the pressures of school.

"The freshman football player has absolutely no life," Barnett said. "His only life is practice and classes. The first 90 days of college is no fun."

Not even for Harrington Darnell Autry, born into a U.S. Air Force family stationed in Weisbaden, Germany. It took plenty of convincing to keep Autry, who chose NU over ASU, UCLA, Colorado and Syracuse because of the school's unparalleled theater program, in Evanston.

Suddenly, Autry had forgotten Barnett's original pitch to him the previous year.

"You can go to a school that's been good for a long time, and they can pretty much probably win without you," Autry recalled Barnett saying. Or you can go to a school where you can make your own path, and be as important to this school as building a foundation.

"That's what I bought into, and I believed it," he said. "I had a lot of faith in it. He's also a player's coach. He came to my house and he wasn't all uptight. I'd met a couple of coaches, and they were kinda like real businesslike. He seemed laid back. He wanted to know about me and my family."

All that was forgotten in the winter of 1994-'95. Autry was looking at airline schedules to Phoenix.

"I'm outta here, I'm gone," Autry remembered telling people.

"But people like Rob Johnson told me he loved me, wanted me to be here. And he told me I was making a big mistake, the biggest mistake of my life."

His parents said the same thing. Barnett's thoughts were along the same line. Autry listened and decided that leaving was not a risk worth taking.

"It was cured this summer, whether or not we'd have won or not," said Autry. "I know now what my role is. I'm doing this for me, having fun for me. I hurt myself a lot my freshman year, closed myself down to a lot of things."

Rather than run from Northwestern, he'd run for Northwestern. Along with the theater major he wanted, only NU recruited him as a tailback. The other four schools recruited him as a safety, though, at 5-foot-11, 212 pounds and with 4.4 speed, why they were thinking he couldn't be a major-league running back is unclear.

Just as he had learned in the winter of his freshman year that transferring wouldn't be the smartest thing in the world, he was learning as a sophomore how to run in college.

"He'd be the first to tell you he should have scored on a long (46-yard) run against Air Force if he'd carried the ball in his proper arm," said Barnett. "He made a couple misreads, didn't follow blocking schemes.

"He's an intuitive, instinctive player. One day he'll misread a play and run for a touchdown, and I'll say, 'Great instinct.'"

Among other things, Barnett, careful to not overcompliment his star player to preserve the team-first atmosphere that had been fostered, had been won over by Autry's enthusiasm.

"Darnell brings an excitement to a huddle that's different than anybody I've been around other than Eric Bieniemy," he said. "You just want to play for Darnell, and that's a real credit to his personality and his upbringing."

"I'd drink molten lava for Darnell," said guard Ryan Padgett, not at all bashful about lavishing praise. "He'll break three or four tackles if he has to. We just like watching him once he gets into the open field. We'll put our money on him against the DB any day. He really sets up your blocks."

In other words, uses the block and then slashes past the defender. In contrast, Dennis Lundy, whom Autry backed up in 1994, crashed through and over the line.

"If (Dennis) didn't see a hole, he'd just run up your back," said Padgett. "Darnell will juke one way, so your guy goes, then you can just keep him going, and Darnell will cut it back."

Autry figures that any break would lead to an opening, both in football and in acting.

"I'll take anything," he said of a possible

Hollywood career. "I'll be the first guy to die in a horror movie, I don't care. In the background, behind the credits, it doesn't matter. You've got to start somewhere.

"I've got tons of goals in my life. This is a stepping stone along the way. I'm close to the goals I have in college, but not close to the goals I have in life. I know football's not my life. I have a lot of important things to do."

Autry's football skills would be on display in the Metrodome. It would be Autry vs. Darkins.

Mostly, it would be Autry.

It would be Autry left.

It would be Autry right.

It would be Autry up the middle.

It would be Autry 28 times, Autry for 169 yards, Autry for three touchdowns as Northwestern, 2½-point favorite, erased an 11-point deficit to post a 27-17 prime-time win over the Gophers before 50,504 fans under the Teflon roof in Minneapolis.

As far as the Gophers were concerned, Autry was already starring in a horror story. Call it "Footsteps in the Night," or (as they used to say in those Rocky and Bullwinkle cartoons), "The Man Who Ruined Homecoming."

"It was as big a win as we could have had this year, based on the circumstances," said Barnett. "It was very special to our program. One of the hardest jobs that a coach has is coming off a huge win like that, and still getting his players down to earth and refocused, and for the players to get themselves down to earth and refocused."

In one way, the game made a believer out of Barnett.

"For the first time, watching our team, we had the same kind of speed, the same kind of size, the same kind of everything that anybody else has in this league," he said. "I just thought we executed some things very well. I was impressed with the sharpness of our team."

Maybe it was the lights in the Metrodome. To casual observers, NU had looked really good against Notre Dame, and even better against Michigan the week before. But it was overcast at Ann Arbor.

Autry scored on an 18-yard run in the second quarter, following which a pass from Steve Schnur to D'Wayne Bates tied the game 14-all. He scored on an 11-yard run in the third quarter that moved NU ahead 21-14. And, last but not least, he took off on a career-long 73 yard flight, an odyssey which culminated in a crash into the right side of the end zone along with defender Rodney Heath.

"I was trying to be as patient as I could," said Autry, who raised his season touchdown total to eight, seven on the ground. "The front guys just took care of business, and I just followed them."

Autry's running took care of the offense, along with Schnur's more than respectable total of 190 air yards on 13-of-23 passing. And the defense did what it had done for all but one of the season's first 20 quarters. It forced turnovers. Two of Minnesota's three giveaways turned into 10 Northwestern points.

"We made stupid mental errors," said Gopher quarterback Cory Sauter. "That's what kills you."

Sauter found out firsthand how Northwestern's defense could tighten its grip as the game proceeded. He was untouched in the first half, and sacked a half-dozen times in the second half.

"We saw them emptying their backfield in the second half," said inside linebacker Tim Scharf. "To us, that was a sign that we'd pretty much stopped Darkins and they were going to go to the pass."

"We felt our defense had them under control right at the end of the first half," said Barnett. "On offense we felt there were some ways we wanted to move the ball. We kept bouncing the counter (to the outside, trying to turn the corner), and we finally got Darnell to take it up inside. When he did, he broke the long run."

NU's comeback began in the second quarter, after the Gophers had taken a 14-3 lead on the strength of the first first-quarter touchdown allowed all year by the Wildcats, and a second-quarter punt-block of Paul Burton by Sean McMenomy. Darkins, who would gain just 75 yards on 25 carries, made Minnesota's margin 11 points with a 6-yard dash.

"The defense took control of the game after the second (Gopher) score," said Barnett. "They never let Darkins get into any rhythm."

"I think our mood changed a lot once we got behind," said Bates.

The Gopher lead lasted only 7 minutes 26 seconds. A fumbled punt return by Heath set up a 29-yard field goal by Sam Valenzisi, and shortly thereafter, a Darkins fumble gave NU the ball again. That drive climaxed with Autry's first score.

"To fall behind like we did, and come back as fast as we did, our kids showed a lot of poise in that situation, and our defense played relentlessly," said Barnett.

"They definitely came out on a mission," said Darkins. "They're very good."

Autry's night ran his string of 100-yard plus games to seven over two seasons, tying the school record established by Mike Adamle in 1970. Whether this meant Autry had a future as a host on "American Gladiators" was not immediately known, but it pushed his season total to 936 yards on 187 carries, averages of 5.00 yard-per-rush and 156 yards-per-game.

It wasn't a perfect night for Autry. His fourth-quarter fumble led to Minnesota's only points of the second half, a 47-yard field goal by Mike Chalberg. That prevented the defense from collecting another second-half shutout to go with the blankings it recorded against Air Force and Indiana, but otherwise, it was no big deal.

What was a big deal was obvious. Northwestern's fourth win in a row (an achievement not accomplished since 1962, when NU started 6-0) moved it to 5-1 overall and 3-0 in the Big Ten, while Minnesota dropped to 3-2, 1-1, the Rose Bowl hopes of the Gophers dashed.

NU's weren't. The Wildcats, up to No. 11 in both the AP writer-broadcaster poll and the CNN/USA Today coaches poll after the game, kept their half-game lead on Ohio State (which knocked Wisconsin out of the undefeated-in-the-league department) and Iowa, both 2-0 in the Big Ten.

To Northwestern's students, this was a reason to throw a party. About 1,000 fans turned out at Dyche Stadium at about 1 a.m. to welcome the team back from the Twin Cities.

"It was crazy! If I was a little younger, I'd have stayed," said Barnett, a youthful 49.

And for the first time, people started to wonder what would happen if NU and Ohio State tied for the league title. Thanks to the 11-team Big Ten's eight-game conference slate, the Wildcats and Buckeyes wouldn't meet in 1995 (or, for that matter, 1996). Both teams would play Iowa, which meant the Hawkeyes were, in theory, in the best position of all, able to help decide their own fate.

Close inspection of the Big Ten's Rose Bowl tiebreaker system found that even though Northwestern hadn't gone to the game since

Cornerbacks Rodney Ray (#15) and Chris Martin (#16) enjoy the Wildcats' success over Minnesota. (Larry Ruehl/Daily Southtown)

1949, another tiebreaker preceded it. Instead, the best record in nonconference games (not including the Kickoff Classic, which OSU played in and won) would take precedence. This year, it would determine the Rose Bowl representative, because the Buckeyes, who looked unbeatable, were 3-0 in nonconference tiffs, the Wildcats 2-1. There was that Miami game again, hanging over their heads.

Barnett wasn't worrying that far ahead. He was just interested in getting his team to play more consistently on offense. He thought the Cats were lining up on too many third-and-long situations, and blamed it on erratic play on first down.

"We just keep scratching and clawing," said Barnett. "We may not be real pretty, but we're sort of alley cats."

MINNESOTA VS. NORTHWESTERN

Saturday, October 14, 1995 at H.H.H. Metrodome, Minneapolis
Weather: 72° Wind none Cool
Attendance: 50,504

SCORE BY QUARTERS	1	2	3	4	SCORE
Minnesota (3-1)	3	11	7	6	27
Northwestern (3-1)	7	7	0	3	17

First Quarter

		NU	MN
NU	3:49 Sam Valenzisi 20-yard field goal (8 plays, 77 yards, 3:15 TOP)	3	0
MN	0:30 Paul Kratochvil 4-yard pass from Cory Sauter (Mike Chalberg kick) (6 plays, 57 yards, 3:19 TOP)	3	7

Second Quarter

MN	13:08 Chris Darkins 6-yard run (Mike Chalberg kick) (2 plays, 12 yards, :54 TOP)	3	14
NU	9:47 Sam Valenzisi 29-yard field goal (4 plays, 6 yards, 1:35 TOP)	6	14
NU	5:42 Darnell Autry 18-yard run (D'Wayne Bates from Steve Schnur) (3 plays, 39 yards, :56 TOP)	14	14

Third Quarter

NU	3:57 Darnell Autry 11-yard run (Sam Valenzisi kick) (9 plays, 66 yards, 5:11 TOP)	21	14

Fourth Quarter

NU	12:21 Darnell Autry 73-yard run (kick failed) (2 plays, 79 yards, :50 TOP)	27	14
MN	8:51 Mike Chalberg 47-yard field goal (5 plays, 4 yards, 1:12 TOP)	27	17

Big Ten Standings

1. Northwestern (3-0-0)
2. Ohio State (2-0-0)
3. Iowa (2-0-0)
4. Michigan (1-1-0)
5. Minnesota (1-1-0)
6. Michigan State (1-1-1)
7. Wisconsin (1-1-0)
8. Penn State (1-2-0)
9. Illinois (1-2-1)
10. Purdue (0-2-1)
11. Indiana (0-3-0)

AP Top 25

1. Florida St.
2. Nebraska
3. Florida
4. Ohio State
5. Southern Cal
6. Tennessee
7. Kansas
8. Kansas St.
9. Colorado
10. Michigan
11. Northwestern
12. Oregon
13. Auburn
14. Virginia
15. Oklahoma
16. Texas
17. Notre Dame
18. Iowa
19. Penn St.
20. Washington
21. Alabama
22. Texas A&M
23. Stanford
24. Wisconsin
25. Texas Tech

TEAM STATISTICS

	NU	MN
First Downs	17	23
Rushing	5	6
Passing	9	16
Penalty	3	1
Rushing Attempts	35	33
Yards Gained Rushing	203	99
Yards Lost Rushing	11	48
Net Yards Rushing	192	51
Net Yards Passing	200	303
Passes Attempted	25	50
Passes Completed	14	29
Had Intercepted	1	1
Total Offensive Plays	60	83
Total Net Yards	392	354
Average Gain per Play	6.5	4.3
Fumbles: Number-Lost	1-1	3-2
Penalties: Number-Yards	2-19	9-70
Interceptions: Number-Yards	1-0	1-3
Number of Punts-Yards	7-224	6-243
Average Per Punt	32.0	40.5
Punt Returns: Number-Yards	1-8	4-25
Kickoff Returns: Number-Yards	1-29	5-83
Possession Time	24:10	35:50
Third-Down Conversions	2 of 12	10 of 20
Sacks By: Number-Yards	6-40	0-0

Scores of interest

Ohio State 27, Wisconsin 16
Penn St. 26, Purdue 23
Iowa 22, Indiana 13
Florida St. 72, Wake Forest 13
Nebraska 57, Missouri 0
Florida 49, Auburn 38
So. Cal. 26, Wash. St. 14
Tennessee 41, Alabama 14
Kansas St. 23, Okla. St. 17
Oklahoma 24, Texas 24
Oregon 52, Calaifornia 30
Stanford 28, Washington 28
Notre Dame 28, Army 27
Virginia 44, Duke 30
Texas A&M 20, SMU 17
Texas Tech 63, Arkansas St. 25

Darnell Autry in the safety of the end zone after his 32-yard touchdown run. (Art Vassy/Daily Southtown)

Chapter 12
FULL-HOUSE DOMINATION

"That didn't look like Cinderella out there to me."

—Gary Barnett

NORTHWESTERN'S WIN at Minnesota was its fifth of the year, as many victories as the Wildcats had managed in the previous two seasons combined, and more than any Wildcat squad had posted since 1971, when Alex Agase's next-to-last NU team went 7-4.

The team was beginning to catch on. The Chicago-area media, always happy to jump on a bandwagon, suddenly discovered the Wildcats. Those camera crews that came out after the win over Notre Dame, then disappeared after the loss to Miami, had returned for good. Reporters began to come out in larger numbers for practices.

Never mind Michael Jordan. The Wildcats were "in," a feel-good story. The real-life version of "Revenge of the Nerds," somebody called it on a sports talk show.

Actually, by now reality had begun to blend with fantasy. The October 21 game with Wisconsin would not only be the sixth game in seven outings to be televised (ESPN2 would do the honors), it would be the first sellout of 49,256-seat Dyche Stadium in 12 years. Not since Rose Bowl-bound Illinois played at NU in 1983 had the facility been full to the brim.

The only thing that made it less than tremendous for NU supporters was that they'd have company. As usual when Wisconsin visited, thousands of red-clad Badger fans would tag along. In 1994, when Wisconsin also played at NU, 46,437 people, most of them from north of the border, turned out for the game.

That did not sit well with the Wildcat players.

"I remember last year when we had a full crowd for Wisconsin, and I was in a huddle on the sideline," defensive tackle Matt Rice mused. "I heard the crowd go crazy, looked up, and we'd fumbled. Later, there was a roar, and I thought, 'Great, we scored a touchdown.' It was an interception.

"It would be great to have the crowd rooting for us."

Gary Barnett, who watched crowds come back at Colorado while he was an assistant to Bill McCartney, talked about the advantage of a full home stadium frequently.

"If we can create an atmosphere at home where it's a tough place to play for everybody else, then it'll make a difference," Barnett said after the win at Notre Dame. "We have not had the home crowd as a factor because we haven't had the numbers or that kind of enthusiasm. If (beating ND) can create that, then it'll make a big difference. If it doesn't, it won't make any difference whether we're home or away.

Kicker Sam Valenzisi is helped up after making a tackle. Later, he'd go down for the season. (Art Vassy/Daily Southtown)

"That's part of where we have to go in this program. If we're going to compete in this league, then we have to create an atmosphere here that's like the other schools in the Big Ten. That means it's got to be a hard place to play."

He too remembered how Wisconsin fans had taken over Dyche the previous season.

"We came out, kicked off to them, held, they punted to us, we got a penalty on a punt return, got the ball on about the 4-yard line, and the crowd noise from their crowd was so loud in our stadium, we jumped offsides and ended up turning the ball back to 'em down there.

"From then on, it was like sharks to blood. They were after us and we never regained our composure. I hope we have a friendly crowd in our stadium."

And if not?

"We've had two away games in a row. I'm sure we can handle the crowd."

Against Wisconsin, the atmosphere, and probably with more of a purple tint than in meetings past, would be there. So would the 24th-ranked Badgers, at 2-2-1 overall and 1-1 in the Big Ten, and with a veteran quarterback, to say the least, in 25-year-old Darrell Bevell, someone who played a vital part in the win at Penn State.

"It's going to be tricky playing him," said Wildcat linebacker Tim Scharf. "You've got a guy who can move the chains on you. You don't want to blitz a lot on a guy like that."

Wisconsin head coach Barry Alvarez had set up an offense where the precision passing game Bevell excelled at—he'd completed 65.9 percent of his passes coming into the game, just behind Ohio State's Bobby Hoying—actually set up the running game. Since Alvarez' arrival, the Badgers were 26-7-3 in games where they ran for over 200 yards.

"At the Big Ten luncheon, Barry said he had the most talent he ever hard," said Barnett. "Couple that with a 25-year-old quarterback, a guy two years away from retirement."

Wisconsin's offense had something else going for it. It was careful with the football. Bevell had thrown five interceptions, but the Badgers had fumbled only once.

At the same time, here was NU, with a plus-10 turnover ratio. The Wildcats had given the ball away six times, but had taken it away 16 times. The plus-10 ratio was tops in the conference, in large measure because of a ball-hawking defense. For that, Barnett credited his defensive staff, headed by defensive coordinator Ron Vanderlinden.

"They use every minute trying to find a way to stop any particular player," he said. "We do a good job with our film work, our computer work, with our scheme. Those guys work until 10 o'clock, constantly looking for a way, all day Thursday and Friday, just looking for another little thing that'll help us.

"What scheming does is it allows you to get a guy in the right place. Then he's got to make the play. Everybody asks, 'What are you doing different?' We're not doing anything different than we've ever done here. Not one single thing.

"Players are playing better, and there's a higher level of trust, maybe, than there's been. We've got some guys who can make plays. Hudhaifa (Ismaeli) makes plays. Casey Dailey makes plays. Chris Martin's making plays. Fitz (Pat Fitzgerald) makes plays.

"You can put a lot of guys there, but they don't always make plays. Now, we've got guys who are making plays."

In the first six games, NU's defense had allowed more than one score in a quarter only twice: in the second quarter at Notre Dame, where the Fighting Irish put up nine points, and in the final quarter against Miami, where the Redskins' 23-point surge dealt NU its only loss.

In 12 of the other 22 quarters, the Wildcat defense had pitched a shutout, including the second half against Air Force and Indiana. They'd only allowed one touchdown, by Michigan, in the third quarter. This was a team that, to this point, knew how to adjust at the half.

The Wildcats had, to this juncture, shown remarkable focus for a team that hadn't been to these heights with these players.

"Our guys aren't acting like they haven't been through it," Barnett said. "They're handling it well. This week, I'm more concerned about them being relaxed and fresh than I am anything."

Two seasons earlier, Alvarez had guided the similarly-unfamiliar Badgers to the Rose Bowl, bringing back to Camp Randall Stadium the Wisconsin fans who had gone duck-hunting on Saturdays. Minus the duck calls, he saw a similarity in Northwestern's rise.

"I know what Northwestern's done," said Alvarez. "A number of their players who are seniors or juniors, they've started and played two or three or four years. While they didn't have success, they were competitive.

"Now, they're veterans. They know what it takes to win. You develop a confidence that way. I guess the trick is beating the so-called powers in the league, and they've done that."

That made the meeting more than an important game for this season. It could also be seen as a test on where each program was going. For the Badgers, beating Northwestern would keep their Rose Bowl hopes alive. For the Wildcats, victory was necessary to sustain the momentum generated by the wins over Notre Dame and Michigan.

"This particular game becomes, as any coach would tell you when you've got a string going and are sitting on top of the league, this game becomes critical," said Barnett. "Because

Wide receiver Brian Musso hangs on to the ball while Badger defender Jason Suffle hangs on to him. (Art Vassy/Daily Southtown)

Linebacker Geoff Shein's big hit on Wisconsin tight end Matt Nyquist ensures an incompletion. (Art Vassy/Daily Southtown)

it's the one we're playing, it's critical."

And because it was Wisconsin, and a winning season could be had, and maybe a bowl, and the place would be jammed, and, was there anything else? Well, Northwestern was the No. 14 team in the country, playing at home, on Homecoming, against a lesser-ranked team with a lesser record. So which team was favored? Wisconsin, by two points.

Barnett talked about that privately, not publicly, during the course of the week. He didn't have to say much.

Then came Saturday morning, and lousy weather. The temperature had dropped to 40 degrees. The wind blew out of the west, bringing with it light rain.

Still, the fans came. By the 11:30 a.m. game time, Dyche Stadium was awash in humanity. So was Central Street and the roads funneling into Central Street, which is the only way to get to Dyche Stadium. The Wildcats' success had not only generated a sellout crowd, it had generated a mammoth traffic jam, the largest seen in years in Evanston.

Eventually, everybody made it in.

Badger fans soon wished they weren't there. This wasn't like 1993 in Madison, a 53-14 Badger romp, or 1994 in Dyche, a 46-14 pasting of NU.

This was the opposite.

This was Wildcat domination, start to finish.

Northwestern won 35-0, a rousing hour-long display of what they'd been up to so far this season. In annexing their sixth victory, the Wildcats scored early and late, scored almost at will.

The Badgers offense and Wildcats defense combined to make it a rout. Wisconsin turned the ball over seven times. NU took advantage, scoring 26 points off five of the gifts. That performance earned the Wildcat defense, en masse, the Big Ten's defensive player of the week award.

At the same time, the Wildcat defense, playing the shark role, held Wisconsin to 101 yards on the ground. Bevell's passing game looked good on paper (15-of-23, 193 yards), but two interceptions that the NU offense turned into 10 points made the paper worthless.

The Wildcat fans roared every NU score, every Badger miscue. Rice, who had heard the cheers going the wrong way in 1994, loved every second of it.

"Fantastic!" he exclaimed. "They drowned out the Wisconsin fans so much. I didn't hear a peep out of 'em all day."

This wasn't a competition, it was a parade, and the Cats were leading it. They led 10-0 after a quarter, by 13 at the half, added six more points in the third quarter, and 16 more before time ran out.

"Wow, what a game," said a giddy, nearly breathless Barnett before the largest group of reporters at an NU home game in at least 15 years. "Our defense was just relentless to produce seven turnovers.

"I knew we were going to play hard. We felt like this was a game that we needed to earn some respect. We felt like we'd earned attention around the country, but to be ranked 11th, playing the 24th-ranked team, have a sellout and be a two-point underdog, that's not much of a show of respect."

This outcome demanded respect, not to mention banner headlines. The Wildcats were more than real. They were dangerous, a team not to be trifled with.

"People just sorta thought we were Cinderella, and that sooner or later, the glass slipper was gonna come off," Barnett said. "That didn't look like Cinderella out there to me."

The Wildcats didn't arrive in a horse-drawn stagecoach, but there was a touch of magic to the game. At 1:02 p.m., just as the Wildcats took the field for the second half, the first snowflakes of the season began to fall in Evanston. The place went up for grabs. It reminded many of the NFC Championship game for the 1985 season, when the Bears' Wilber Marshall picked up a loose ball and ran it 52 yards for a score as snow began to fall at Soldier Field. A sign, perhaps?

The win did, after all, clinch a winning season for the Wildcats for the first time in 23 years.

It was the first shutout by an NU squad since a blanking of Princeton in 1986, the first against a Big Ten since the infamous 0-0 tie at Illinois in 1978, and the first shutout win over a conference foe since 1975, when Indiana fell 30-0.

It also made Northwestern, the one-time doormats of college football, eligible for a postseason bowl. The thought of that quickly brought Barnett, who said "endorphins are running rampant through me," down to earth a bit.

"I think we probably have to win seven to be assured of a bowl," he figured. "Who knows? If we play the way we did today, we're hard to beat. We've been pretty consistent the last 5-6 weeks. And given the people we've beaten, we would have a chance to play heads up with anybody.

"This was the most meaningful win. It assured a winning season for the first time in years, and that's what we came here to do. I'd like to be in a corner of the locker room now to watch the kids celebrate."

One thing was sure. If a football fell on the locker room floor, a Wildcat would fall on it so it wouldn't get away.

The defensive game plan called for keeping Wisconsin tailback Carl McCullough from turning the corner. If he was forced to run between the tackles, he wouldn't go far. That

Wisconsin safety Leonard Taylor is in hot pursuit of Darnell Autry. Ryan Padgett (75) and James McCaffrey form a mobile cheering section. (Art Vassy/Daily Southtown)

Offensive tackle Ryan Padgett was too late to stop Badger end Tarek Saleh from sacking quarterback Steve Schnur. (Art Vassy/Daily Southtown)

worked. He was held to 74 yards on 23 carries. And, with Bevell forced to throw deeper than he would have preferred, the passing game eventually misfired.

"We did what we set out to do," said Barnett. "From the time the whistle blew, the kids attacked. Special teams were outstanding, our offense opportunistic, but our defense was stifling."

Right from the start, he might have added. Wisconsin freshman Aaron Stecker contributed the game's first two turnovers. He muffed the first punt of the game, allowing the Wildcats to take over on the Badger 27. It led to the first score, Steve Schnur's 1-yard plunge on the drive's second fourth-down conversion. Barnett, with no clue as to what was to come, eschewed a field-goal in favor of going for the touchdown.

"The theme today in chapel was risk-taking," he explained. "There's a difference between taking a chance and taking a risk. We didn't take a chance on fourth down. We took a risk."

Wisconsin soon took a powder.

"It was really disappointing," said Alvarez. "Northwestern defeated us every way they could. Things started with that punt and snowballed from there."

The avalanche was set off by Stecker. If his muffed punt return wasn't enough, he took the next kickoff, and promptly fumbled it on the Badger 20. Sam Valenzisi, amazingly, missed a field-goal attempt a few plays later - his first miss after a school-record 13 straight successful tries—but the die had been cast.

Stecker felt awful about it, saying, "I feel I let the team down."

It was a team effort on Wisconsin's part. The third turnover came before the first quarter was history. Soon, the Badgers were history.

Actually, Stecker nearly averted the shutout. On their final drive, with Wisconsin's second-team offense against NU's second-team defense, the Badgers made it all the way to the 1. It was fourth-and-goal, with time for only one play. Stecker got the handoff, ran to the left, near the overflowing NU student section. He ran out of room and was dropped by Chris Rooney for a 2-yard loss, guaranteeing the first Wildcat shutout in Dyche Stadium in 105 games.

"Guys were flying to the ball," said safety William Bennett. "They were swarming. And the balls were just laying on the ground."

"Coach (Vanderlinden) came up with a good scheme and we ran it to a T," said linebacker Pat Fitzgerald, who led with 10 tackles.

The defense was so dominant, Darnell Autry's two touchdowns were nearly overshadowed. Originally, it appeared that Autry's string of 100-yard rushing games had ended. He was first credited with 81 yards on 26 carries.

However, there was much clamor in the press box about a third-quarter swing pass to him from Steve Schnur that Autry turned into a 32-yard score.

Was the pass really a pass? Or did it go backwards, which would turn Autry's receiving yardage into rushing yardage? Since Dyche Stadium's press box, rebuilt in 1961, didn't have a television in it—not even a 1961-vintage Philco—nobody was sure.

It wasn't until Monday that Northwestern sports information director Brad Hurlbut ruled Autry had rushed the ball. That meant he had 113 yards on 27 carries, eight 100-yard games in a row, and, in 1995, 1,049 yards in just seven games. No Northwestern back had gotten to the 1,000-yard mark more quickly. He needed just 242 yards in the final four games to snag the single-season rushing mark from Bob Christian, who ran for 1,291 yards in 1989, a year the Cats went 0-11.

The Wildcats winning 35-0 wasn't the most unlikely thing that could have happened all day. The most unlikely thing that could have happened was Valenzisi, always pleased to be able to smack someone, getting injured while celebrating someone else's stop on one of his kickoffs. That happened.

Early in the fourth quarter, Autry had scored on a 3-yard pitch to the left, a play set up by Mike Warren's interception of Bevell. NU led 26-0, with all but three points coming off Badger turnovers. Dyche was in an uproar.

It soon quieted. Cecil Marin took Valenzisi's kickoff on the 2, but slipped after taking one step and was buried. Back at about the 20, Valenzisi jumped into the air. When he came down, he came down hard, and sprawled on the turf. Either on the way up or the way down, he blew out the anterior cruciate ligament and tore some cartilage in his left knee, his "plant" leg. The season was over for the No. 1 placekicker in the country.

It was hard to tell at the time. Gamely, Valenzisi, a one-time walk-on who had driven himself to become a second-team All-Big Ten selection in 1994, refused to be carried off. Nor would he walk off. He insisted on trotting off to the sideline, and he did so, to a roar from the crowd, albeit while listing to one side.

Quarterback Steve Schnur is helped after the Badgers got to him. (Art Vassy/Daily Southtown)

110 PURPLE ROSES

A trio of Wildcat defenders, including linebacker Pat Fitzgerald, corral Badger tailback Carl McCollough. (Art Vassy/Daily Southtown)

"I told him to be businesslike, but ... " Barnett said, in disbelief at the way Valenzisi was injured.

Backup kicker Brian Gowins, suddenly in the spotlight, hit a 40-yard field-goal later in the game, but missed an extra-point attempt. In the minutes after the game, he still hoped Valenzisi would return the following week against Illinois.

"He said he hurt it on the kick, and ran down the field on adrenaline," Gowins said. "When he was sitting on the cart, Sam assured me that he'd be back next week, that the doctors had him there just as a precautionary measure."

For the first time, NU would have to deal with a season-ending injury. Long snapper Paul Janus, hurt early in the Miami of Ohio game, had come back two weeks later, increasing his activity each week. But Valenzisi would be a spectator the rest of the season.

Rodney Ray was in better shape. Like Valenzisi, a fifth-year senior, Ray was knocked out in a first-half collision. He was deemed ready to return in the second half, but held out because of the score.

Otherwise, it was a great day to be a Wildcat. NU would climb into the top 10, to the No. 8 position, in the new AP poll—finally ahead of Michigan—and was still a half-game ahead of Ohio State atop the Big Ten. What's more, Iowa's loss to Penn State meant it was shaping up as a two-team run for the Roses.

"We're pretty good right now," said Barnett. "And that crowd! That was sweet, wasn't it? I'm going to be smiling all night."

WISCONSIN VS. NORTHWESTERN

Saturday, October 21, 1995 at Dyche Stadium, Evanston, IL
Weather: 40° Wind W12 Cloudy with light rain
Attendance: 49,256 (sellout)

SCORE BY QUARTERS	1	2	3	4	SCORE
Wisconsin (2-3-1)	0	0	0	0	0
Northwestern (6-1)	10	3	6	16	35

First Quarter

		NU	WN
NU 7:22 Steve Schnur 1-yard run (Sam Valenzisi kick) (9 plays, 27 yards, 4:44 TOP)		7	0
NU 2:39 Sam Valenzisi 32-yard field goal (4 plays, 6 yards, 1:20 TOP)		10	0

Second Quarter

		NU	WN
NU :56 Sam Valenzisi 26-yard field goal (11 plays, 71 yards, 4:24 TOP)		13	0

Third Quarter

		NU	WN
NU 13:21 Darnell Autry 32-yard run (2-pt conversion pass failed) (3 plays, 36 yards, 1:25 TOP)		19	0

Fourth Quarter

		NU	WN
NU 13:34 Darnell Autry 3-yard run (Sam Valenzisi kick) (3 plays, 5 yards, :50 TOP)		26	0
NU 11:03 Brian Gowins 40-yard field goal (4 plays, 7 yards, 1:32 TOP)		29	0
NU 7:29 Levelle Brown 38-yard run (kick failed) (4 plays, 62 yards, 2:02 TOP)		35	0

TEAM STATISTICS

	WN	NU
First Downs	20	12
Rushing	7	8
Passing	12	3
Penalty	1	1
Rushing Attempts	40	45
Yards Gained Rushing	139	223
Yards Lost Rushing	38	12
Net Yards Rushing	101	221
Net Yards Passing	220	79
Passes Attempted	30	16
Passes Completed	18	8
Had Intercepted	2	1
Total Offensive Plays	70	61
Total Net Yards	321	300
Average Gain per Play	4.6	4.9
Fumbles: Number-Lost	5-5	0-0
Penalties: Number-Yards	3-25	5-29
Interceptions: Number-Yards	1-0	2-64
Number of Punts-Yards	5-185	5-226
Average Per Punt	37.0	45.2
Punt Returns: Number-Yards	2-12	2-14
Kickoff Returns: Number-Yards	7-84	1-19
Possession Time	29:12	30:48
Third-Down Conversions	6	4
Sacks By: Number-Yards	1-1	1-11

Big Ten Standings

1. Northwestern (4-0-0)
2. Ohio State (3-0-0)
3. Michigan (2-1-0)
4. Iowa (2-1-0)
5. Michigan State (2-1-1)
6. Penn State (2-2-0)
7. Minnesota (1-2-0)
8. Illinois (1-2-0)
9. Wisconsin (1-2-0)
10. Purdue (0-3-1)
11. Indiana (0-4-0)

AP Top 25

1. Florida St.
2. Nebraska
3. Florida
4. Ohio State
5. Tennessee
6. Kansas
7. Colorado
8. **Northwestern**
9. Michigan
10. Oregon
11. Auburn
12. Notre Dame
13. Southern Cal
14. Kansas St.
15. Texas
16. Penn St.
17. Washington
18. Alabama
19. Texas A&M
20. Virginia
21. Syracuse
22. Texas Tech
23. Oklahoma
24. UCLA
25. Iowa

Scores of interest

Ohio State 28, Purdue 0
Michigan 34, Indiana 17
Penn State 41, Iowa 27
Florida State 42, Ga. Tech 10
Nebraska 49, Kansas St. 25
USC 10, Notre Dame 10
Kansas 38, Oklahoma 17
Colorado 50, Iowa St. 28
Auburn 34, W. Michigan 13
Virginia 16, Texas 16
Alabama 23, Mississippi 9
Texas A&M 24, Baylor 9
Stanford 42, UCLA 28
Texas Tech 31, Rice 26

Punter Paul Burton joins his teammates in getting ready for action. (Scott Strazzante/Daily Southtown)

Chapter 13
DRIVEN TO VICTORY

"We're definitely going to try to run the table."
—Darnell Autry

TWO DAYS AFTER beating Wisconsin, Gary Barnett couldn't stop talking about the 35-0 outcome.

"The momentum of that game was one like I've never been a part of," he said. "I'm certainly glad I was on the side of the field I was instead of on Coach (Barry) Alvarez's, because that can be so disheartening to have so many things happen to you the way they had happened to them.

"Part of it, we created, and part of it was luck."

All of it was helpful. Northwestern was ranked No. 1 in the country—in turnover margin. In 1994, it was minus-11. Now, the Wildcats boasted a plus-16 margin.

"What's happening is, your team, once you start getting a feel for turnovers, you start looking for ways to manufacture them," Barnett said. "You're tuned in.

"A couple of years ago, we'd have been happy just with the tackle. Now, we're going down and tackling and ripping the ball out. It becomes a competitive thing between your players."

Then the offense would take over. Through seven games, NU had scored after 18 of 23 turnovers, tallying 98 of their 197 points.

Not bad. But not good enough for offensive guard Ryan Padgett. He wanted more.

"The focus this week is to come into our own as an offense," said Padgett. "Against Illinois, it'll be a great challenge."

The offense wasn't a spectacular unit on a par with, say, Florida. But, putting up 28 points a game, it was more than just efficient. With Autry running the ball behind a stout offensive line, the Wildcats had a unit that was dependable, and one built for the bad late-season weather that's very much a part of the Big Ten.

The Wildcats would take their aggressive defense, their opportunistic offense, their dangerous special teams, their 6-1 record, their 4-0 conference reading, their No. 8 ranking in both polls and their five-game winning streak into a game where all the numbers and many of the trends were meaningless.

It was the week of the Illinois game, a rivalry game.

At least, it is to Northwestern. In Champaign, the year-in, year-out rivals of the Fighting Illini were considered Michigan, Ohio State, and, in recent years, Iowa. Sure, the Sweet Sioux Tomahawk trophy was always at stake, but Northwestern?

"I think they consider it a rivalry more than we do," Illini head coach Lou Tepper had said a few years earlier.

Steve Schnur prepares to hand off behind Justin Chabot's blocking. (Larry Ruehl/Daily Southtown)

Barnett certainly thought it was a rivalry, saying, "No matter what our record was, this team would be pointing towards Illinois. That's just the way it falls every year. You can throw all the records out. It always has been that way."

Illinois, with linebackers Simeon Rice and Kevin Hardy, whom Barnett pegged as first-round NFL draft picks, leading the defense, was supposed to have a big season. Through six games, there were big questions. Illinois was 3-3, just 1-2 in conference, and had scored only 99 points, an average of 16.5 per game.

It was a record the Illini would have liked to throw out. They were stuck with it, and many thought the offensive inconsistency came because of the revolving door on the offensive coordinator's office. Paul Schudel, the new man in that position, was the fourth in five years. It did not make for an easy time at the quarterback position, and already, Scott Weaver had replaced Johnny Johnson as the starter.

"The hardest position to play in any sport, at this level, is quarterback," said Barnett. "What you have to know, what you have to see, what you have to react to is why. I'd love for any of you guys to go out there and try that. You wouldn't believe what it's like."

Barnett, in comparison, had made only one coaching change on his staff since arriving four years earlier. Only Jerry Brown, who replaced Kevin Ramsey as the defensive backs coach in 1993, wasn't around for the first season.

"For me, personally, it's critical," Barnett said. "It's been the most important thing to be able to keep these guys. When they all came here, I asked them for a two-year commitment, and now it's the fourth year for eight of the nine. Most of them have turned down jobs at other places in order to stay here. I think much of that is the families. The wives are critical in the coaching profession. My wife's done a great job of making sure we're part of a close-knit family. I've tried to pay attention to the needs of our families as well. That wasn't always true for us. In the early stages at Colorado, we worked extremely long hours. I knew when I got here, the track record of assistant coaches had been horrendous."

A measure of Barnett's consideration became public at the postseason victory banquet. He didn't just introduce his assistant coaches. He introduced their wives.

Ron Vanderlinden, the soft-spoken architect of Northwestern's defense, was already at Colorado when Barnett arrived there. And he was the first person to come along when Barnett left for NU.

"From Day 1, Gary was always a guy who you respected what he had to say," Vanderlinden explained. "He chose his words carefully at all times. He was always a fun, engaging guy who everybody liked. I had a lot of respect for his football knowledge, but most importantly, he's a terrific guy.

"I believe that the first mark of leadership is a man who can lead himself, and Gary was always a self-starter. I had confidence he'd be a good recruiter, be good with alumni."

Like Barnett, Vanderlinden had some misgivings about leaving Colorado.

"We'd just won our third straight Big Eight championship," he said. "We'd just built a $12 million football building, and Boulder's a great place to live. There weren't a lot of guys anxious to leave. But I came in and saw that everything was here you needed to win. There was no reason you couldn't win here. It just had to be attacked in the right manner."

Attack was the operative word. The Illini would come to find that out.

By this, the eighth game of the season, the starting lineup had changed slightly from the opener. At defensive tackle, Joe Rieff was ahead of Ray Robey, though Robey was still seeing plenty of action. Geoff Shein had jumped ahead of Tim Scharf at one of the linebacker spots. And Justin Chabot got the call ahead of Chad Pugh at an offensive guard spot.

One change Barnett hadn't planned was using Brian Gowins as a field-goal kicker instead of Sam Valenzisi. That was necessitated by the always-chatty Valenzisi's season-ending injury.

"Before, he was responsible for himself," said Barnett. "Now, he's responsible for Brian. I fully anticipate him being even more vocal than he's been, which none of us want, but we can live with it."

The stretch run would begin in Champaign on Saturday, October 28, which, like seven days before in Evanston, was not conducive for much more than running the football. A stiff wind howled out of the northwest. The 48-degree temperature combined with the gale to make underdressed fans sitting in Memorial Stadium, one of the grand stages in college sport, wish they had dug their long underwear out of storage.

Illinois, more than the wind, blew Northwestern back in the early going. The Illini, before 20 minutes had gone off the clock, had raced to a 14-0 lead.

The way they moved ahead two touchdowns was the most impressive thing. They drove on Northwestern, first with the 25 mile-per-hour wind at their back, then against it.

Weaver's 1-yard fourth-and-goal plunge 5:19 into the game had opened the scoring, but a bizarre third-down pass had kept the drive

Cornerback Rodney Ray prepares to lower the boom on Illinois receiver Jason Dulick. (Larry Ruehl/Daily Southtown)

alive. He fired over the middle, but a pair of players fighting for the ball, NU safety William Bennett and UI wideout Jason Dulick, collided as the pass came in. The ball caromed 30 feet into the air and came down into the hands of Rob Majoy at the Wildcat 31. He wasn't stopped until reaching the NU 8.

If that was a harbinger of bad tidings for Northwestern, Illinois' third possession was even more telling. Starting on their 3, the Illini moved methodically downfield. An offense that had been erratic all season was gobbling up yardage against a defense that didn't yield much. Throw out the record books, indeed.

Twice, Weaver found receivers for first-down yardage on third and long. Ty Douthard and Robert Holcombe alternated in crashing through the line or going around end. It was Holcombe who scored, using the block of Martin Jones to go around left end from the NU 7 on the 16th play of the drive. Brett Scheuplein's kick gave Illinois a 14-0 lead.

Northwestern hadn't been behind this much all season. The Wildcats had trailed Minnesota by 11 and made that up, but the Illini were looking far more formidable.

The subsequent possession brought a glimmer of hope. Quarterback Steve Schnur hit Brian Musso for 16 yards and a first down on a third-down situation, the first such conversion in four tries. On the next play, Darnell Autry, to this juncture penned in, broke loose for 14 yards behind Toussaint Waterman's kickout block. The drive stalled and Gowins was called in to try a 49-yard field-goal. Wind-aided, the line shot was good, barely clearing the crossbar, and the lead had been trimmed to 14-3.

Less than four minutes later, it was 14-10. The Wildcat defense stiffened. NU got the ball back on its 27, and three snaps later, in large part because of Schnur's 21-yard completion to D'Wayne Bates, was at the Illini 46. Autry ran to the 34 on the next play, and from there, Schnur found Bates again. When senior defensive back Tyrone Washington went for the interception, there was nobody to stop Bates. The 34-yard TD reception, coming on a play Schnur convinced Barnett and offensive coordinator Greg Meyer was there for the taking, brought NU right back into the game.

"Coach gives us leeway," said Schnur. "They weren't getting a real good jam on D'Wayne, and that's what they need to do. D'Wayne had noticed it earlier and brought it to my attention."

Schnur then told Barnett what was available, and got the green light.

"That's sort of the way we've been operating all year," said Barnett. "We listen to players quite a bit. He wanted to throw it down there so we let him throw it down there."

Both defenses came to the fore now. It be-

D'Wayne Bates' 34-yard touchdown reception just before the half brought the Wildcats within reach of the Illini. (Larry Ruehl/Daily Southtown)

Driven to Victory 117

Hudhaifa Ismaeli jumps into the arms of Eric Collier after Collier's game-clinching interception of Scott Weaver with seven seconds left. (Larry Ruehl/Daily Southtown)

came a game of punting, of field position, of avoiding mistakes. The crowd of 65,425 and the audience watching the telecast by Creative Sports, the Big Ten's syndicator, waited for the break that surely would decide the game.

It came with 11:42 to play, when the against-the-wind punt of Brett Larsen from the Illini 31 went only to the NU 42. That was set up, so to speak, by the move Barnett made at the half. The Wildcats had won the toss before the game and deferred their choice to the second half.

"I had a big decision to make," he said. "I asked our defense if they could keep 'em off the board, because I felt our offense had to have the wind in the fourth quarter. So we took the gamble."

Linebacker Danny Sutter remembered Barnett doing more than asking.

"I'm putting my faith in you guys," Sutter recalled him saying. "I have total faith in you guys. I'm going to let them have the wind."

NU held all through the third quarter, Illinois running only 11 offensive plays. When the defense held again early in the fourth, Larsen was forced to punt into the wind.

The Wildcats, who had started their previous three drives at no better than their own 16, would take over in excellent field position. They had to go 58 yards for a touchdown.

In the first huddle of the drive, Schnur was direct. "Guys, this is it, it's do-or-die time." he said. "The momentum has changed. The defense is doing their job. We've gotta score."

Autry, with 106 yards already, would go up the middle for six more on the first play, then bolt through the same hole for seven, then crash through for another half-dozen yards. The ball was quickly on the Illini 39.

Something had changed, and it was where the Wildcats were sending their fullback.

"They had Rice and Hardy on the same side," Barnett explained. "Hardy was mirroring our fullback. They always had an extra guy at our point of attack. We went to our spread formation, and that balanced 'em up, and that's what we ran most of the second half."

Hardy kept mirroring Matt Hartl even when Autry ran the other way. That meant one less player for the line to block and one less player for Autry to run away from. It, and trying to cut off Rice, who finished the day with only three tackles, got the offense going against the No. 14 defense in the country.

"It was a chess game in the press box because of what we had to do to solve it," said Barnett. "We never got it really solved, but we were able to make some plays to be able to make it. We didn't outsmart anybody, just found a way to get a hat on everybody.

"This was a war."

And NU was on the attack. Schnur dropped back to pass, finding Bates running a turnout

118 PURPLE ROSES

Brian Gowins, Faraji Leary, and Kevin Buck (l to r) celebrate their come-from-behind win. (Larry Ruehl/ Daily Southtown)

route near the left sideline. He got by a diving Washington and gained 19 yards.

Now the ball was on the Illinois 20. There was little doubt who would get the football. The only question was whether Illinois could stop Darnell Autry.

The answer was not quickly enough. He carried the ball six straight times, including a two-yard pickup on third-and-1 behind the block of Paul Janus.

Schnur was stopped next to the goal-line on a third-and-goal sneak attempt from the 1, but that merely gave Autry, who had carried the ball nine times in 11 snaps, a breather. On the drive's 12th play, he went over left tackle for the score, tight end Darren Drexler laying out Hardy to clear the way.

Schnur had called that play as well. You'll find it called "Toss 39" in the Wildcat playbook.

"This was not like Wisconsin, where they had a little cushion there," said Schnur. "They were loaded up inside."

"We were going to go for it regardless," said Barnett. "We were two inches from the goal line. I was thinking sneak, and Steve said, 'I can't get it.' So we went with the toss."

With 6:14 left, Northwestern led 17-14. The Wildcats would fend off a final Illini surge, one that partially misfired when Weaver was sacked after failing to call time out following a run up the middle by Holcombe. Still, it wasn't over until Eric Collier picked off Weaver's pass for Dulick in the end zone with seven seconds left.

Barnett was right. It was a war. The War of 17-14.

Northwestern had done it again, coming from behind on the road to post as impressive a victory as one by three points could be. Not bad for a team that was, once more, an underdog, this time by one point, in the eyes of oddsmakers who didn't believe what they had seen in the season's first seven weeks.

Believe this: NU was 7-1, its best start since 1936, the last Big Ten title year, 5-0 in the Big Ten, about to move up to No. 6 in both polls, and, without a doubt, headed for a bowl game for the first time in 47 years.

"I told 'em we're going somewhere warm for Christmas," said Barnett in Memorial Stadium's visiting team interview room, a space that holds a dozen people comfortably and now had three times that many jammed into it. "I don't have a guarantee, but I have pretty good percentages.

"I'm really proud of our guys for persevering. We could have let this one slip away. We knew going into this thing it was going to be just like that. I could have predicted the whole thing. Our guys just hung in and hung in."

Autry had another big day, with 151 yards on a career-high 41 carries pushing his season total to 1,200, with averages of 150 yards a game and 4.71 per carry. His name was starting to crop up in talk for the wide-open Heisman Trophy. Barnett, trying to keep the team attitude intact, played that talk down.

"I don't even have a vote," he said. "I have no idea. He's the best tailback on our team. I think he showed that he can hang in there and hammer against a pretty good defense, but he had a lot of help, too. He played very physically."

Enough so to be holding a packet of aspirin after the game.

"It felt like 40 carries or whatever," Autry said. "I've got my ice bags waiting for me."

Autry, always cool, was more interested in talking about the ever-growing bowl possibilities. NU had stayed the half-game ahead of Ohio State, which led Iowa 56-0 late in the first half and coasted to a 56-35 victory. NU's 17-14 margin probably didn't look as impressive to scoreboard-watchers, but it meant just as much.

"I think we've pretty much locked ourselves into a bowl game now," said Autry. "We're definitely going to try to run the table."

"This was a pretty special win," figured defensive tackle Matt Rice. "Special because we really had to fight and claw to get it. You appreciate things more when they're hard to come by. Sweet? It is pretty sweet. Sweet Sioux."

The Wildcat faithful were thinking of Pasadena. (Art Vassy/Daily Southtown)

Driven to Victory   121

ILLINOIS VS. NORTHWESTERN

Saturday, October 28, 1995 at Memorial Stadium, Champaign, IL
Weather: 48° Wind W15-25 Cloudy with light drizzle
Attendance: 65,425

SCORE BY QUARTERS	1	2	3	4	SCORE
Northwestern (7-1-0)	0	10	0	7	17
Illinois (3-3-0)	7	7	0	0	14

First Quarter
			NU	IL
IL	9:41 Scott Weaver 1-yard rush (Scheuplein kick)			
	(9 plays, 56 yards, 3:52 TOP)		0	7

Second Quarter
IL	10:42 Holcombe 7-yard rush (Scheuplein kick)			
	(16 plays, 97 yards, 6:33 TOP)		0	14
NU	8:12 Brian Gowins 49-yard field goal (8 plays, 42 yards, 2:30 TOP)		3	14
NU	4:40 D'Wayne Bates 34-yard pass from Steve Schnur (Brian Gowins kick)			
	(5 plays, 73 yards, 1:36 TOP)		10	14

Third Quarter
no scoring

Fourth Quarter
NU	6:14 Darnell Autry 1-yard rush (Brian Gowins kick)			
	(12 plays, 58 yards, 5:38 TOP)		17	14

TEAM STATISTICS	NU	IL
First Downs	16	15
Rushing	7	5
Passing	5	10
Penalty	4	0
Rushing Attempts	45	43
Yards Gained Rushing	163	142
Yards Lost Rushing	10	35
Net Yards Rushing	153	107
Net Yards Passing	117	198
Passes Attempted	19	32
Passes Completed	8	18
Had Intercepted	0	3
Total Offensive Plays	64	75
Total Net Yards	270	305
Average Gain per Play	4.2	4.1
Fumbles: Number-Lost	2-0	0-0
Penalties: Number-Yards	1-15	9-77
Interceptions: Number-Yards	3-15	0-0
Number of Punts-Yards	7-204	6-244
Average Per Punt	29.1	40.7
Punt Returns: Number-Yards	3-18	1-2
Kickoff Returns: Number-Yards	1-5	2-34
Possession Time	28:06	31:54
Third-Down Conversions	3 of 15	7 of 18
Fourth-Down Conversions	1 of 1	2 of 3
Sacks By: Number-Yards	2-24	0-0

Big Ten Standings

1. Northwestern (5-0-0)
2. Ohio State (4-0-0)
3. Michigan (3-1-0)
4. Penn State (3-2-0)
5. Iowa (2-2-0)
6. Michigan State (2-2-1)
7. Wisconsin (2-2-0)
8. Minnesota (1-3-0)
9. Illinois (1-3-0)
10. Purdue (0-3-1)
11. Indiana (0-5-0)

AP Top 25

1. Nebraska
2. Florida St.
3. Florida
4. Ohio State
5. Tennessee
6. **Northwestern**
7. Michigan
8. Notre Dame
9. Kansas St.
10. Colorado
11. Kansas
12. Penn St.
13. Texas
14. Southern Cal
15. Washington
16. Alabama
17. Texas A&M
18. Arkansas
19. Oregon
20. Syracuse
21. Auburn
22. UCLA
23. Texas Tech
24. Virginia
25. Oklahoma

Scores of interest

Penn St. 45, Indiana 21
Ohio St. 56, Iowa 35
Wisconsin 45, Michigan St. 14
Michigan 52, Minnesota 17
Nebraska 44, Colorado 21
Florida 52, Georgia 17
Tennessee 56, S. Carolina 21
Kansas 41, Kansas St. 7
Oregon 24, Arizona St. 35
Auburn 28, Arkansas 30
Notre Dame 20, Boston Col. 10
Southern Cal 21, Wash. 21
Texas A&M 31, Houston 7
Texas Tech 34, N. Mexico 7
Oklahoma 13, Missouri 9
UCLA 33, California 16

Linebacker Tim Scharf leads a host of Wildcats in standing up tailback Chris Eberly. (Art Vassy/Daily Southtown)

Chapter 14
THEY DIDN'T PLAY POSSUM

"Often, television used to come here because of the opposition. Today, we're here because of Northwestern."
—ABC's Keith Jackson, high atop Dyche Stadium

ON THE FIRST WEEKEND of September, Northwestern beat Notre Dame.

On the first weekend of October, Northwestern beat Michigan.

On the first weekend of November, Northwestern would face Penn State.

Against Notre Dame, the Wildcats went in as virtual unknowns to the country, and, if not taken lightly by Notre Dame, were at the least not prepared for by the Irish in the fashion they had needed to prepare.

Against Michigan, the Wildcats came in as a known factor, but not as a team with a reputation for playing great football consistently.

Against Penn State, there would be no chance for a surprise. There would be no chance to catch the Nittany Lions napping. Joe Paterno, who, it was believed, was coaching there when William Penn was still trying to tell the difference between Altoona and Harrisburg, not only thought Northwestern's success was good for college football, but had seen it coming. He pinned the reason for the rise in fortune squarely on the shoulders of Gary Barnett.

"He's a very strong person, very sound judgment-wise," Paterno said. "I've been very impressed. You could see the leadership Gary provided. I felt very confident he could get it done. He never does 'get rich quick' kinds of things. They had a scheme and stuck with it, both on offense and defense."

The scheme had become evident. Have Darnell Autry run the ball behind an offensive line that could block all day, and rely on a dynamite defense to disturb the opposition to no end.

That was the plan in 1994, and, to a degree, it worked. Northwestern had the ball for all but 19 seconds in the first quarter, but trailed 14-0 after 15 minutes. The Wildcats had the ball for 41:37 in all, and lost 45-17, even though Autry had run for 171 yards. The difference was a quartet of NU turnovers. Penn State scored off each of them.

This year, the tables had turned. NU was holding on to the ball, and forcing turnovers, which is why the Big Ten standings were turned upside down.

The Wildcats were a team that had accomplished more than any Northwestern outfit in 23 years, since the 7-4 team Alex Agase coached in 1971. Their No. 6 ranking in the AP writer/broadcaster poll and the CNN/USA To-

124 PURPLE ROSES

Fullback Mike McGrew and a teammate create running room for Darnell Autry by shoving Penn State's Jim Nelson aside. (Art Vassy/Daily Southtown)

day coaches poll was the highest since the Wildcats' similar 1963 preseason standing.

A bowl was a lock. And Barnett, looking for a motivational edge, wondered out loud if the players were satisfied.

"Our team now has to make a decision," he said. "Do we get better and go for the whole thing, or do we just ride it out? As a team, we can sit back and say, 'All right, we're in a bowl game. Let's just rest on this.' Or we could have a run at the whole thing.

"To do that, we've got to get better fundamentally. We really have to work harder than we have. And that's a tough decision, because we've been working hard already. But we're going to have to reach out a little bit farther, I think, in order to be able to do that."

The message to his players was obvious: Don't be satisfied. Autry, in talking about trying to run the table after the win at Illinois, had already indicated they weren't satisfied. But with four of the five goals on the list achieved, and No. 5, the Rose Bowl, doubtful because of the tiebreaker edge Ohio State enjoyed, Barnett needed a theme for the week. Besides, without an indoor practice facility, practice wasn't exactly a joy in November.

"When you're sitting in a nice room it's easy to say, 'Yeah, let's go for it all.' But when it's 41 degrees tomorrow outside, and it's raining, and the indoor facility's a year away, and we've got 2½ hours of practice and they've got a midterm, then maybe they don't.

"This is a decision our team has to make."

It was a decision that had already been made. The Wildcats, having come this far, weren't about to take it easy. Why settle for being good when being great was possible?

Pat Fitzgerald wasn't settling for anything. One of the most motivated Wildcats, the junior had moved into a starting role with the departure of Hugh Williams, but not before winning a war for the position with sophomore Don Holmes. He had quickly become precisely what defensive coordinator Ron Vanderlinden had seen watching him play for Sandburg High School in southwest suburban Orland Park.

"I saw a guy that made plays," Vanderlinden recalled. "I saw an intensity about him. I saw a game where the other team took the ball right down to the goal line, and I saw a fire, saw him get really excited. I was standing right down by the end zone, and saw him make two really nice plays right on the goal line. What we needed at that time was to bring in guys who could play with confidence and make plays. You can recruit guys who have ability and potential, but in the end, it's performance. And Pat performed."

Through the first eight games of the season, Fitzgerald had made 103 tackles, with a high of 18 at Michigan. He had led NU in tackles in every game except against Indiana, when William Bennett's 10-tackle performance edged him by one.

Twice he'd been named the Big Ten's player of the week on defense, sharing the honor with Penn State's Kim Herring on one occasion, and getting it solo on another. And, of course, he was a part of the NU squad's being named player of the week after the shutout of Wisconsin.

So what was Fitzgerald, who had both the grades and the talent to go anywhere, doing at Northwestern? The answer was simple.

"It was close to Orland Park, so my parents would be able to see all of my games," said Fitzgerald, who has kept close ties to the Sandburg program. "When coach (Gregg) Brandon recruited me, he asked me a question at the beginning of the recruiting process: 'Give me three reasons why you want to go to a school.' I said, 'Cause it's close to home, has a good education and a good football program.' When it came down for me to make my decision, he asked me that same question, and that's exactly what it came down to."

Northwestern, with Evanston about 75 minutes from Orland Park on non-game days, was close, closer even than Notre Dame, which had been after Fitzgerald until abruptly cancelling his official visit. The academics at NU, ranked No. 13 in the country by *U.S. News and World Report,* were unquestioned. As for the Wildcats having a good football program, when Fitzgerald committed in the winter of 1992-'93, after Barnett's first season at the helm, there was still little evidence of that to outsiders.

In Barnett, Fitzgerald said, "I saw someone who was sincere and honest. He was a coach I could believe in, where in some other coaches I'd dealt with it was like, 'Well, you can come in and start right away,' and all this stuff. Coach Barnett said, 'You'll have a chance to play. I'm not going to tell you you'll start or what your role's going to be, but you'll have a chance.'

"That's all I wanted. I believed in him."

Barnett, while tabbing the term "trite," called Fitzgerald "a coach on the field."

"Fitz knows as much as Vandy can teach him," said Barnett. "He's like a sponge. He just absorbs all that stuff and then he's able to let everybody know.

"What Fitz is going to teach our younger linebackers is what happens when you sit down, you watch enough film and you listen and absorb what he tells you. There's so much information that is given out by coaches that's left on the floor in the meeting rooms. Fitz doesn't leave any of it on the floor."

Nor Autry, someone Paterno knew his defense, which was allowing only 108 rushing

Darnell Autry on the move for some of his 139 yards. (Art Vassy/Daily Southtown)

yards per-game, would have to contend with.

"Autry's certainly there with anybody in the conference as a tailback," Paterno said. "The kid at Ohio State (Eddie George) has got a lot more help. He doesn't have to carry it 40-some times a game like Autry does. This Autry kid is like the fullback at Purdue (Mike Alstott), except Autry doesn't have to block.

"You don't stop him. You try to slow him down. You try to create some second-and-12s and make them throw the ball a little bit. Nothing against Northwestern's quarterback, but Autry's the kid who really makes you stay up nights."

Besides, as much as Barnett talked about spreading out the offense and having Steve Schnur pass more, the Lions had collected 33 sacks, including 17 in the last two weeks, "more sacks than Dominick's," in Barnett's view.

The game would be played on the ground, as generic a brand of football as Penn State's vanilla uniforms.

The only thing that was unsure was the status of NU guard Ryan Padgett. The standout had sprained his left ankle when Autry clipped him against Illinois and was considered doubtful for the game.

"They're not fancy winning," Paterno went on. "It's not a very intricate offense. Nobody carries the football except Autry, and he's very careful with it. They play to win by one point, play disciplined. They're fun to watch. I won't have any fun this Saturday. They remind me a lot of my good teams."

This edition of the Nittany Lions wasn't exactly a bunch of slouches. Since a 17-9 loss to Wisconsin, they were averaging 34 points a game. With Mike Archie and Curtis Enis alternating at tailback and fullback Jon Witman a regular contributor, they didn't have to depend on just one position, as NU did.

Likewise, the Lions had a one-two punch at receiver similar to Michigan's. The Wolverines had Amani Toomer and Mercury Hayes. Penn State quarterback Wally Richardson had Bobby Engram and Freddie Scott to throw to. "It's the best offense we've played," said Barnett without exaggeration.

"Penn State is Penn State," said Wildcat linebacker Danny Sutter.

Because Penn State was Penn State, Penn State was listed as a five-point favorite (a figure that jumped to seven points just before the game, and was even higher in Pittsburgh), and this time, Barnett could understand why.

"I looked, and Penn State has 15 *Parade* All-America first-teamers or *USA Today* players of the year in their first 22 guys," he said. "I looked through our media guide, and I didn't find any. On paper, it's not much of a matchup. It's a mismatch. But we haven't gone by much of that stuff anyway."

Mismatch or matchless, the meeting of No. 6 Northwestern and No. 12 Penn State was not only big enough to lure ABC to Dyche Stadium —a place the network did not have on its short list of venues to visit back in September—for the first time since 1983, it was of such enormity that Keith Jackson, the voice of college football, would handle the play-by-play, working with Bob Griese and Lynn Swann.

Jackson could have been excused if he needed a guide to get to Evanston. He hadn't called a game at Dyche Stadium since 1958, when Washington State visited NU and he was their radio voice. In all of ABC's visits since, Jackson had been assigned to a different game.

The network exposure also meant a 2:30 p.m. starting time, and that meant bringing in the portable lights of the Musco Mobile Lighting, Ltd., of Oskaloosa, Iowa. Three of Musco's diesel-powered lighting units, each with a boom rising 140 feet above the landscape, would be positioned around Dyche Stadium.

They had been used before at Dyche for early-season night games in the late 1980s, but this was different. This was going to be a happening.

Chicago had caught Wildcat fever. Pennants and purple "N" flags were beginning to appear in shop windows in Evanston, places like Wilbert T. Findley Insurance and Harold's True Value Hardware. Souvenir sales were picking up. Ross Kooperman, owner of The Locker Room, a small shop filled to the brim with Wildcat goodies across Central Street from Dyche, was beginning to see a steady stream of foot traffic from panting pursuers of priceless purple paraphernalia. Scalpers appeared on the street in greater numbers before the game. The Wildcats, on the outs for a generation, were very in.

"Look at the madness that's been created," Fitzgerald had said a fortnight earlier.

They Didn't Play Possum

He hadn't seen anything yet. When Northwestern took the field against Penn State on November 4, the roar from the crowd could not only be heard, it could be felt on the field and in the stadium. Unlike the Wisconsin game, where thousands of fans were Badger backers, this was, save for about 2,000 Nittany Lion rooters, a Wildcat crowd. It might have been 30 degrees, but 69-year-old Dyche Stadium was about to boil over.

On Thursday night, Barnett had told his players, "November is a new season. Champions are crowned in November."

They listened, then went out and proved him right. The offensive line blocked. Autry ran like a deer. Fitzgerald made tackle after tackle. The clock ran down, then out on Penn State. Northwestern, with Autry scoring three touchdowns, won 21-10, becoming the first team since Michigan State to beat Notre Dame, Michigan and Penn State in the same season.

The Spartans had managed that trifecta twice, in 1951 and 1965, *Bloomington Herald-Times* writer Bob Hammel had discovered.

Northwestern had equaled the achievement, and spectacularly.

"We must be pretty good or we probably couldn't do those things," said Barnett before dozens of reporters from across the country.

What they and millions of viewers in the eastern half of the U.S. had seen was a performance by an offensive line that moved the Penn State defensive line where it needed to move it, giving Autry room to run from the start. A "stone wall," Barnett called it.

Smartly, offensive coordinator Greg Meyer ordered a series of passes to tight end Darren Drexler on the first drive, opening things up. The combination of Schnur-to-Drexler, Autry on the ground, and an ill-timed pass interference penalty by Lion cornerback Mark Tate all contributed to the Wildcats scoring on the game's opening drive, a 14-play, 73-yard match that ended with Autry going around left end from the 1 on third-and-goal.

"Their offensive line played hard, and he's a tough kid," admitted Paterno. "They're good. People just don't seem to want to admit they're good. They were better than we were today. They're a very intelligent football team."

Three possessions after NU's first score, the Wildcats were on the move again. Triggered by Brian Musso's 23-yard punt return to the Lion 34, it took only five plays, one of them a 16-yard pass from Schnur to Musso on third-and-6, to get into the end zone. It was Autry again, this time turning it up at left end and using D'Wayne Bates' seal block on Tate to find his way to the second touchdown of the day.

That sent the fans into a frenzy, and what happened next might have sent a few into shock. The Lions took over on their 22 after Stephen Pitts' 21-yard kickoff return, but had the ball for only 11 seconds. Richardson, look-

Darnell Autry stretches for yards while in the grasp of a Penn State defender. (Art Vassy/Daily Southtown)

Cornerback Chris Martin ties up Nittany Lion Brian Milne as Eric Collier comes in to finish him off. (Art Vassy/ Daily Southtown)

ing for Engram deep near the right sideline, was picked off by Martin, who returned the ball 24 yards to the Penn State 39.

The Wildcats had a chance to go up by an even larger margin, but Brian Gowins missed a 44-yard field goal to the right.

Now, with less than five minutes left in the half, it was Penn State's turn. The Lions finally moved the football, going 73 yards in 11 plays, Richardson hitting tight end Keith Olsommer over the middle in the end zone from the 5 to cut Northwestern's lead to 14-7.

All season, Northwestern had excelled in making defensive changes and shutting down teams in the second half. Against Illinois, for instance, they had limited the Illini to 78 yards, including minus-1 yards on the ground, and held them off the scoreboard after the band played. It was Northwestern's fourth "half-shut-out" of the year.

Penn State would move the football. Penn State would move it a lot. But Penn State would not get into the end zone, and only a miscue by Matt Stewart on a punt—the ball bouncing off his foot when he couldn't get out of the way, and into the waiting mitts of Penn State's Chuck Penzenik—allowed the Lions to get close enough to score a field-goal.

Brett Conway made it from the 24-yard line 6:28 into the third quarter, cutting NU's lead to 14-10.

Quickly, after holding the Cats to three plays and a punt, Penn State was on the march again, starting at its 25.

Presently, it was third-and-4 on the Lion 31. Richardson hit Engram, who was playing with a sore hand, in the left flat for 11 yards and a first down. Soon, it was third-and-3 on the Wildcat 41. Richardson hit Olsommer over the middle for the three yards needed. Before long, it was third-and-5 at the NU 33. Richardson went to the air again, and under pressure, found Jon Witman, the fullback, in the right flat for exactly five yards.

The Lions were inside the NU 30, and driving. After Curtis Enis ran for three yards, Richardson hit Engram over the middle for 18 yards. Now it was first-and-goal. The Wildcat defense had to come through, or it was curtains.

Enis got the call and broke over left tackle for three yards, but a penalty flag fluttered through the air. Lion center Barry Tielsch held on the play, and the 12-yard walkoff moved the ball back to the 19.

With that, the Wildcat defense turned it up. Hudhaifa Ismaeli stormed in and sacked Richardson for an 8-yard loss on the next play.

That ended the third quarter, and it gave the Wildcat defense, on the field for all but 30 seconds of it, a much-needed breather.

"Tired? Yeah, we were tired," said defensive end Casey Dailey.

"But you don't feel it during plays. Just between plays."

Breather or not, the Richardson-Engram connection was working again on the first play of the fourth. Engram got away near the right sideline for 17 yards. Now it was third-and-goal on the 10. Richardson looked to Freddie Scott for the seventh time on the day. Scott had caught four passes already, but this time, in the left corner of Dyche Stadium's north end zone, the pass would fall incomplete.

Conway came in to attempt a 27-yard field goal. He kicked it from the right hash-mark, and kicked it straight. According to the official under the crossbar, it just missed to the outside of the right post. Penn State's 17-yard drive, which took 8:17 off the clock, had gone for naught.

"I thought it was good, actually," said Fitzgerald, whose announced 20-tackle performance was trimmed to a still-robust 17 after coaches reviewed film.

"We had a chance, and they hung in there and did what they had to do," said Paterno. "The field goal? I can't tell. The kids thought it was good. That was the best defense we've played against this year."

The Wildcat offense, quiet since early in the second quarter, had to come up big now, or risk letting an exhausted group of NU defenders back on the field. And, aided by Tate's second pass-interference penalty of the game, it did the job.

This time, on third-and-5 at the NU 25, Tate hit Bates before Schnur's pass got there, a 14-yard penalty that gave NU a first down.

On the next snap, Schnur, who was never sacked, hit Bates for 11. Two plays later, Dave Beazley ran a reverse to the right, gaining 25 yards. Autry slashed over right end for 11 more, getting to 1,297 yards for the season to break Bob Christian's rushing record.

There was no time for back-slapping. Two plays later, Autry ran for 22 more to get over 100 yards on the day. Then he got over the goal line, bolting over right tackle from the 1. There was bedlam in Dyche Stadium.

It was a tough day for Tate. His first interference penalty led to Autry's first touchdown, he was blocked by Bates as Autry sped by to his second score, and now, this flag would keep a drive alive that climaxed in Autry's third touchdown of the day, the one that put the game away.

Yes, there was 11:03 left, but the Wildcat defense, blitzing more now, was resolute down the stretch. For the game, NU held Penn State to 232 yards, a shade over half the Lions' 449.3 yard season average.

With seven minutes left, Barnett, tickled with the way the defense was playing, said to himself, "I think we can win this game now."

Rabid Wildcat fans tried to dislodge the goalposts but they held as well as NU's defense. (Art Vassy/ Daily Southtown)

The Lions never got past the 50, turned the ball back with 3:07 remaining, watched the Wildcats run out the clock, and then watched thousands swarm onto the field under the lights and a nearly-full moon.

"It's a possum moon," Keith Jackson had said along the way. He and Griese had also lavished compliment after compliment on the Northwestern players, coaches and program. It was a 3½-hour promotion for Wildcat football, the kind of publicity that money can't buy, and something sure to pay off down the road in recruiting.

As might some of Paterno's postgame comments, especially when he said of NU's rise to prominence, "I think it's good for the Big Ten conference and good for college football. Anytime you see a team play the way they're playing, you've got to admire 'em. They've got great team cohesion and great leadership and they're doing a great job coaching.

"They don't have a lot of glamour athletes, except for Autry. They're like some of the good teams I had some of those years. Nothing very fancy, they don't win big. They just go out and win. They plod along in there, and don't look spectacular doing it. But they're my kind of football team."

There could be no higher praise from Paterno.

"That they're this good, maybe this surprises me," he added. "But that's what happens when things start to go your way. You get confidence and momentum."

Northwestern was definitely rolling. The Cats were 8-1 now, 6-0 in the Big Ten compared to Penn State's 6-3, 3-3 mark and hanging-in Ohio State's 9-0, 5-0 record. NU's seven-game winning streak was its first since 1936, its most recent Big Ten title year.

To Barnett, one of the keys to the victory was simply taking the ball and scoring at the start of the game, rather than deferring after winning the toss, as is his usual stratagem.

"Thursday, I told the kids if we won the toss, we were going to take the ball, much like Wisconsin did, keep their offense off the field, and hope to get an extra drive with our offense," Barnett explained.

Ryan Padgett, incidentally, was there from the start, wearing a plastic boot on his tender left ankle for stability.

"The first drive always sets the tone," said center Rob Johnson. "After you (score), you feel you can score on every possession."

NU didn't do that, but they did enough. Autry's 139 yards, moving him to 1,339 yards for the season, and three touchdowns were enough. The 21 points were, as it turned out, more than enough.

"You have to stop now and give our kids credit," Barnett said of the Notre Dame-Michigan-Penn State trifecta. "We're a pretty good football team. If we don't turn the ball over and only have to play against one team, then we've got a chance.

"Who knows what this team can do?"

There was plenty left to shoot for, including a Big Ten title. That, though, could be accomplished only by winning out against Iowa and Purdue and hoping Ohio State would stumble in one of its last three games.

Now, NU was going into uncharted waters historically. The Wildcats had never won eight in a row.

Then again, they'd never had a team like this, and certainly no defense like this in the modern era. When it had to, it repulsed a Penn State attack that had been churning out yardage for a month.

"We knew we had to get back to fundamentals, which we didn't do last week," said Fitzgerald. "We knew we had to stop their running attack. We got our pads lower and started flying around and playing like we usually do. Instead of sitting there waiting for someone to make a big play, we went out and made the big play.

"When we have success is when we're flying around with confidence and we're making big plays."

Fitzgerald was not about to take credit for his big day.

"Guys like (Matt) Rice and Dailey and (Ray) Robey and (Keith) Lozowski are in front of me, and keep me free," he said. "I've been saying all year, the way our D line plays, that's the way our defense plays."

Along with everything else, the Wildcat players got inspiration from the pregame introduction of the parents of Marcel Price, the would-be sophomore who had been shot and killed in Nashville, Tennessee, over the summer.

"It wasn't meant to be (a motivating factor)," said Barnett. "We really tried to have the Prices up at an earlier game. This wasn't planned. We had not done anything with that all year. Marcel was a special player and had a special place on our team. That's a private thing, and we've tried to keep it that way."

Regardless, it motivated.

"It was an emotional kick in the pants," said Johnson. "To finally see his parents, it was emotional, especially for me."

Speaking of emotion, Iowa was next.

"Iowa is a game that this team wants so much that I can't put it into words right now for you," said Barnett. "They've wanted it for 12 months."

Now, they only had to wait seven days.

Chris Martin hauls down Penn State's Chris Eberly for a loss. (Art Vassy/Daily Southtown)

Northwestern fan frenzy. (Art Vassy/Daily Southtown)

They Didn't Play Possum

PENN STATE VS. NORTHWESTERN

Saturday, November 4, 1995 at Dyche Stadium, Evanston, IL
Weather: 30° Wind W9 Mostly sunny
Attendance: 49,256 (sellout)

SCORE BY QUARTERS	1	2	3	4	SCORE
Penn State (6-3-0)	0	7	3	0	10
Northwestern (8-1)	7	7	0	7	21

First Quarter
		NU	PS
NU	8:47 Darnell Autry 2-yard run (Brian Gowins kick) (12 plays, 73 yards, 6:13 TOP)	7	0

Second Quarter
| NU | 8:07 Darnell Autry 10-yard run (Brian Gowins kick) (5 plays, 34 yards, 2:27 TOP) | 14 | 0 |
| PS | 0:48 Keith Olosommer 5-yard pass from Wally Richardson (Brett Conway kick) (11 plays, 73 yards, 4:08 TOP) | 14 | 7 |

Third Quarter
| PS | 8:32 Brett Conway 24-yard field goal (6 plays, 15 yards, 2:49 TOP) | 14 | 10 |

Fourth Quarter
| NU | 11:03 Darnell Autry 1-yard run (Brian Gowins kick) (9 plays, 80 yards, 3:43 TOP) | 21 | 10 |

Big Ten Standings

1. Northwestern (6-0-0)
2. Ohio State (5-0-0)
3. Michigan (3-2-0)
4. Michigan State (3-2-1)
5. Penn State (3-3-0)
6. Iowa (2-3-0)
7. Illinois (2-3-0)
8. Wisconsin (2-3-0)
9. Purdue (1-3-1)
10. Minnesota (1-4-0)
11. Indiana (0-5-0)

AP Top 25

1. Nebraska
2. Ohio St.
3. Florida
4. Tennessee
5. **Northwestern**
6. Florida St.
7. Kansas St.
8. Notre Dame
9. Colorado
10. Kansas
11. Texas
12. Southern Cal
13. Michigan
14. Virginia
15. Arkansas
16. Alabama
17. Oregon
18. Texas A&M
19. Penn St.
20. Auburn
21. Virginia Tech.
22. Washington
23. Syracuse
24. Clemson
25. San Diego St.

TEAM STATISTICS	PS	NU
First Downs	15	16
Rushing	7	10
Passing	8	4
Penalty	0	2
Rushing Attempts	38	43
Yards Gained Rushing	139	184
Yards Lost Rushing	36	16
Net Yards Rushing	103	168
Net Yards Passing	129	96
Passes Attempted	29	16
Passes Completed	18	10
Had Intercepted	1	1
Total Offensive Plays	67	59
Total Net Yards	232	264
Average Gain per Play	3.5	4.5
Fumbles: Number-Lost	0-0	2-1
Penalties: Number-Yards	7-65	5-35
Interceptions: Number-Yards	1-0	1-24
Number of Punts-Yards	6-234	4-142
Average Per Punt	39.0	35.5
Punt Returns: Number-Yards	1-1	5-47
Kickoff Returns: Number-Yards	4-71	3-62
Possession Time	33:53	26:07
Third-Down Conversions	8 of 17	5 of 11
Sacks By: Number-Yards	0-0	5-29

Scores of interest

Ohio St. 49, Minnesota 21
Michigan 25, Michigan St. 28
Nebraska 73, Iowa St. 14
Florida St. 28, Virginia 33
Florida 58, N. Illinois 20
Tennessee 42, S. Mississippi 0
Notre Dame 35, Navy 17
Kansas State 49, Oklahoma 10
Colorado 45, Oklahoma St. 32
Kansas 42, Missouri 23
Texas 48, Texas Tech 7
USC 31, Stanford 30
Washington 22, Oregon 24
Syracure 31, Virginia Tech 7
Auburn 38, NE Louisiana 14
UCLA 37, Arizona St. 33

Hudhaifa Ismaeli gets away from Iowa's Sedrick Shaw en route to a 31-yard fumble return touchdown in the fourth quarter. (David Banks/Daily Southtown)

Chapter 15
A RED-LETTER GAME

"We're smelling roses, but we have a game to prepare for."
—cornerback Chris Martin

THE POSITIVE SHOCK waves reverberating around Northwestern from the win over Penn State, what center Rob Johnson called "one for the scrapbook," continued well into the next week.

On Sunday, the Wildcats, 8-1 for the first time since 1904, climbed into fifth place in both polls, their highest placement since a No. 1 ranking for two weeks in 1962.

On Monday, Pat Fitzgerald was named the Big Ten's defensive player of the week for the third time in seven weeks, and WBBM-TV announced it would follow the syndicated broadcast of Saturday's game with Iowa with a special, Bears-style, postgame show, a first in NU history.

By Tuesday, it was known that Darnell Autry, who had been the conference's offensive player of the week way back against Notre Dame, was up for a greater honor. He'd be on the cover of *Sports Illustrated*, the first time that had happened to an NU player in 33 years. The magazine would hit newsstands the next day, and be in mailboxes around the country by the end of the week.

By Wednesday, the campus was crawling with reporters from national publications. The Wildcats had gone beyond the sports realm. It was one thing for the *Los Angeles Times* to send a staffer to the NU-Penn State game. Now *People Weekly* had a reporter in Evanston.

The phone lines were buzzing, old Wildcats calling the current crop.

"They were saying, 'You guys have done what we never did!'" Barnett said. "Have a winning season? 'No, play in front of a full crowd at Dyche!'

"I'm convinced we would not have won the game if not for the crowd," he said. "For the first time since I had a chance to coach here at Northwestern, what I saw Saturday was what I'd hoped it could become. That was a home-field advantage with a raucous home crowd into college football. I just can't think that there can be any better situation for a home team to experience than what we experienced Saturday.

"It was ours, it was purple and it was loud."

And welcome.

"There's no place I'd rather play right now than Dyche Stadium," said quarterback Steve Schnur. "I used to like playing on the road, because there were big crowds."

Somehow, the players took all the extra attention in stride. Barnett, using subtle motivation, had gotten his players up for games emotionally, but kept them on track mentally. Often, he spoke of their intrinsic motivation.

"Remember, after the fourth win, everything's

been new to these guys," Barnett said. "They haven't had four wins trying to get five before, and haven't had five trying to get a winning season. They haven't had six trying to get to a bowl game before. Then they haven't had seven, trying to beat Penn State, to beat Penn State, Michigan and Notre Dame in the same year.

"They've pretty much guided themselves. It's the difference between driving a stick and an automatic. I've got an automatic and am trying to stay out of the way. After the Notre Dame game, I realized we were on overdrive."

The attention went all the way to Hollywood. Northwestern alum Charlton Heston was crowing about the Cats. Found by ESPN at a party and asked to comment on the team's rise, he went back to his role as Moses, and intoned, "Behold the power of the Lord!"

For WLUP-FM talk maven Jonathon Brandmeier, Heston left a message on Schnur's answering machine:

"You guys are no longer the Mildcats, you're the Wildcats. Go all the way, guys!"

Meanwhile, back on the field, here came Iowa, the team the Wildcats had grown to hate.

It was a curious feeling, actually. The coaching staff, led by Gary Barnett, professed wanting to emulate the Hawkeye program, known for its continuity in the staff and dedication to detail. But the players were ticked off at assorted sins committed by the Hawkeyes, from head coach Hayden Fry on down, over the years.

So, when the schedule that would hand on the wall in the Nicolet Center auditorium, the names of 10 teams were in purple. One was in red.

Iowa. The date: November 11.

Johnson was seeing red.

"We don't want to win, we want to hurt them," Johnson had said.

Fighting words. Words guaranteed to go up on the bulletin board in Iowa City.

Words that the Wildcats would have to back up. Why were the Cats so perturbed at the Hawkeyes?

"Iowa's big for us for many reasons," said cornerback Chris Martin. "We don't really care for 'em."

Twenty-one straight losses was a big reason. NU hadn't beaten Iowa since 1973, and in terms of a streak, the run by the Hawkeyes exceeded the 19-win run Michigan enjoyed going into the 1995 season.

The margins of recent victories played a part. Iowa won 56-14 in 1990, which was too far back for any current player to feel the sting from, but won by an identical score in 1992, when this year's seniors were freshmen. In

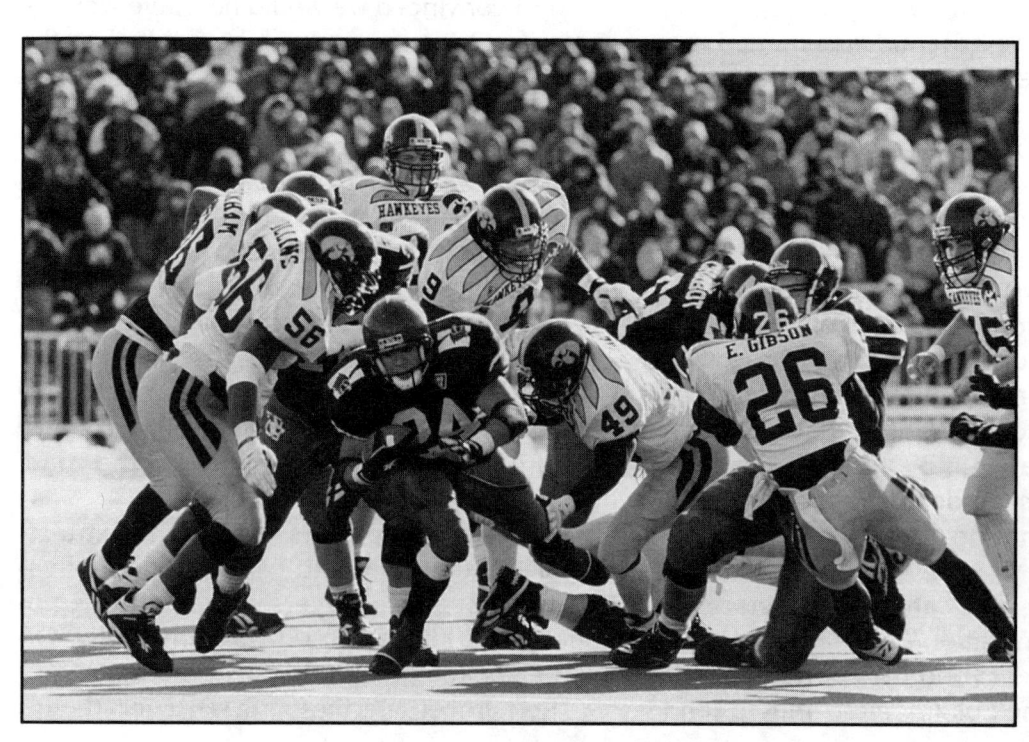

It took eight Hawkeyes, with a ninth looking on, to bring down Darnell Autry on this play. (David Banks/Daily Southtown)

Wildcat safeties Eric Collier and William Bennett team up to bring down Iowa back Sedrick Shaw. (David Banks/Daily Southtown)

1994, the Hawkeyes rolled to a 49-13 victory, Iowa piling up 602 yards of total offense.

Moreso, it was the way the points piled up that got under the skins of the Wildcats.

"We've been flat-out embarrassed by them the previous three years, and not just the score," said Johnson. "Ever since I've been here, they've done some really embarrassing things to our team, whether intentional or unintentional. We've been looking forward to this game for a long time. I think you're going to see a very motivated Wildcat team this week in practice, and a very, very motivated team on the field next week.

"I think they ran an onside kick back for a touchdown one year. That's how ridiculous it's been for the last four years. Hayden Fry has done a great job of preparing his kids to beat the pants off us. And they have, and now it's our opportunity to gain some revenge, and this is definitely a revenge game for us. Guys have been talking about this game since before the season started."

Mostly, it was the seniors. But there was a trickle-down effect.

"It filters down from them to me," said Autry, a sophomore. "I was here last year, and things just broke down completely when we played them. The seniors have been through some embarrassing losses."

One of them, senior quarterback Steve Schnur, chose his words carefully.

"I don't know if they've run it up against us," he said. "They've just scored a lot of points. Sometimes, you can't help but score. And we didn't score much."

Schnur's opposite number, Iowa quarterback Matt Sherman, was a dynamo the season before, hitting 19 of 24 passes for 331 yards and three touchdowns.

Barnett tried to cool the ardor of his players, but had to admit they were chomping at the bit.

"We went into the locker room (Saturday), and even before we started singing the fight song, which we do after every victory—we've all learned the words this year, and we've got some seniors who didn't know the words until this year—the talk was about Iowa.

"Last year, we felt like we embarrassed ourselves. Nothing to do with Iowa. They played very well, but it was our own doing."

Barnett, who used to recruit the St. Louis and Kansas City areas when he was with Colo-

"Throw it to me," tight end Darren Drexler seems to be saying. (David Banks/Daily Southtown)

rado, talked mostly about how he wanted his program to look like Fry's program.

"When I first got here, I looked at the programs we'd be playing every year, and felt that Iowa was probably the program we would most like to be like," he said. "We didn't have Michigan on the schedule every year. But we did have Iowa. Hayden Fry has done an unbelievable job of resurrecting that program, taking it from the ashes. It was dead for a while.

"As a coaching staff, we really admire what Iowa's done. And our players, even though we've been on the short end of it, have admired the way Iowa's been able to punish us over the years. So this is not a game that anyone has to worry about us looking beyond. We've been waiting to get to this one for a long time."

Fry tried to be careful in his response, and was on the Big Ten's telephone hookup on the Tuesday before the game. He said things like, "When you've lost 21 straight years, you try to find reasons," and denied running up the score.

"We've scored quite a few points through the years, but it's been by running the football unless we threw for five or six touchdowns early. When you get into the fourth quarter, I've got my second- and third-team people in there. I've never tried to run up the score on anybody in my life.

"Sometimes, the other team has something to do with it."

That was tepid compared to Fry's comments on Wednesday, before his usual gathering of regular reporters in Iowa City. There, he essentially challenged the Wildcats to prove they were good.

"Across America in sports, you're going to have teams jump up and do well from time to time. But that's not the barometer to judge. You need to do it over the long haul and see how long you're really competitive.

"I think Northwestern's players are just feeling their oats. Whatever is in their craw is in their craw. So be it."

The Cats were certainly more concerned with Iowa than they were with a possible national championship. That, though, was a possibility, however remote. All kinds of things had to happen, and in the right sequence, for the fifth-ranked Cats to make their way into the Bowl Alliance as the sole at-large selection.

First off, Notre Dame had to drop out of the top 10. Otherwise, presuming an eight-win season, the Fighting Irish would be the at-large Alliance selection to go with the champions of the Southeastern, Southwest, Big Eight, Big East and Atlantic Coast conferences.

If ND wasn't an automatic bid, it could still be picked anyway, but other schools, including Northwestern and Tennessee, which probably wouldn't win the SEC but was ranked higher than longshot Arkansas, would be eligible for selection.

So the No. 5 Cats would have to be picked, and along the way to that selection, hope that enough teams above them fell to allow them to sneak into the Fiesta Bowl.

One team that had to keep winning for this to happen was second-ranked Ohio State. Top-ranked Nebraska, which had jumped over Florida State before the Seminoles had fallen to Virginia, could keep winning, and probably would. But No. 3 Florida and No. 4 Tennessee would have to lose for the Wildcats to get a

A Red-Letter Game

Fiesta Bowl date with the Cornhuskers. And if Ohio State lost, the Wildcats, presuming wins over Iowa and Purdue, would go to the Rose Bowl.

There wasn't a national title available there, but Pasadena, rather than the more likely Florida Citrus Bowl, is where the Wildcats wanted to go.

"It's the ultimate for us," said Johnson.

Almost as big as beating the Hawkeyes.

Iowa came into the game hurting, an unIowan three-game losing streak having dropped their record to 5-3 overall and 2-3 in the conference.

"We're probably dealing with a wounded animal," said Barnett.

The Hawkeyes were even more wounded after the game. Northwestern, winning a school-record eighth straight game, administered a 31-20 whipping, treating the Hawkeyes as coldly as the 26-degree weather. The plus-1 wind chill, created by the northerly wind howling up to 30 miles per hour—enough to stir up whitecaps on Lake Michigan, the early-morning heavy snow on the north side of the Chicago area, not even the local telecast of Creative Sports' syndicated production would keep Dyche Stadium from being filled for a third straight home game. The mob of 49,256, warming itself on coffee, hot chocolate and more potent liquids, stayed until the happy ending.

It could have been happier. The Wildcats, trailing 20-17 at the half, took over, as usual, in the second half, but lost junior middle linebacker Pat Fitzgerald, their leader, to a broken lower left leg and ankle in a third-quarter pileup.

There was an audible gasp from the crowd when the PA announcer reported it was Fitzgerald lying on the icy AstroTurf.

"I was gasping too," said linebacker Danny Sutter, part of the collision that Fitzgerald couldn't avoid.

"He'll miss the bowl game, I'm sure," said Barnett of Fitzgerald, NU's leading tackler. "We lost one heck of a football player. We all have to play a little bit better."

Northwestern, play better? Here was Barnett, challenging his players again.

Iowa created a challenge from the start. While NU took a 3-0 lead on Brian Gowins' 50-yard field goal, the Hawkeyes came right back with a 17-play drive highlighted by four third-down conversions and capped by Sedrick Shaw's 1-yard plunge over left tackle with 8:03 left in the first half.

Less than five minutes later, the Hawkeyes stole a page—and a football—from the Wildcats. Steve Schnur's pass to fullback Matt Hartl from the NU 23 went through Hartl's hands. Tom Knight grabbed it at the 28 and zipped

Danny Sutter, Pat Fitzgerald, and Mike Warren combine for a stop on Iowa tightend Scott Slutzker. (David Banks/Daily Southtown)

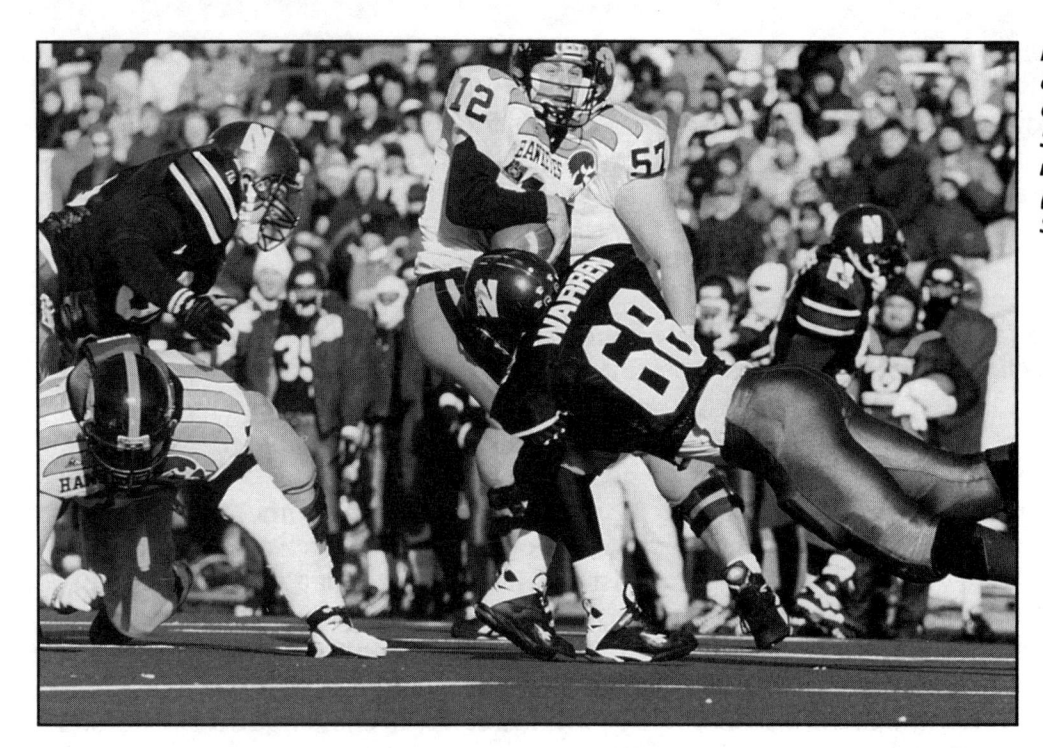

Left end Mike Warren clobbers Hawkeye Quarterback Matt Sherman, one of four registered by NU. (David Banks/Daily Southtown)

straight down the sideline, untouched by any Wildcat. It was 14-3, and the majority of the crowd was silent. Iowa had the lead and the momentum.

The latter was Iowa's for only one play. Adrian Autry's 18-yard return and a personal foul on the Hawkeyes gave NU the ball at its 44. Darnell Autry and the offensive line went to work. Autry went around left end and wasn't stopped for 27 yards, the first play in a five-play sortie that wrapped up with Schnur hitting tight end Darren Drexler over the middle with a pass that didn't appear to be more than a 10-yard gain until Drexler began carrying Iowa defenders toward the end zone. They all got there, the 21-yard strike cutting the Hawkeye lead to 14-10.

Autry didn't think it was his carry that woke the team up as much as it was the guys in front of him.

"The offensive line said enough is enough," said Autry. "I followed them."

It wouldn't stay that way for long. The Wildcat defense stopped the Hawkeyes in three plays, forcing Nick Gallery to punt. He had the wind at his back, but that proved to be a mixed blessing. Gallery lined a low three-hopper up the middle of the field, a 48-yard punt that Brian Musso grabbed at ground level at the NU 40. He took off, took two steps to the right, eluded Tim Dwight, and was on the go when Chris Martin hammered Gallery. Musso, who had managed an 86-yard return against Indiana that fell just short of the end zone, made it in this time, a 60-yard score.

"It was spectacular and timely," said Barnett.

"To me, every punt return is a chance to score," said Musso.

In a flash, the Wildcats had moved ahead 17-14. The two touchdowns had come in 1 minute 39 seconds.

This, though, was not going to be as easy as that. Iowa came back to score on its next possession, Sherman connecting with Scott Slutzker, who was chased by Eric Collier for what seemed to be a half-mile. Actually, it was a 39-yard touchdown pass with 1:31 left in the half. Iowa, on the game's third lead-change, was ahead 20-17 after Zach Bromert's extra-point try failed.

"We just wanted to focus on the fact we'd given up two easy touchdowns," said Barnett of his halftime thoughts. "I really felt it was going to come down to whether our offensive line was going to block what they were doing to us."

Iowa's lead lasted just 6:23. The Wildcats took over—took command, actually—with their first drive of the third quarter. With smooth efficiency, without needing a third down, the Cats, led by the offensive line, grabbed a 24-20 advantage, Autry diving around right end from the 3 for the score behind blocks by Hartl and guard Justin Chabot. Along the way, Schnur had hit D'Wayne Bates for a 22-yard pickup and Bates had run a reverse that gained the same yardage.

Now, Iowa was forced to come from behind, and in the second half—all season, Northwestern's half. For a time, it appeared they would. A drive that commenced on the Iowa 18 with 8:27 left in the third quarter went on and on and on. This was Penn State all over again. Twice, Sherman found receivers for the necessary yardage on third down, and twice, the Hawkeyes ran for what they needed and more on fourth down.

But, early in the fourth quarter, now with the wind against them, the drive bogged down. Sherman had guided Iowa to the NU 21, but slipped for a nine-yard loss, and a pair of passes fell incomplete. After 18 plays and 10:04 on the clock, Iowa had come up with nothing.

The Hawkeyes wouldn't threaten again, committing two turnovers down the stretch, the first when Sherman's pass to split end Demo Odems was intercepted by Martin.

"We're smelling roses, but we have a game to prepare for," said Martin, thinking ahead not only to the finale against Purdue, but to the possibility, pending an upset of Ohio State, of a trip west.

Northwestern's last score came when Sherman's completed pass to tight end Derek Price was stripped away by Rodney Ray and picked up by Hudhaifa Ismaeli, who ran 31 yards to the end zone with 2:56 remaining.

"Winning in this conference is hard," said Barnett. "Iowa came out stoked up, played very physical on both sides of the ball. They really controlled the line of scrimmage. Their defense caused us some problems we never really did get straightened out."

The dominance of NU's defense again was on display in the second half. Along with their fifth "half-shutout" of the year, they held Iowa to 123 yards in the second half, and only 38 on the ground. Fifty-two of those 123 yards, and 29 of the rushing yards, came on the 18-play drive that came up empty.

Fitzgerald's injury occurred during the long drive. He was moving to his left, trying to line up Shaw, and was hit by a Hawkeye lineman. Fitzgerald got up and again gave chase to Shaw, but almost instantly, he became part of the collision between Iowa left tackle Jeremy McKinney and Sutter. McKinney crashed into Sutter, Sutter fell on Fitzgerald's lower back, and all three hit the ground in a heap.

It was Fitzgerald who didn't get up. Dyche Stadium empty was never quieter than it was

Eric Collier watches as Northwestern's medical staff tends to fallen linebacker Pat Fitzgerald in the third quarter. (David Banks/ Daily Southtown)

for the next few minutes, the crowd realizing the implications of losing Fitzgerald.

"He's a huge loss," Sutter said. "Everybody's going to have to step up and make the plays he's been making."

Sophomore Don Holmes, who had lost the position battle to him in spring drills, was already gearing up.

"We'll try to keep things rolling, keep moving forward," said Holmes. "It's not pressure. In practice, I've been getting the snaps. It's just making the plays on the field."

For Fitzgerald, who was tracked down at Evanston Hospital by *Daily Southtown* columnist Phil Arvia, it was a sad end to a delightful season. He underwent surgery the morning after the game, but still was expected to miss the bowl game.

"I'm disappointed for myself, because I've had some success here," Fitzgerald told Arvia. "But I got a guy who's been waiting, chomping at the bit to get some playing time and he's going to have his day in the sun now.

"I just want to get this crap over with and get in his ear as quick as I can. I'm going to be killing myself, but as long as these guys find a way to get me a ring, I'll be happy."

Holmes had four tackles in the game's last 20 minutes. Fitzgerald had collected 10 in his time on the field.

Other than Fitzgerald's injury, it was a good day to be a Wildcat. The record was improved to 9-1 overall and an astonishing and unprecedented 7-0 in the Big Ten. NU had won a school-record eight straight games since the loss to Miami. The Cats would stay fifth in the polls, but a measure of their national notice came when representatives from the Fiesta and Sugar bowls sat side-by-side, watching just in case everything went NU's way.

Not everything did around the Big Ten. Ohio State vanquished Illinois, Eddie George gaining a school-record 314 yards in the Buckeye's 41-3 romp over Illinois. OSU, 6-0 in the league and 10-0 overall, looked unbeatable.

Autry's 110-yard day, his 11th straight 100-yard-plus outing, raised his season total to 1,449 yards, 144.9 a game and 4.49 per carry.

"He's an exceptional running back, a great back," said Fry, gracious in defeat. "To my knowledge, he didn't fumble today, and our defense really got after him.

"I compliment a fine Northwestern team and effort today. They are just a heck of a football team."

Fry, in the following days, would write Fitzgerald.

"He's probably the inspirational leader in defense," said the veteran coach. "I greatly appreciated his comments during the week, when some of the Northwestern guys, in their enthusiasm, said a few things that weren't very complimentary about Iowa.

"He had the poise and leadership ability to emphasize they got caught up in their enthusiasm after the Penn State game. I really appreciate that as a coach. He had the cool and poise to put everything in the proper perspective.

"I tried to encourage him to continue being the leader for the Wildcats, because it's obvious he's not going to be recovered (in time to play in a bowl). I just can't say enough about the young man. He's not just a tremendous football player, but he's obviously a tremendous person."

One who would have to watch Northwestern's bid for the Big Ten championship from the worst possible place: the sidelines.

IOWA VS. NORTHWESTERN

Saturday, November 11, 1995 at Dyche Stadium, Evanston, IL
Weather: 26° Wind N30 Overcast
Attendance: 49,256 (sellout)

SCORE BY QUARTERS	1	2	3	4	SCORE
Iowa (5-4)	0	20	0	0	20
Northwestern (9-1)	3	14	7	7	31

First Quarter
		NU	IA
NU	6:24 Brian Gowins 50-yard field goal (8 plays, 25 yards, 3:21 TOP)	3	0

Second Quarter
		NU	IA
IA	13:03 Cedric Shaw 1-yard run (Zach Bromert kick) (17 plays, 80 yards, 8:21 TOP)	3	7
IA	8:25 Tom Knight 28-yard interception return (Zach Bromert kick)	3	14
NU	6:44 Darren Drexler 21-yard pass from Steve Schnur (Brian Gowins kick) (5 plays, 56 yards, 1:41 TOP)	10	14
NU	5:05 Brian Musso 60-yard punt return (Brian Gowins kick)	17	14
IA	1:31 Scott Slutzker 39-yard pass from Matt Scherman (kick failed) (8 plays, 80 yards, 3:34 TOP)	17	20

Third Quarter
		NU	IA
NU	11:08 Darnell Autry 3-yard run (Brian Gowins kick) (8 plays, 69 yards, 3:52 TOP)	24	20

Fourth Quarter
		NU	IA
NU	Hudhaifa Ismaeli 31-yard fumble return (Brian Gowins kick)	31	20

TEAM STATISTICS

	IA	NU
First Downs	18	11
Rushing	10	6
Passing	6	5
Penalty	2	0
Rushing Attempts	50	38
Yards Gained Rushing	186	134
Yards Lost Rushing	41	28
Net Yards Rushing	145	106
Net Yards Passing	158	82
Passes Attempted	24	12
Passes Completed	16	6
Had Intercepted	1	1
Total Offensive Plays	74	50
Total Net Yards	303	188
Average Gain per Play	4.1	3.8
Fumbles: Number-Lost	3-1	0-0
Penalties: Number-Yards	5-34	4-46
Interceptions: Number-Yards	1-28	1-0
Number of Punts-Yards	6-224	6-245
Average Per Punt	37.3	40.8
Punt Returns: Number-Yards	1-4	1-60
Kickoff Returns: Number-Yards	4-40	4-63
Possession Time	34:55	25:05
Third-Down Conversions	9	1
Sacks By: Number-Yards	3-18	4-34

Big Ten Standings

1. Northwestern (7-0-0)
2. Ohio State (6-0-0)
3. Michigan (4-2-0)
4. Michigan State (4-2-1)
5. Penn State (3-3-0)
6. Wisconsin (3-3-)0
7. Iowa (2-4-0)
8. Illinois (2-4-0)
9. Purdue (1-4-1)
10. Minnesota (1-5-0)
11. Indiana (0-6-0)

AP Top 25

1. Nebraska
2. Ohio St.
3. Florida
4. Tennessee
5. **Northwestern**
6. Florida St.
7. Kansas St.
8. Notre Dame
9. Colorado
10. Texas
11. Southern Cal
12. Michigan
13. Virginia
14. Arkansas
15. Kansas
16. Oregon
17. Alabama
18. Texas A&M
19. Penn St.
20. Virginia Tech.
21. Auburn
22. Washington
23. Syracuse
24. Clemson
25. Miami

Scores of interest

Ohio St. 41, Illinois 3
Michigan 5, Purdue 0
Wisconsin 34, Minnesota 27
Michigan St. 31, Indiana 13
Nebraska 41, Kansas 3
Florida 63, S. Carolina 7
Florida St. 28, N. Carolina 12
Kansas St. 49, Iowa St. 7
Colorado 21, Missouri 0
Texas 52, Houston 20
USC 28, Oregon St. 10
Virginia 21, Maryland 18
Arkansas 24, SW Louisana 13
Texas A&M 17, Rice 10
Auburn 37, Georgia 31
Va. Tech 38, Temple 16

Larry Guess' expression and the number on his uniform tell it all: Northwestern's No. 1 in the Big Ten. (Scott Strazzante/Daily Southtown)

Chapter 16
CHAMPIONS!

"They're the best 'team' in the Big Ten. Ohio State has the best athletes, but they're the best 'team.'"
—Purdue defensive tackle Jayme Washel on Northwestern

IN THE LOBBY of the John C. Nicolet Football Center, hanging high from the ceiling, center stage, there's a Tournament of Roses banner, the stylized red rose centered on a field of arctic white.

It has been there since Gary Barnett arrived, a permanent reminder from him to every Northwestern coach and player, to every visitor to the 7-year-old complex, that dreams can come true and are worth pursuing.

After 10 games, this 112th and best team in the history of Northwestern football was still striving to reach its fifth and ultimate goal, a trip to Pasadena.

No previous NU team had earned 10 victories in a season, much less nine in succession. A win over Purdue on November 18 would enable this group to reach both standards simultaneously.

It would also earn Northwestern, in the Big Ten's centennial season, at least a share of the 100th conference championship.

Northwestern's last title had come in 1936. It was truly ancient history. Not only were none of the current squad's players alive then, many of the parents of those players had not yet been born. The only living link from then to now was the presence of 79-year-old Bob Voigts, a sophomore tackle (and Big Ten honorable mention) on that team and coach of NU's 1948 Rose Bowl squad, at home games.

The 1936 championship was NU's fifth, and the only one it didn't share with another Big Ten team. Now, with the Cats in position to win it all, there was a good chance they'd have to share again. Ohio State was still there, still unbeaten, still hanging in. And a shared title with the Buckeyes would mean a trip to Orlando for the Florida Citrus Bowl. While Orlando is a warm place to visit, the Florida Citrus Bowl, known as the Tangerine Bowl in its early days, has none of the prestige, history or glory that the Rose Bowl represents.

There is no Florida Citrus Bowl banner hanging anywhere in Nicolet Center.

"I personally want to go to the Rose Bowl," said center Rob Johnson. "For a kid growing up in the Midwest, the ultimate dream is going to college, playing Big Ten football, winning the Big Ten and going to the Rose Bowl. It'll take care of itself in the next couple of weeks. All we can do as a team is go out and play as hard as we can against Purdue, then sit back and wait to see what happens.

"Winning the Big Ten would be the culmination of five years of effort for me and the other fifth-year seniors on this team. We've been beating our heads against the wall trying to get this thing turned around, and finally seeing all the fruits of our labor come to an incredible head like this is an unbelievable experience."

To get to Pasadena, there was no other option but to beat Purdue.

"For me, I want to play in the Rose Bowl because it represents the top bowl in our league, and that's what you set your goals on," said Gary Barnett. "That's the only reason I want to play in the Rose Bowl, because it's the top bowl in the Big Ten. If it were the whatever other bowl, that's the one I'd want to go to. After that, if I can't, I want to play against the best team we can play against, which, at this point in time, would look like Tennessee."

Before any bowl, Northwestern had to beat Purdue. A loss, and the Wildcats would go to the Citrus for certain, barring an unlikely pair of losses by Ohio State.

"We knew the Purdue game was going to be important when we talked in our coaches meetings in August," said Barnett. "I don't think any of us would have guessed we would be in this particular situation, but did feel, as we looked over that schedule, that the Purdue game was going to be a big game.

"It might decide our sixth win in a season where we were trying to get over the hump. Now, it's even bigger than just the sixth win. It's even more significant than that."

Infinitely so. Now, it was the difference between a fine season and a measure of immortality.

It was up to the Boilermakers to play Spoilermakers.

"Purdue is probably the best 3-5-1 team we've ever seen," Barnett said, noting the Boilermakers' narrow losses to Notre Dame, Penn State, Michigan and Michigan State. "Then you're looking at a completely different scenario."

Northwestern had faced passing teams, option teams, and balanced teams, but in Purdue, the Wildcats would be up against the best fullback in the country in Mike Alstott, who had prepped at Joliet Catholic Academy, southwest of Chicago. At 6-foot-2, 240 pounds, Alstott presented a massive problem. The senior was 16 yards away from breaking Purdue's career rushing record of 3,315 yards, set by Otis Armstrong.

"He's tough to bring down," Barnett said. "You want to know Purdue, watch 'em maul Wisconsin. That'll keep us up six more nights."

Alstott had run for 204 yards, his career high, against the Badgers. Only blizzard conditions at Michigan the following week had held him to 19 yards on 11 carries.

"We have a great deal to play for, no question about it," Barnett said. "As I told our guys

Wildcats head coach Gary Barnett leads his troops onto the field for the finale against Purdue. (Scott Strazzante/Daily Southtown)

Sunday, we're six days away. We can spit wooden nickels for six days."

Between then and Saturday, Barnett and his assistants who had played on or coached on championship teams had an idea. At a team meeting, they showed the team their own championship rings, symbols of what could be theirs.

By game time Saturday, another 2:30 p.m. start for ABC's benefit, the Wildcats were 3½-point favorites, not a large margin for the No. 5 team in the country going against a sub-.500 team. People still didn't believe.

The next three hours proved that whatever nervousness the players felt had turned into eager anticipation, with copious preparation resulting in superior execution. Besides, there were rings to play for.

The stage, Purdue's Ross-Ade Stadium, was the same one where Barnett had won his first game as NU's head coach. Located, perhaps tellingly, just off Northwestern Avenue in West Lafayette, it wouldn't be full on this chilly Saturday, and it wasn't Dyche Stadium, but in the crowd of 47,172 fans, there were about 5,000 Northwestern rooters, almost all of them wearing purple, to cheer their heroes on. One of those 5,000 was Voigts, there in the cold and dampness to see this Northwestern team do what the team he played on 59 years earlier had done.

They cheered all day and into the night. Northwestern won at least a share of the Big Ten championship in convincing, dominating fashion, a 23-8 victory over Purdue not telling the whole story of how one-sided the game became.

"It's indescribable!" said cornerback Chris Martin, one of the key players on this 10-1, 8-0 powerhouse. "This is something I dreamed of. I knew we could make it happen. I believed, and our teammates believed, and I think it showed."

Martin had started it with his interception of Boilermaker quarterback Rick Trefzger at the Wildcat 24 midway through the first quarter.

Purdue, via the rushes of Alstott and tailback Corey Rogers and a pair of passes, had moved from its 34 to the NU 35. Now, Trefzger got greedy, and went for tight end Jon Blackman

Purdue's Chike Okeafor gets airborne in an effort to stop tight end Shane Graham. (Scott Strazzante/Daily Southtown)

in the right flat. The ball was off target, behind Blackman and to his left, right where Martin was.

"I guess he was running a hot route and the quarterback tried to go to him, and I just stepped in front," said Martin.

The next place Martin was was in the end zone. He ran the pickoff back 76 yards for a touchdown, and Northwestern led 7-0.

On the next four series, Purdue ran three plays and punted.

On one occasion in those series, Alstott dragged three Wildcat defenders, gained nine yards, taking the rushing record from Armstrong in the process. The game was stopped, he was given the ball, and allowed to run to the other end of the field to give the ball to his parents. It was a marvelous gesture, a moment of sentimentality rarely seen these days in big-time athletics.

"Giving that ball to my mom and dad was really special," Alstott said. "But after that moment, it was a disappointing game. Things didn't go our way."

Giving the ball to Alstott had been special all season. But against NU, he carried it only

Linebacker Pat Fitzgerald, his broken left leg and ankle in a cast, watches the Wildcats warm up. (Scott Strazzante/Daily Southtown)

13 times for 71 yards, a big reason Purdue's offense bogged down. His first carry of the second quarter didn't come until about six minutes remained. Whatever Purdue head coach Jim Colletto was thinking, it was the wrong thing to think.

"I thought the defense dominated the entire game," said Barnett. "This is a tremendous day, a wonderful day for our program. It means we've done something that hasn't been done around here since 1936. It means respectability. It means we're a big-time football program with big time football players. We're just real happy. It may not have been real pretty, but it's ours. Co-champions, at least."

The Wildcat offense, which Barnett wanted to become a big-play attack, finally showed signs of that. Late in the second quarter, Steve Schnur hit D'Wayne Bates in mid-stride on a crossing pattern, allowing Bates to turn upfield smoothly and accelerate past safety Jamel Coleman and linebacker Chike Okeafor. The 72-yard strike gave NU a 14-0 halftime lead.

It took only 83 seconds of the third quarter for the Wildcats to put the game out of reach.

The Wildcat defense, by now setting up shop in the Purdue backfield on nearly every play, and taking advantage of the Boilermakers forgetting about Alstott, forced a punt from the Purdue 25. Rob Deignan barely had the snap in his hands before a purple wave of players came at him.

Martin blocked the punt, then went after Deignan when he grabbed the ball on a carom. Touissant Waterman slapped the ball out of Deignan's hands, and Mike McGrew fell on the football in the end zone. It appeared to be a Northwestern touchdown, but was called a safety.

No matter. NU led 16-0, and was getting the ball back. On the first play, Schnur did the logical thing. He called Darnell Autry's number. Autry had 92 yards to this point, and wanted more.

He gained 60 more. Big blocks by the usual suspects in the offensive line opened the hole, and after some nifty maneuvering down the left sideline, he was ridden out of bounds at the Boilermaker 1. Schnur's sneak made it 23-0, and made the rest of the game academic.

Most of the second half was still to be played, but it was obvious that Purdue's offense was no match for the third-best scoring defense in the country. The Wildcats were in the rare position of knowing they had accomplished what many had considered impossible, if they had considered it at all, and were able to celebrate that accomplishment even as the game was winding down.

"When we got to six minutes, I knew we were gonna win the game, because I didn't think they were going to move the ball on our defense," said Barnett. "I'd been looking forward to those last six minutes for 11 weeks."

"It felt good as time was clicking down," said Autry. "It felt great. We, as a team, before the season, set some goals. We accomplished all our goals, and obviously, we need some help for the Rose Bowl, but we've had a hell of a season.

"At first, we were excited about big wins and stuff like that. After a while, you noticed that people were not getting as excited. It was like, 'OK, business as usual. We're going to go out there, win the game, and go out afterwards.' That's how it is every game. Go out there, get the job done, and then you're done.

"We've done everything we wanted to do. Let's get the bowl game going."

Everything? Autry thought there was one more thing NU could do.

"I thought we could go undefeated," he said.

Maybe the feeling of exhilaration was why the last few minutes were a little sloppy, and why Edwin Watson, on a 3-yard plunge, was able to avert the shutout for Purdue after a Paul Burton punt was blocked by Chris Koeppen. Otherwise, it was all NU, churning out yardage. Autry, with a career-high 226 yards on 32 carries, finished the regular-season with a school-record 1,675 yards on 355 carries. He, linebacker Pat Fitzgerald and kicker Sam Valenzisi, the team's three most-heralded players, were the symbols of the shrugging off of 59 years of frustration.

Northwestern, at 5:33 p.m. Chicago time on the 18th day of November, had done it. As the clock ran down, the index fingers went into the air. The Wildcats, mocked for years as losers, were the Big Ten champions!

Said Gary Barnett to his players, "What do you say we go meet the crowd!" And here came hundreds, then thousands of Wildcat fans, young and old, onto the field, swarming around the players.

"Big Ten champs! Big Ten champs!" the mob shouted over and over, celebrating so long and so heartily the Purdue band's postgame show was delayed.

Before the season started, most of the spectators probably had never heard of Ryan Padgett or Chris Martin or Matt Rice, or perhaps not even Steve Schnur or Darnell Autry. Now, everyone was on a first-name basis.

Before the season started, only the players had believed. Only they had high hopes, had expected victory. Now, they had pushed over that rubber tree plant, and become champions. Now, everybody believed.

"I wasn't here 60 years ago," said Autry. "I know it means a lot to us. Everybody comes up and says, 'Thank you. It's been so long, so long.'

"We've done a lot for the people at our school and done a lot for each other."

Fitzgerald had watched the game while leaning on crutches on the sideline, his broken left leg in a cast. He and Valenzisi, the sparkplug kicker who had started his career as a walk-on and risen in the eyes of his teammates to the role of captain, could only cheer, celebrating as best they could as the points mounted up and the clock wound down.

"It was tough," Fitzgerald said over the din of the locker room. "I wanted to be out there so bad."

Fitzgerald was not forgotten by the fans. He received a standing ovation from the NU con-

The unrelated Autrys, Adrian (32) and Darnell (24), cheer on the fans cheering them. (Scott Strazzante/Daily Southtown)

Linebacker Danny Sutter and his cohorts wrap up Purdue's Mike Alstott. (Scott Strazzante/Daily Southtown)

tingent when he arrived on the field, and thanked the thousands by waving his Big Ten Centennial cap over his head.

By game's end, he and the rest of the team were wearing 1995 Big Ten Champion caps, complete with the school's "N" logo in the middle.

"Chicago's a tough media market, but these guys have been Cinderellas in the city for the last six weeks," said Big Ten commissioner Jim Delany before presenting the Wildcats the Big Ten's championship trophy. "Those cities aren't easy to turn people on. The Miracle Mets did it in New York in '69, and the Wildcats did it in Chicago in 1995.

"Northwestern does it the right way. It's nice to see them climb the ladder of success. And they did it in the centennial year, a year when we've been as good top-to-bottom as we've been in many years.

"It's the best story in college football in the last decade at least. They earned at least a co-championship in the toughest conference in the country."

The locker room was a madhouse, jammed with players thrilled to go forward with another rendition of "Go 'U' Northwestern," the trophy presentation by Delany—still without a plaque, because nobody knew if the Wildcats would own the title outright or share it with Ohio State—and, eventually, a mob of reporters.

Over in one corner was Schnur, the unheralded quarterback, saying, "If you look around, I don't know if everyone here realizes what we've done. But it's a great feeling regardless. It's crazy! It's been a long road. Every one of these guys is deserving of what we've done this season. I'd be lying if I'd told you I expected this."

"We played this way all year," said safety Eric Collier.

"Everything came together, finally," said defensive tackle Matt Rice. "Everything at the right time. Thank goodness we didn't blow it. We didn't think that until afterwards."

Since this was a college locker room, nobody was spraying champagne around. The hardest stuff to be found was a six-pack of Ocean Spray. It quickly disappeared.

Finally, the Cinderella tag could disappear as well.

"The glass slipper's broken," Barnett had said on the field. "She threw it against the wall, smashed it to pieces."

One of the many signs in the crowd was a classic.

"CATS PURR-FECT," it read.

For Barnett, there was work to do. There was this sign in the football offices that had the Wildcats' previous championships listed.

"It says 1-9-9-question mark," said Barnett. I'm gonna go paint that in with a '5' now."

A few minutes later, the celebration still going on, Gary Barnett was out of his coaches clothes and in a suit, standing with his wife Mary and a friend. He whispered a few encouraging words in Pat Fitzgerald's ear, then surveyed the scene with a small smile of quiet satisfaction on his face.

Amazing, wasn't it, what could be accomplished when victory was expected.

In the game's dying minutes, when it was obvious the Wildcats would win, NU safety William Bennett received a surprise. There was Trefzger, Purdue's quarterback, coming over to him at the end of a long day.

"I thought he was coming over to talk trash," said Bennett. "He said, 'I hope you guys go to the Rose Bowl and you win it—win it for us and yourselves.' I thought it was great."

Indeed, compliments fairly gushed from the Boilermakers.

"They say if you get a Northwestern degree, you're set for life," said Trefzger. "They're the smartest defense I've ever seen. They knew our calls. They knew what our adjustments were. They're a sound team, deserving of the ranking."

The praise came from both sides of the ball.

"I wish they were really bad sports, because I really wanted to hate them," said Boilermaker defensive tackle Jayme Washel. "But I couldn't help admiring them. They're a good team. They're the best team in the Big Ten. Ohio State has the best athletes, but they're the best team."

Now, all Northwestern's purr-fect team could do was wait for a week, when Michigan would host Ohio State.

Center Rob Johnson, who had stirred it up before the Iowa game, had only two words to say: "Go Blue!"

That had a ring to it.

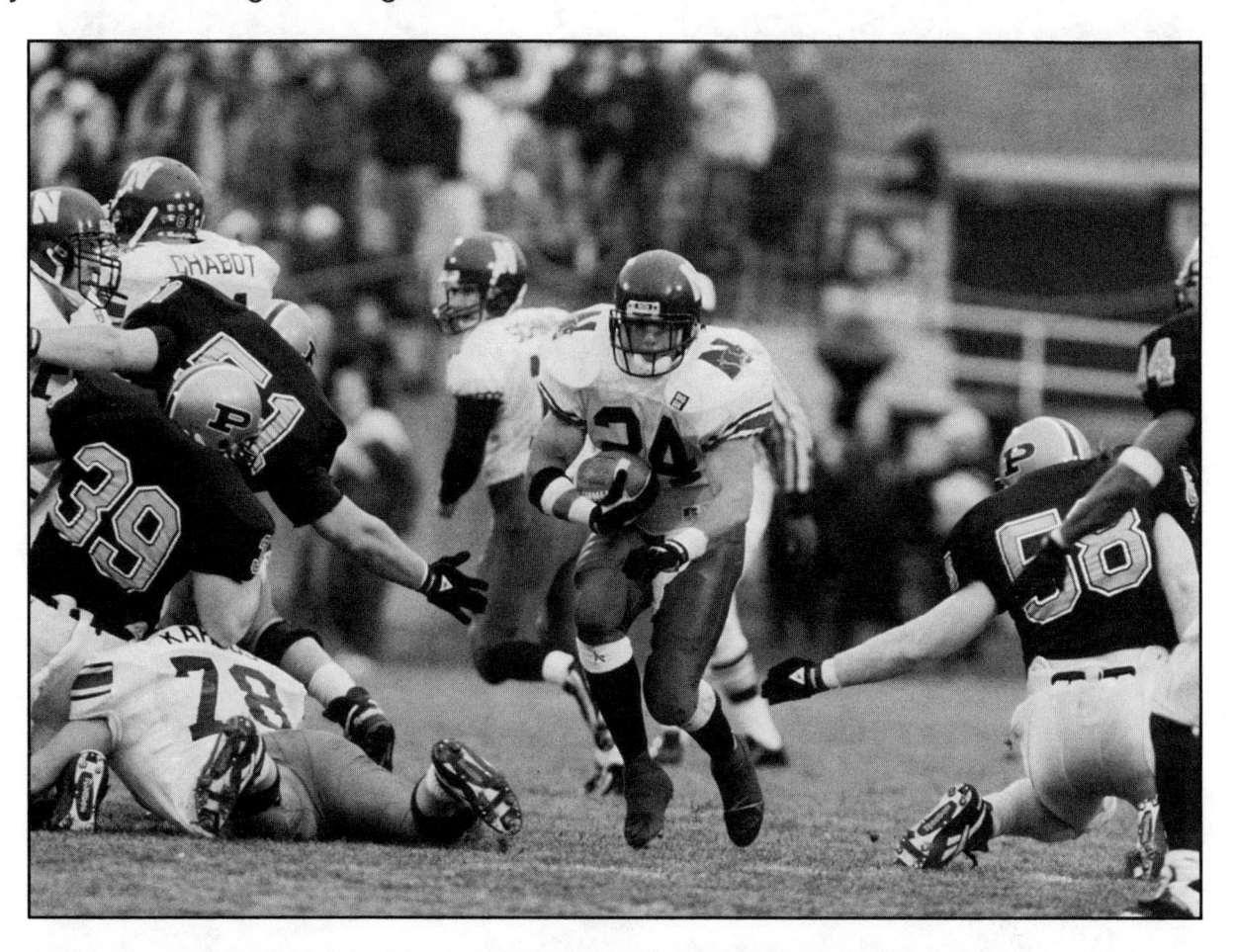

Here's how to gain 226 yards. A huge hole, formed in part by Brian Darro's block, gave Darnell Autry room to elude Aaron Hall (39) and Craig Williams (58). (Scott Strazzante/Daily Southtown)

152   PURPLE ROSES

Defensive tackle Matt Rice is in the spotlight after the romp over the Boilermakers. (Scott Strazzante/ Daily Southtown)

NORTHWESTERN VS. PURDUE

Saturday, November 18, 1995 at Ross-Ade Stadium, West Lafayette, IN
Weather: 39° Wind NW8 Overcast
Attendance: 47,172

SCORE BY QUARTERS	1	2	3	4	SCORE
Northwestern	7	7	9	0	23
Purdue	0	0	0	8	8

First Quarter — NU IA
NU 7:47 Chris Martin 76-yard interception return (Brian Gowins kick) — 7 0

Second Quarter
NU 3:10 D'Wayne Bates 72-yard pass from Steve Schnur (Brian Gowins kick)
(4 plays, 87 yards, 0:50 TOP) — 14 0

Third Quarter
NU 13:53 Safety credited to team — 16 0
NU 13:37 Steve Schnur 1-yard rush (Brian Gowins kick)
(2 plays, 61 yards, 0:16 TOP) — 23 0

Fourth Quarter
PU 10:30 Edwin Watson 3-yard run (Mike Alstott pass from Rick Trefzger)
(2 plays, 9 yards, 0:40 TOP) — 23 6

TEAM STATISTICS

	NU	PU
First Downs	14	16
Rushing	7	9
Passing	7	7
Penalty	0	0
Rushing Attempts	44	38
Yards Gained Rushing	242	160
Yards Lost Rushing	31	37
Net Yards Rushing	211	123
Net Yards Passing	158	178
Passes Attempted	21	37
Passes Completed	12	22
Had Intercepted	1	2
Total Offensive Plays	65	75
Total Net Yards	369	301
Average Gain per Play	5.7	4.0
Fumbles: Number-Lost	2-1	5-1
Penalties: Number-Yards	1-10	2-15
Interceptions: Number-Yards	2-76	1-19
Number of Punts-Yards	6-198	7-223
Average Per Punt	33.0	31.9
Punt Returns: Number-Yards	3-47	3-26
Kickoff Returns: Number-Yards	2-54	4-51
Possession Time	29:33	30:27
Third-Down Conversions	4 of 13	3 of 15
Fourth-Down Conversions	0 of 2	1 of 5
Sacks By: Number-Yards	2-16	0-0

Big Ten Standings

1. Northwestern (8-0-0)
2. Ohio State (7-0-0)
3. Michigan State (4-2-1)
4. Michigan (4-3-0)
5. Penn State (4-3-0)
6. Iowa (3-4-0)
7. Wisconsin (3-4-0)
8. Illinois (3-4-0)
9. Purdue (1-5-1)
10. Minnesota (1-6-0)
11. Indiana (0-7-0)

AP Top 25

1. Nebraska
2. Ohio St.
3. Florida
4. **Northwestern**
5. Tennessee
6. Florida St.
7. Notre Dame
8. Colorado
9. Texas
10. Kansas St.
11. Kansas
12. Oregon
13. Virginia Tech.
14. Penn St.
15. Texas A&M
16. Auburn
17. Southern Cal
18. Michigan
19. Virginia
20. Washington
21. Alabama
22. Syracuse
23. Arkansas
24. Clemson
25. Miami

Scores of interest

Ohio St. 42, Indiana 3
Florida 38, Vanderbilt 7
Tennessee 34, Kentucky 31
Florida St. 59, Maryland 17
Kansas St. 17, Colorado 17
Notre Dame 44, Air Force 14
Texas 29, Texas Christian 19

Gary Barnett can't take his eyes off the action in Michigan's upset of Ohio State. (David Burns/Daily Southtown)

Chapter 17
A TALE OF TWO CITIES

"Michigan is nobody. I guarantee we're going to the Rose Bowl."

—Ohio State flanker Terry Glenn

HOW DO YOU get ready for a football game that decides your fate when it's one you're not playing in?

This was Northwestern's quandary in the days after beating Purdue. Now, the Wildcats had to play the waiting game.

Football players don't like to play the waiting game. They like to play.

It was Ohio State and Michigan who would play. Northwestern would play the role of innocent bystander. In the season of their first Big Ten football championship in 59 years, a game between the 100-year-old conference's traditional powers would decide the bowl destination of the Wildcats.

Finally, after a season of consulting media guides, fiddling with slide rules, and guessing what poll voters might do, it came down to this:

—If Ohio State won, the Buckeyes would go to the Rose Bowl, and Northwestern would play in the Florida Citrus Bowl.

—If Michigan won or forced a tie, Northwestern would go to the Rose Bowl, sending Ohio State to the Citrus.

What could be simpler?

What could be more nerve-wracking?

At least the Buckeyes were able to play on November 25. The Wildcats, some of them in Evanston and the rest of them scattered across the country, could do nothing but watch. Or try to watch. Or try not to watch.

NU center Rob Johnson wanted to go to the game in Ann Arbor.

"I'm going to get to that game somehow and wear all the blue and gold I can," he said, presumably meaning maize and blue.

About two dozen players figured to watch in the Nicolet Center auditorium, the same place they'd watched game films all season long. The place they'd first met before going to Kenosha. The place they'd tried to figure out what had happened after losing to Miami of Ohio. The place they'd kept their wits about them the rest of the season, when the rest of the students on campus and long-suffering Wildcat fans were losing theirs.

Many players would go home for the Thanksgiving holiday. Darnell Autry would fly off to Tempe, Arizona. Casey Dailey was headed to Los Angeles. And Chris Martin of Tampa was scouting about for tickets to the Florida-Florida State game.

When they weren't making plans, the Wildcats could reflect a bit on their amazing season, a 10-1 campaign and 8-0 rumble through conference play that now had them ranked No. 4 in the Associated Press writer/broadcaster poll and the CNN/USA Today coaches poll, thanks to Tennessee's narrow win over Kentucky. The unimpressive Volunteers dropped to No. 5.

The shuffle brought Northwestern a hair closer to a national championship. Notre Dame's win at Air Force had locked the Fighting Irish into the Bowl Alliance, but if No. 1 Nebraska lost to Oklahoma, No. 2 Ohio State lost to Michigan and No. 3 Florida lost to Florida State over the Thanksgiving holiday, NU could be No. 1 going to the postseason, and other permutations moved the Cats to No. 2 or 3. Crazy, sure, but the season hadn't exactly been sane to this juncture.

"We don't have any control over it," said Gary Barnett. "It's speculation. If it happens, it happens because some guy didn't do this or that guy didn't do that. It's in someone else's control. If it was something we could control, I'd sure feel like we were involved in it, but we're not.

"Are we the best team in college football? I don't know. I know we're a good team. What we've demonstrated in this whole process is that a team will beat a group of talented guys, and that's sort of how we've represented ourselves, and pretty much what we're about."

When the NCAA statistics came out the Monday after the Purdue game, NU pawprints were all over them.

"To see that our defense was No. 1 in the country in points scored against them was very fitting," said Barnett. "It's really been the key for us. That's probably the most important stat kept by the NCAA as far as winning and losing goes."

Northwestern allowed only 12.7 points per game, shutting opponents out in the second half five times. It would have been six times, but for a blocked punt that Purdue used to set up a touchdown on Saturday. Otherwise, the Wildcats were perfect again.

"Our defense has played just outstanding, especially Saturday night," Barnett said. "Our defensive linemen, Larry Curry, Matt Rice, Ray Robey, Mike Warren, had outstanding games. The kind of pressure they put on and the way they were able to handle the run versus the No. 1 rushing team in the conference was really impressive."

The Wildcats allowed only 140 points, 211 fewer than the season before, and the fewest given up by an NU team since the 124 allowed in a nine-game season in 1963. This year's average of 12.7 improved on the 1963 average of 13.7. NU's defense was impressive in stopping almost every kind of offense there is, from Notre Dame's balanced attack to Air Force's wishbone to the grind-it-out games most Big Ten schools employ. It also shut down every big-name receiver it faced, from Derrick Mayes to Mercury Hayes.

"I think probably the feeling that best describes maybe the bus trip home and everything since then is fulfillment," said Barnett. "You feel real fulfilled that a group of guys sat down and set their sights as high as we set our sights, or goals, and with all the adversity, went out and got it done. As a human being, I don't know that there's anything more gratifying or fulfilling than to set your goals as high as we set ours and to reach them."

The only downside coming out of the finale was the status of wide receiver Toussiant Waterman. He suffered a lacerated kidney during the game, was hospitalized in West Lafayette after the game, and wouldn't be released until November 27. He'd miss the bowl game, but was expected to be fine for spring football.

It was only the third major injury of the season to a Wildcat player, which in itself was good news. While Northwestern had depth, it didn't have to go too deep in too many places too many times.

Barnett turned his attention to Michigan-Ohio State, and tried to play the role of politician.

"We want to go, as we've said before, to the bowl that represents the highest standard in the Big Ten, and of course, that's the Rose Bowl. But in no way do we want to take anything away from the fact we may get an opportunity to go the Citrus Bowl."

He wasn't convincing. That sign on the wall behind him in the Nicolet auditorium with the team's goals on it didn't say "Citrus Bowl" at the top. It said "Rose Bowl." And he knew it, and so did everyone else.

Ohio State vs. Michigan. The phrase brings to mind Bo vs. Woody. "The Victors" vs. the devilishly intricate Script Ohio. Big Ten championships being decided year after year on the

A Tale of Two Cities   157

final weekend of the season, either on the banks of the Olentangy River in Columbus, or in the largest stadium in football, at what Woody Hayes called, disdainfully, "That school up north."

Michigan-Ohio State is three yards and a cloud of dust. It's Hayes punching an ABC cameraman during a game. It's Glenn "Bo" Schembechler throwing down his headset. It's the Buckeyes going for a two-point conversion in 1968 after scoring to go ahead 48-14, only because, Hayes said, "I couldn't go for three." And getting that conversion.

The Ohio State-Michigan game was moved to the end of the Big Ten season in 1935. This would be the 33rd time the contest would help decide the conference championship. Never, however, had the Northwestern Wildcats been a part of the story. Now, it was Maize and Blue and Scarlet and Gray and Purple and White.

"Obviously, this game's one you throw records away," said Barnett. "It always has been. It'll be a great, great athletic event, a great happening in Ann Arbor.

"Which team's better? I don't know. If Michigan wins, we'll go to the Rose Bowl, and if Ohio State wins, they'll be a great representative of this conference, because they are truly a great football team. My choice for coach of the year was John Cooper, because he's had the pressure and the schedule that demanded of him to play at this particular level, and he'd pulled it off."

Everybody else was tabbing Barnett as the coach of the year, both in the conference and nationally. But Barnett was right about everything else. Michigan-Ohio State was one of the fiercest rivalries in college football.

It would burn white-hot, this 92nd renewal, courtesy of Buckeyes wide receiver Terry Glenn. In the course of the week, one traditionally reserved for saying nothing but nice things about the other guy, Glenn, Ohio State's leading receiver, went the other way.

"Michigan is nobody," Glenn blurted out. "I guarantee we're going to the Rose Bowl."

That couldn't be stapled to the bulletin boards in Schembechler Hall quickly enough. Wolverines head coach Lloyd Carr, the interim tag removed from his title a fortnight before, didn't have to come up with a rah-rah pregame speech for his 18th-ranked 8-3 club now. Glenn had done it for him.

The loose-lipped receiver was right in one way. Nobody would get in the way of No. 2 Ohio

Pat Fitzgerald applauds a Michigan maneuver while waiting for Northwestern's bowl fate to be decided. (David Banks/Daily Southtown)

State's Rose Bowl trip. Nobody in the blurry form of Michigan's Tshimanga Biakabutuka, who would run for 313 yards, the best day in the century-long history of the series. Nobody in the form of the Wolverine defense, which would shut down Ohio State back Eddie George and put the clamps on Glenn as well.

All that nothing by those nobodies added up to a 31-23 Michigan victory over the Buckeyes, who were favored by 8 1/2 points before the game and shocked to be headed to the Florida Citrus Bowl after it.

And in Evanston? Roses mysteriously appeared in the hands of the Wildcat players at the end of the game, after Ohio State quarterback Bobby Hoying's last pass ended up in the hands of Michigan's Charles Woodson with 48 seconds left. Somebody fired up a boom box. The song? "Go 'U' Northwestern."

Northwestern, nobodies themselves in the eyes of many before the season began, was headed west, as the undisputed champions of the Big Ten, to Pasadena to play in the 82nd Rose Bowl against Southern California. This was better than a dream. This was sweet reality.

"We're alone at the top, and it's incredible!" said offensive guard Brian Kardos. "This was absolutely phenomenal."

"When we were 3-7-1 (last year), nobody was in here," said linebacker Pat Fitzgerald. "But the sweet thing is, we did it right. Who woulda thunk it?"

By this point, maybe not even Barnett, not on a logical level. But he, like the rest of the Wildcats, believed.

"I believe in destiny," Barnett said, not far from where a large blue Michigan flag, complete with a yellow block "M," hung near the screen. "I don't deny there's a little fairy dust around.

"I'm happy for Larry Curry," added Barnett, remembering his misfiring long snaps in the Miami game, the loss that had haunted Northwestern ever since. Now, with the Wildcats Pasadena-bound, the loss to Miami was moot.

Pasadena-bound. What was it Barnett had said back in the winter of 1991-'92?

"We came here and made a promise one day, we'd take the Purple to Pasadena, and we're going," he smiled.

There was unbridled joy at the end, but watching the drama play out was torture.

"It was hell," said Ryan Padgett. "It was second-and-5, a meaningless play, and you were on the edge of your seat."

Padgett was with Johnson, not in Ann Arbor, but at Johnson's family's summer home near Michigan City, Indiana.

"Our tickets fell through," said Johnson. "So we watched there (Michigan City), and I'm telling you, I thought the floor was going to fall through. It's not a nice feeling, watching. It's hard to just sit back."

In Oxford, Ohio, Justin Chabot was going through the same thing.

"I ended up not watching a lot of the game," he said. "I tried to stay relaxed."

That turned out to be impossible in Nicolet Center. While only injured kicker Sam Valenzisi and Barnett were in the auditorium in the minutes before the game, more players began to trickle in. Fitzgerald hobbled in. Dave Beazley, who had been in his apartment, had to watch with his teammates. Shane Graham and Kardos got good seats up front. In came punter Paul Burton, whose father Ron, the All-American at NU, believed Michigan would win.

Soon, alumni began to show up. They sat, stood, paced, nibbled on pizza and chewed on fingernails while watching the big screen, which displayed ABC's picture from Ann Arbor, and, occasionally, from the very room they were in.

In Ann Arbor, monitors in the press box displayed the same picture. Reporters who, at the start of the season, traveled to Champaign to cover the Michigan-Illinois game and ended up watching Northwestern-Notre Dame on television, were now at the game Northwestern was watching, and watching Northwestern watch as well. Rod Serling would have loved it.

What the Wildcats, the cross-country audience, and the 106,288 spectators in Michigan Stadium saw was a demonstration of heart and achieving against the odds that was, well, worthy of the 1995 Wildcats.

It started on Michigan's first play, when Biakabutuka slammed off right tackle, broke a pair of tackles and gained 22 yards. On the next play, he ran around left end, broke one tackle and gained 19 more yards. While the Wolverines wouldn't score on that drive, the trend was clear. The Wolverines were mad. Glenn and his teammates would be treated more coldly than the mid-40s weather and pay for his injudicious comments.

First, Ohio State would get on the board via Josh Jackson's 37-yard field goal. It would be the Buckeyes' only lead of the day, and would last only 1 minute 55 seconds.

The Ohio State defense would never be able to contain Biakabutuka. He'd gain 16 yards, then 44 more, on his first two carries in the next drive, which set up Brian Griese's 4-yard touchdown pass to Clarence Williams with 5:34 left in the first quarter.

Ohio State cut the 7-3 lead to 7-6 on a 21-yard field-goal by Jackson early in the second quarter, but Remy Hamilton's 38-yarder expanded the difference back to four points five minutes later. And Biakabutuka kept running wild, shining brighter than the late-November sun. In the first half alone, he had 195 yards, and seven carries of at least 10 yards.

Only sloppy play by the Wolverines was keeping Ohio State in the game. The second interception of Griese in the opening half led to Jackson's third field goal, a 37-yarder, with two seconds left before the intermission. It was 10-9, and long-time watchers of the Ohio State-Michigan series remembered a game in 1974, where four Buckeye field goals gave OSU a 12-10 win and a Rose Bowl berth.

Valenzisi, watching back in Evanston, remembered, even though he was in diapers in 1974. An Ohio native, he was off in a corner, finding it impossible to root for Michigan, even under these circumstances.

"There's too much of my father in me," he said.

Michigan scored on its first drive of the second half, Biakabutuka gaining 41 of the 49 yards, Griese crashing through from about four feet out to move the Wolverines ahead 17-9. But the lead was neither large nor solid. The afternoon's third interception of Griese, this time by defensive end Mike Vrabel, set up Eddie George's l-yard plunge with 1:14 left in the third quarter.

Michigan led 17-15. It seemed that this Ohio State-Michigan game would, like most Ohio State-Michigan games do, go down to the final seconds.

No, it wouldn't. Not with Biakabutuka on the loose, it wouldn't.

Not with him doing the dirty work to set up Williams' 8-yard dash off left tackle early in the fourth quarter. And not with Williams returning the favor, setting up Biakabutuka's 2-yard plunge with 7:55 left. That gave Michigan a 31-15 lead, which meant Ohio State would have to score three times to beat the Wolverines.

That just wasn't going to happen, especially with Cooper having junked the usual game plan—give it to George —in favor of a passing game, and doing it when the Buckeyes trailed by nine. George, who finished with 104 yards, didn't carry the ball in the final 13:04. A late TD pass from Hoying to Buster Tillman only made the margin of Michigan's victory less impressive.

One point would have been enough. Carr, like Gary Moeller before him and Schembechler before him, would beat Ohio State on his first attempt. Wolverine historians compared it to the 1969 game, when Schembechler, in his first season, guided an average Michigan team to a 24-12 upset, and, not incidentally, the Rose Bowl.

Watching the final minutes was excruciating. The clock seemed stuck on nine minutes, then eight, then seven, and hey, how come Ohio State was running so many plays?

"Show the clock," Barnett implored to the screen at one point. It came up: 3:46 left.

"Holy smokes," he said.

Michigan wouldn't get roses this time. But they succeeded in jabbing thorns in the side of the Buckeyes, and that was satisfaction enough. As one blue-clad Wolverine fan said to someone dressed in Buckeye gear while exiting Michigan Stadium, "We can't go, so you can't go either!" He didn't have to say where.

Northwestern could and would go, for the first time in 47 years.

"We weren't worried about other teams," said Biakabutuka, who gained 1,724 yards in his junior season. "We were worried about ourselves, about our seniors."

Glenn's outburst made the worries go away.

"Terry Glenn said some things we didn't appreciate," Biakabutuka went on. "We proved to him that Michigan wasn't on the bottom. I thought the Notre Dame game two years ago was the greatest game I'd been a part of. But this is.

"It's the greatest feeling when you can prove somebody wrong."

"Saying Michigan was nobody!" said Griese. "That's disrespecting your opponent. This win says we have character. Nobody had faith in us but us."

That could have been said by Barnett or his players. Carr, a teammate of Barnett's at Missouri almost 30 years earlier, was near tears, his voice breaking, as he met reporters.

"I don't think anybody in the country gave us much of a chance, but I told our kids it's not important what the other people think but what the people on our side believe," said Carr. "And we believed."

At 11-1, and 7-1 in the Big Ten, the Buckeyes were still a fine team. They just weren't going to Pasadena, and that realization hit home hard.

Glenn, standing in his underwear 45 minutes after the game in which he caught four of the 12 balls thrown his way (with all the receptions in the first half), dropping a pair and seeing another pair get intercepted, didn't want to leave the locker room. Hoying called it "the toughest day I'll have to live with for the rest of my life. It's going to be something I might never get over. I can't explain it."

Cooper lost more than the game. He also lost the $60,000 in incentives that he'd have pocketed for beating Michigan in a nine-win season and going to the Rose Bowl. If Ohio State had won the national championship, there would have been even more.

Two days after the game, somebody asked Barnett how to spell Biakabutuka. He quipped in return, "T-I-M T-D. T-H-A-N-K Y-O-U."

On that Saturday, there was still a formality to be taken care of. Tournament of Roses president Bud Griest was in Ann Arbor, three dozen roses in hand, ready to invite the Buckeyes in person. That not being possible, ABC wired him for sound and connected him with Barnett in Evanston so he could issue the invitation to the Wildcats electronically.

Barnett played the moment for all it was worth.

"I want to ask our guys if they want to go to Pasadena," he said, turning to his players.

"Yeaaaa!" they exclaimed.

Out on Central Street, a steady stream of cars, horns honking and purple "N" flags waving, drove along. Just as at the start of the season, the students were home, off campus. But this time, the community was celebrating. They did everything but throw a parade.

That could wait until New Year's Day, when one was already scheduled.

In Pasadena.

Darnell Autry, a Big Ten first-team selection as a sophomore, will be opposing defenses' No. 1 target in 1996. (Scott Strazzante/Daily Southtown)

Chapter 18
REFLECTION AND REWARD

"We did it."
—captain William Bennett

"IN YEARS PAST," said Northwestern athletic director Rick Taylor at the start of the football awards banquet, "we could have held this in a McDonald's and had a Happy Meal."

Not after the season just completed. It was Monday, November 20, two days after the Wildcats had beaten Purdue, five days before they'd know their bowl destination was their ultimate destination: the Rose Bowl, and about 600 Cat fanciers descended upon the Omni-Orrington Hotel in downtown Evanston for the annual bash.

Taylor wasn't far off. In the previous several years, the Grand Ballroom was more than big enough to accommodate the 400 or so attendees. This year, with Wildcat fever high, the banquet expanded to use the hotel's other two dining rooms as well, with extra seating in the Grand Ballroom for the presentation of the awards and speeches, and the showing of a highlight film.

That was another difference. This year, there was highlight after highlight after highlight on the highlight film. It ended with Frank Sinatra's rendition of "High Hopes," the first inkling the general public had that this season had, in a way, been set to music.

Some NU football banquets in years past had been downright funereal, and none since 1971 had a winning team to honor. After the 0-11 seasons, hemlock was the drink of choice at the bar. One or two soirees had thrown off sparks, notably the 1980 banquet, when head coach Rick Venturi said he wouldn't quit. He was fired the next morning.

This one would be joyous, upbeat, filled with laughter and mirth. There were congratulations all around. Darnell Autry, clutching a Michigan cap when he entered the lobby, signed copies of his *Sports Illustrated* cover appearance, the first for an NU player since the Parseghian years. He had not heard, until reporters told him, of the *SI* cover jinx.

"What jinx?" Autry said, asking for details. It didn't jinx him, thus putting him in company with a very select group, including, oh, Kathy Ireland.

Autry would be one of many Wildcats honored in the course of the night.

Taylor wanted to assure those who had been attending Northwestern games for years that only the won-loss record was different.

"Success is not measured by what you've achieved," said Taylor. "Success is measured by where you've come from. I think the fact

Defenders Casey Dailey (36), Joe Reiff (94), and Matt Rice (95) all will be back for more in 1996. (Scott Strazzante/Daily Southtown)

we've come so far in such a relatively short period of time, this success is far greater than anything I've experienced, and I've been fortunate enough to be around a little bit.

"This has brought great pride to Northwestern, but understand that nothing about this great university has changed. We don't have to fall back on, 'Yeah, but we have good academics.' The 'Yeah, but' days are over.

"We now have a football team that I certainly hope the academic arm of the university can match in the future," Taylor said to the happy crowd. "We're fourth and academics is 13th. Ooh, I'll hear about that one tomorrow."

University president Henry Bienen, who took over at NU at the start of the year and revealed upon his arrival that he was a big sports fan, laughed heartily.

"It's wonderful to have a great football program, and it's wonderful to be successful," said Bienen. "The most important thing was that we did it our way. We turned the football program around and had great success with athletes who were students. When you hear our students, our coaches on television, you know you're at a real university."

The ballroom was festooned with purple and white balloons and a huge bowl-bound banner. What bowl, nobody knew yet. What was missing was the "Expect Victory" banners NU fans had become accustomed to. Taylor explained why.

"What would you do other than expect victory?" said Taylor.

"Would you expect a tie, expect to lose? Victory was so obvious, we sort of, as a department, let it go, and we're very glad the football team, the players and coaches, have given us the charge now to come up with something really catchy we can use for our marketing next year.

"The beauty (of this season) is that the people here, the players and coaches, fit Northwestern, and Northwestern fits them. If there's a common denominator to the remarks I've heard over this past year from our alumni, it's how well our players and coaches represent Northwestern. That's the thing I'm most proud of."

The newcomer awards, presented by the Northwestern Gridiron Network, were first, with D'Wayne Bates collecting the offensive award and Josh Barnes the defensive award.

Fifth-year senior center Rob Johnson, whose 44-start streak would extend to a record 45th in the Rose Bowl, received the George W. Ballentine Award, given to the player exhibiting superior leadership.

Sam Valenzisi, another fifth-year senior, collected the Thomas Airth Spirit Award. And fourth-year senior William Bennett was presented with the Carnig Minasian Citizenship Award.

The Marcel Price Award, a new honor named for the would-be sophomore who was shot and killed in midsummer, was presented to fifth-year senior Rodney Ray.

Then it came time for the most valuable player awards. Northwestern recognizes both the offense and defense, selected by the staff, then an overall MVP, voted by the players.

There wasn't much doubt that Darnell Autry would win the offensive MVP award. His school-record season of 1,675 yards rushing and 15 touchdowns, with only one turnover in 376 carries and receptions, made that a lock.

Who, though, would win the defensive MVP award? Pat Fitzgerald? Ray or Chris Martin, the cornerbacks? Defensive tackle Matt Rice?

Everybody won. In a fitting departure from tradition, the coaching staff named the entire defense the defensive MVP. The gesture earned a standing ovation.

"One more time, now," said defensive coordinator Ron Vanderlinden.

Finally, Autry was voted Northwestern's most valuable player by his teammates.

The honor made him eligible for the *Chicago Tribune*'s Silver Football, since 1924 the Big Ten's MVP award. Autry came in third behind winner Eddie George of Ohio State and runner-up Mike Alstott of Purdue, a pair of seniors.

In the ensuing weeks, more honors came to Northwestern football than had come in decades.

The Big Ten teams were announced first, and a school-record-tying six Wildcats made the media's all-conference first team: Autry, Johnson, offensive guard Ryan Padgett, Valenzisi, Fitzgerald and Martin. The only other time a half-dozen Northwestern players had been so honored was 1970. There had only been five first-teamers from NU since 1989, though two, punter Paul Burton and guard Matt O'Dwyer, were selected in 1994.

Four more NU players, offensive tackle Brian Kardos, Bates, Rice and defensive back Hudhaifa Ismaeli, made the second team, while safeties William Bennett and Eric Collier, cornerback Rodney Ray and quarterback Steve Schnur received honorable mention.

Fitzgerald, whose 13-tackle per-game average was tops in the league, and whose total of 130 tackles in 10 games was better than anyone but Wisconsin's Pete Monty (137) managed in 11 or 12 games, was selected the defensive player of the year by reporters, and Barnett the conference's coach of the year.

The Big Ten's coaches, who can't vote for members of their own teams, also picked Autry, Padgett, Valenzisi, Fitzgerald and Martin to their first team. Fitzgerald was unanimous, meaning he was on all 10 ballots aside from NU's, and named the defensive player of the year.

Johnson was on the second team with Ismaeli and Collier, while Bates, Kardos, Rice and Schnur were honorable mention selections.

Next, national honors started to flow in. On December 7 in Orlando, Barnett was named national coach of the year, and Fitzgerald given the Chuck Bednarik Trophy as national defensive player of the year, winning over finalists Illinois' Kevin Hardy and Simeon Rice.

"The irony of this award," said Barnett of his honor, "is that the person who receives it receives it because someone else does so well. In my case, 95 wonderful young men who made a commitment to pull together, and a coaching staff of the most dedicated role models and great teachers I've ever been around."

The day before, Fitzgerald was named to the AP's All-America Team at one of the four linebacker spots, along with Hardy, Miami's Ray Lewis and Texas Tech's Zach Thomas. Autry and Valenzisi were selected to the second team. It had been 12 seasons since a Wildcat had been a first-team All-America player. Punter John Kidd was selected to the 1983 team.

That left the Heisman Trophy. Autry, while something of a longshot, was one of the five players invited to the Downtown Athletic Club in New York City, along with George, Florida quarterback Danny Wuerffel, Iowa State running back Troy Davis, and Nebraska quarterback Tommie Frazier, for the December 9 presentation.

Many were surprised when George won the Heisman, believing either Frazier or Wuerffel to be the favorite, but his 264-point margin of victory over Frazier left no doubt. Autry's fourth-place showing, with 535 points to George's

Steve Schnur and Darnell Autry formed an effective combination in 1995. (Scott Strazzante/The Daily Southtown)

1,460, was the best placing for a Northwestern player since Otto Graham finished a distant third to winner Angelo Bertelli in 1943.

All that was ahead on the night of the banquet, however. Before Barnett would get a chance to speak, the graduating seniors had their say. It was a mixture of high praise and low comedy.

Sam Valenzisi, the master of ceremonies, saluted his father, Al, the head coach at John Marshall High in Cleveland, by saying, "Dad, you'll always be my coach."

William Bennett surprised a few people when he said that he'd never played on a .500 team, not even in high school, and remembered the first three banquets he'd attended.

"The seniors were unable to say three words: 'We did it!' Before the season, we talked about having a winning season, and here we are 10-1. We talked about going to a bowl, and we're going. Honestly, I didn't think about winning the Big Ten. I knew we'd win a lot of games, I knew we'd go to a bowl, but the Big Ten championship?

"We did it!"

Rob Johnson, introduced by Valenzisi as "the most handsome and intelligent center in the United States," surveyed the house and remembered his freshman year.

"There were about seven people here," he said. "This is wonderful. It's really brought home what we've accomplished."

Chris Martin thanked the fans, "the loyal ones and the bandwagoners."

Rodney Ray went on longer than some Academy Award acceptance speeches go, to which Valenzisi said, "Man, I can't believe you fit all that on one little card."

Finally, Barnett took the floor, and those in the audience were treated to what his players had heard all season.

"Four years ago tomorrow, an opportunity was created for my family to come to Evanston," Barnett began, noting the anniversary of his hiring.

"In our first staff meeting, I said, 'If you can't

see the invisible, you can't do the impossible.' We sorta locked arms and off we went, because we could see it, and we knew we could do it.

"A year ago, at this senior banquet, I talked to the '95 team. What I said to them, I want to read, just as I read last year.

"I said, 'A vision is just a dream until you act upon it.'

"I said, 'We know a person thinks, not when he tells us what he thinks, but by his actions.'

"I said, 'Difficulty is the one excuse that history never accepts.'

"I said, 'Any jackass can kick down a barn, but it takes a real carpenter to build one.'

"I said, 'You must do something you think you cannot do.'

"And I said, 'Nothing splendid has ever been achieved, except by those who dared believe that something inside of them was superior to circumstance.'

"Finally, I said, 'The future is not something we enter, the future is something we create.'

"This isn't anything different, perhaps, that any other coach in America would say to the team he had returning. They're the seeds that you plant, the seeds that you throw out. The difference was, I had fertile soil. You listened. Whether or not you knew you took it to heart, this year is an example that you did.

"You have to have guys who are willing, guys who want to do those things, because those seeds are thrown out to many teams. But it takes a special group of people to take them in, cover them up, nourish them and turn them into something. That's what you've done.

"I can say exactly the same thing to next year's team, '96. I'll say exactly the same words. You too will nurture it and make it grow to what you want it to be.

"This year, people called you relentless, miracle workers, poised, gracious, humble. A Purdue player said of you, 'Ohio State has the best athletes, but they're the best team.'

"Together, we've visualized, we've overcome adversity, we've stalked, we've squeezed, we've stared. We've been trapped in coconuts, and we've counted pennies. Part of that language, only we can understand.

"We've made history. We're one heartbeat. We've become the epitome of team to the nation.

"We're No. 4 in the nation. We're the Big Ten champs. And we're not finished."

Gary Barnett received a standing ovation. It was a happy meal after all.

D'Wayne Bates earned second-team All-Big Ten honors at wide receiver, behind Terry Glenn of Ohio State and Bobby Engram of Penn State. (Scott Strazzante/Daily Southtown)

NORTHWESTERN SEASON REVIEW

RECORD: 10-2-0   (8-0-0) CONFERENCE

GAME-BY-GAME REVIEW

Date	W/L	Rank	Opponent	Score	H/A	Attendance
September 2	W		at Notre Dame (9)	17-15	A	c59,075
September 16	L	(25)	MIAMI (OHIO) (0:00)	28-30	H	26,352
September 23	W		AIR FORCE	30-6	H	26,037
September 30	W		INDIANA	31-7	H	29,223
October 7	W	(25)	at Michigan (7)	19-13	A	c104,642
October 14	W	(14)	at Minnesota	27-17	A	50,504
October 21	W	(11)	WISCONSIN	35-0	H	c49,256
October 28	W	(8)	at Illinois (6:14)	17-14	A	65,425
November 4	W	(6)	PENN STATE (12)	21-10	H	c49,256
November 11	W	(5)	IOWA	31-20	H	c49,256
November 18	W	(5)	at Purdue	23-8	A	47,172

NU was ranked No. 4 in the November 20 AP Poll

82nd Rose Bowl Game

Date	W/L	Rank	Opponent	Score	H/A	Attendance
January 1	L	(3)	Southern California (17)	32-41	N	c100,102

The number in front of the opponent name indicates Northwestern's ranking in the Associated Press Poll entering the game. The number following the opponent's name indicates its ranking. Time indicates time left in games decided late. c-capacity crowd.

REGULAR SEASON STATISTICS

SCORE BY QUARTERS	1	2	3	4	TOTAL	AVG
Northwestern	64	81	57	77	279	25.4
Opponent	17	73	10	40	140	12.7

TEAM STATISTICS	NU	OPP
Total First Downs	169	197
Rushing	86	92
Passing	69	99
Penalty	14	8
Rushing Attempts-Yds	465-1906	451-1507
Rushing Yards per Game	173.3	137.0
Pass Comp-Att-Int	124-228-6	204-365-16
Passing Yards	1559	2034
Passing Yards per Game	141.7	184.9
Punting Number-Yds-Avg	64-2421-37.8	63-2464-39.1
Fumbles-Lost	13-6	31-16
Penalties-Yards	54-454	59-470
Sack by-Yards lost	28-212	8-46
Third Down Conversions	43-147	73-183
Third Down Conversions Pct.	.293	.399
Fourth Down Conversions	7-14	9-22
Fourth Down Conversions Pct.	.500	.409
Avg. Time of Possessions	28:09	31:51

NORTHWESTERN SEASON REVIEW

1995 GAME-BY-GAME STATISTICS

	RUSHING (Carries-Yards-TDs)	RECEIVING (Catches-Yards-TDs)			PASSING (Attempts-Completion-Yards-Int-TDs)
Player	D. Autry	Bates	Musso	Beazley	Schnur
Game					
ND	33-160-0	4-58-1	2-42-0	2-28-1	28-14-166-0-2
MU	35-152-0	5-90-2	0-0-0	1-17-0	26-13-187-1-3
AF	37-190-2	7-110-0	3-29-0	2-16-0	22-16-206-0-0
IU	28-162-2	0-0-0	1-9-0	0-0-0	13-7-45-0-0
UM	26-103-0	2-60-0	0-0-0	1-16-0	23-11-126-0-1
MN	28-169-3	6-100-0	0-0-0	0-0-0	23-13-194-0-0
UW	27-113-2	3-32-0	2-26-0	0-0-0	16-8-79-1-0
ILL	41-151-1	3-74-1	3-38-0	0-0-0	19-8-117-0-1
PSU	36-139-3	4-52-0	1-16-0	0-0-0	16-10-96-1-0
Iowa	32-110-1	2-37-0	0-0-0	2-34-0	12-6-82-1-1
PUR	32-226-0	6-131-1	0-0-0	0-0-0	20-12-158-1-1

1995 FIELD GOALS

Notre Dame
Valenzisi - 37 yds, good, 2nd qtr.

Air Force
Valenzisi - 46 yds, good, 1st qtr.
Valenzisi - 26 yds, good, 2nd qtr.
Valenzisi - 35 yds, good, 2nd qtr.

Indiana
Valenzisi - 40 yds, good, 1st qtr.
Valenzisi - 34 yds, good, 3rd qtr.
Valenzisi - 32 yds, good, 4th qtr.

Michigan
Valenzisi - 29 yds, good, 2nd qtr.
Valenzisi - 28 yds, good, 2nd qtr.
Valenzisi - 32 yds, good, 3rd qtr.
Valenzisi - 22 yds, good 4th qtr.

Minesota
Valenzisi - 20 yds, good, 1st qtr.
Valenzisi - 29 yds, good, 2nd qtr.

Wisconsin
Valenzisi - 29 yds, no good, 1st qtr.
Valenzisi - 32 yds, good, 1st qtr.
Valenzisi - 26 yds, good 2nd qtr.
Gowins - 40 yds, good, 4th qtr.

Illinois
Gowins - 49 yds, good, 2nd qtr.
Gowins - 40 yds, no good, 4th qtr.

Penn State
Gowins - 44 yds, no good, 2nd qtr.

Iowa
Gowins - 50 yds, good, 1st qtr.

Purdue
Gowins - 52 yds, no good, 2nd qtr.

PAT FITZGERALD TACKLES

	Solo	Assist	Total
ND	8	3	11
Miami	8	3	11
Air Force	11	2	13
Indiana	5	4	9
Mich.	10	4	14
Minn.	11	1	12
Wisc.	3	7	10
Illinois	7	7	14
Penn St.	11	6	17
Iowa	4	6	10
Purdue		injured	

Head coaches John Robinson and Gary Barnett chat before Rose Bowl hostilities commence. (Scott Strazzante/Daily Southtown)

Chapter 19
HONOR WITHOUT GLORY

"I'll walk away from this place saying 'What if?' for the rest of my life. That's a horrible feeling to have."

—linebacker Geoff Shein

ON DECEMBER 17, the Northwestern Wildcats left cold Evanston for another world. They left for the Rose Bowl, and for warm weather, palm trees, mountain vistas, 24-hour traffic reports and women in halter tops and shorts.

"Evil things," said Gary Barnett, tongue in cheek, of the latter before the Northwestern contingent shipped out. "There haven't been a lot of girls in shorts and halter tops here lately."

When they arrived in what natives call the Southland, they were a team on a mission. The Big Ten had been convinced, week by week, that the Wildcats weren't a Cinderella team. Most of the rest of the nation still wasn't sure, even though NU was ranked No. 3 in both major polls, and even though the Cats were arriving as the Big Ten champions. They were, after all, the Northwestern Wildcats.

And they were playing Southern California. The Trojans. "America's Bowl Team," and self-billed as such, at that.

Northwestern had been to one Rose Bowl, way back on New Year's Day 1949, so long ago the only national broadcast of the game was on radio, the new medium of television not sufficiently advanced technically then to get a picture out of the Los Angeles basin.

USC had played in 27 previous Rose Bowls, boasting a 19-8 record. The Trojans nearly owned the joint. It was, behind the Los Angeles Memorial Coliseum, their unofficial second home in southern California. The locals knew the way to ring in the new year was to zoom up the Pasadena Freeway, camp out on Colorado Boulevard to watch the Tournament of Roses parade, then get into their second traffic jam of the day on the way to the Rose Bowl to bake in the sun and watch the Trojans take on some Big Ten team just happy to be out of the snow.

Northwestern would be a different animal. Rather than arrive just before or on Christmas, the Wildcats came out more than a week earlier, ran through a stiff series of two-a-days for almost a week, and got into game shape before the usual round of Hollywood-style fun and games began.

"We'll put in the things in the game plan we're sure we're gonna do," said Barnett of the practices at Cal-Irvine.

Not that anyone outside the official Wildcat family would be able to see the important goings-on. Barnett, for the first time since the week of the Illinois game in 1994, closed drills to outsiders.

"There isn't anything cloak-and-dagger about it," he explained. "From one week to another, it's very difficult to make any serious

Darnell Autry (24) and D'Wayne Bates celebrate the first of Autry's three touchdowns. (Scott Strazzante/Daily Southtown)

changes. You are who you are. When a team has a whole month to prepare for you, and you for them, they can pretty well sniff you out. They have a pretty good clue of what to do.

"The coaches that we're dealing with at this level are geniuses in many ways. Realize that we're the No. 3 team in the country, and we're picking the team that was picked to be the No. 1 team in the country. That's pretty elite company. It's not just because of the players, it's because of the coaching staffs that are involved.

"You have a month to search and find out, to scheme, you can do a lot of things. If you want to be unpredictable in this game, which you have to be in order to win, then you can't just expose yourself to the world. I've had stuff leak out at another place, and it was very damaging."

There was one more reason.

"I need to get 'em away from the distractions, the attention. The only time you feel really comfortable now is when they close that gate out there and you're just alone with the guys you've gone to war with for 15 weeks. I couldn't wait to get on the field (for the first practice) with the gates closed and just yell and practice and have a good time."

Northwestern, a local media story, was now a national media story. Dozens of reporters came to the December 15 news conference in Evanston, and the Chicago media moved en masse with the Cats.

So, after the first few minutes of warmups, reporters and camera crews were ushered out, with Cal-Irvine security guards shooing inquiring minds away.

At USC, practices remained open. Head coach John Robinson had run the operation that way in his first stint in charge, and was running it that way again. The open-door policy had risks, but could also pay dividends.

For a select group of about 30 Wildcats, the trip to Pasadena was nostalgic rather than competitive. That group was comprised of members of the 1948 Northwestern team, the first, and, until this season, only previous Wildcat team to play in the Rose or any other bowl.

The '48ers not only went to the Rose Bowl, but won it, coming from behind to post a 20-14 win over California before 93,000 people in the 35th Rose Bowl on New Year's Day 1949. Led by a charismatic coach, coming off an underwhelming 3-6 season the year before, and with a group of seasoned veterans — of World War II — the Wildcats weren't expected to do much in 1948, but were the surprise of the Big Ten.

They went 5-1 in the league and 7-2 in the regular season, with the only losses against Michigan and Notre Dame. Their record wasn't good enough for the Big Ten title, but, with powerhouse Michigan repeating its 1947 championship and the league's rule against back-to-back trips keeping the Wolverines home, the runner-up Wildcats were sent west to play in the third Rose Bowl since the deal locking in the champions of the Pacific Coast Conference and Big Nine had been struck.

Northwestern's coach was Bob Voigts, who was in his second year in charge, and a pupil of Lynn "Pappy" Waldorf, who had coached Voigts at NU in the 1930s. Voigts, in fact, was an All-Big Ten honorable mention selection as a sophomore at guard for NU in 1936, when the Wildcats won the Big Ten championship, the last such achievement until this year.

The group Voigts had to work with was typical of college teams in the late 1940s, a mixture of World War II vets going to school on the GI Bill and standard-age college students. Voigts, 32, was just six years older than his oldest player.

"I didn't know what to expect," said Voigts. "I had no idea. It was a matter of the older guys taking the younger guys and helping us coach them. It worked very well, the older guys telling them what to expect. We wondered when we got 'em together how we were gonna do this, and it worked."

One reason for the success, said Voigts, was a matter of the team's captain, Alex Sarkisian, motivating his teammates.

"He was a character," said Voigts. "Anybody who got a guy like that on his team could figure he's going to have a good team."

The Wildcats, perhaps because Illinois and Michigan had routed their hosts in the first two games played under the pact between the two conferences, were favored against the Golden Bears by up to 14 points in some circles, but hardly dominated. California, which had lost only once in its past 20 games, put up a stiff fight.

From the start it was obvious it would be a close game. It was also filled with big plays, and would quickly be regarded as one of the most exciting Rose Bowls ever. Northwestern opened the scoring in the first quarter when Frank Aschenbrenner ripped off a 73-yard touchdown run, the longest in Rose Bowl history to that juncture, but saw the score matched on Cal's next series, when Jackie Jensen, who'd later star in major league baseball, answered with a 67-yard scamper.

The Cats made it 13-7 in the second quarter when Art Murakowski scored one of the most controversial touchdowns in Rose Bowl history. He scored on a 1-yard plunge — or did he? Cal partisans weren't sure. Murakowski fumbled as he crossed the goal-line, but head linesman Jay Berwanger, the first Heisman Trophy winner, signaled touchdown.

"I'm sure I was across," said Murakowski at the time. "Somebody tackled me from behind and pulled me back. That's when I fumbled."

Sarkisian, the center, recalled the play clearly, even 47 years later.

"I remember very, very vividly," said Sarkisian. "Art ran off right tackle, and after I

Center Rob Johnson in his NU-record 45th straight start, prepares to snap to D'Wayne Bates, usually a wide receiver, in the second quarter. (Scott Strazzante/Daily Southtown)

snapped the ball and made my block, I looked to the right. I could see Art's right leg on the white line, the goal line. When he took the next step is when he fumbled the ball. Berwanger called it a touchdown, and the referee, Jimmy Cain, he was from the Pac-10."

A photo taken from behind the goal line showed Murakowski leaning forward as he fumbled, with Cal end Norman Pressley making the tackle from behind and Murakowski's feet short of the goal line.

The argument raged for days. Everyone from Big Nine commissioner Ken "Tug" Wilson to PCC supervisor of officials Tommy Fitzpatrick chimed in with their two cents' worth. Movies, taken from high above the 50-yard line, were inconclusive. But Waldorf didn't beef.

"If the officials said he was over the goal-line, that's good enough for me," said Waldorf.

There was still more than a half of football to be played, and Cal would take a 14-13 lead with a minute left in the third quarter on Jack Swaner's 4-yard run, capping a 56-yard drive that commenced when the Wildcats fumbled.

A rally was called for, but the Golden Bear defense held fast, as did Northwestern's. The Cats stopped Cal on the NU 12, and with only a few minutes remaining, needed to go 88 yards to score.

The ball would have to be moved on the ground, for quarterback Ron Burson, playing with a sore arm, was 0-for-3 passing. Then came the first surprise. Aschenbrenner hit Don Stonesifer for a 20-yard gain in what would prove to be NU's only completion of the game.

Subsequently, the ball was on the Cal 43. Now came the second surprise. Aschenbrenner went in motion, the first such maneuver of the afternoon by NU.

"That was the key, because he shielded the defensive end, who couldn't see the snap," said Sarkisian. The end came in and (Ed) Tunnicliff got outside."

The snap by Sarkisian didn't go to Burson, but right halfback Tunnicliff, who sped down the right sideline all the way to the end zone. With just 2:59 to play, the Wildcats led 20-14. Waldorf, standing on the Cal sideline, knew what was coming as soon as he saw Aschenbrenner go in motion. He'd helped draw the play up years earlier.

"We practiced against the Tunnicliff play, but it happened anyway," said Waldorf in the Cal locker room.

Southern Cal's Keyshawn Johnson proved difficult for Northwestern's Tucker Morrison and the other Wildcats to hang on to. He finished with a Rose Bowl-record 216 receiving yards. (Scott Strazzante/ Daily Southtown)

The stunner forced Cal to play catchup, and when a flurry of passes failed to connect, the Wildcats were Rose Bowl champions.

"It was a thrill to go to the Rose Bowl then, and now, it's probably a bigger thrill," said Voigts, now 79 and living in Wilmette. "We thought it was supposed to happen. I didn't jump for joy. We took it as it came along."

It didn't come along again. Voigts coached NU eight seasons, and was under .500, at 33-39-1, when he left after the 1954 season. The Wildcats still had some good years, even reached No. 1 in the polls for two weeks under Ara Parseghian, but never made it to postseason action.

Until 1995, that is. And that made Sarkisian and his old teammates happy almost beyond words.

"Ten years after that game, we had our first reunion," he said. "We collectively said the greatest joy the 1949 Rose Bowl team would have would be to sit in the stands at another Rose Bowl game and cheer another Northwestern team to victory."

Thus, not only the 1995 Wildcats arrived in Pasadena. So did some 30 of the 1948 Wildcats, including Voigts, to live out their dream of rooting for their successors in the great stadium at the foothills of the San Gabriel Mountains.

"I think Gary Barnett's a great football coach, and he's got some great kids playing the game," said Voigts. "We had good kids, but they have players that are farther along than we were. They're way advanced. If I had to play a game against them, I'd go hide in the woods."

"We were a big, happy family and this group is," said Sarkisian, comparing the squads. "That's where the similarity ends. These individuals are bigger, stronger Division I football players, great football players."

For Sarkisian, a retired executive for the East Chicago, Indiana, public school system, the success of 1995 made up for all those lousy years in the 1970s and 1980s.

"There was many a year and a game, we'd go to Dyche Stadium, an hour to get there, an hour to get back, and in 25 minutes, we'd be back in the car coming home, because we were getting beat 30 to nothing," said Sarkisian. "I'd turn to my wife and say, 'You know, there's got to be something wrong with me for going up there.'"

Then Gary Barnett arrived. To Sarkisian, Barnett's football's version of "the Messiah." It took one meeting with Barnett to persuade the old captain that Northwestern's long-dormant football program was in good hands.

Said Sarkisian, "When he got through talking, I said to the individuals there, and he was there, 'The only thing we have to do is give this man what he's asking for. Then, if he doesn't win, we'll fire him.' But listening to him, he reminded me so much of Bob Voigts.

"He's a fantastic individual. I'm so tickled that he's our coach. I'm so proud to be able to say I'm a Northwestern man."

One thing hadn't changed from 1949. While the face value of tickets had gone from $5.50 to $75 (and had been $48 for the 1995 game), scalpers were still asking about $60 for tickets. While a shade over half the 100,102 fans who watched the 82nd Rose Bowl were Northwestern fans, there wasn't a huge demand for tickets to the game. And prices dropped precipitously in the last hour before the game, down to 1949 prices.

The real Rose Bowl hoopla got underway on Tuesday, December 26, when the Wildcats traveled to Lawry's, near Beverly Hills, for the "Beef Bowl." They consumed 671 pounds of beef.

"Some of the guys this morning were a little slow moving around," Barnett said of Wednesday morning's practice. That was an early affair, because the festivities continued with the traditional trip to Disneyland.

It was, well, Disneyesque. Mickey and Minnie said hello, Goofy didn't look out of place at all in a referee's shirt, and Darnell Autry, who had been to the park on several other occasions, couldn't wait to go to Magic Mountain.

"I've known Mickey and Minnie for a long time," said Autry, rolling his eyes. "We're real close friends."

For defensive end Casey Dailey, it was a return home of sorts. He'd worked at Disneyland in summers past. Now, he and the rest of his teammates received the ultimate perk at the world-famous theme park. They were allowed to cut to the front of the endless lines to get on rides, all the better for television crews taping the goings-on.

The humor of the day wasn't exactly highbrow. Asked what Disney character the Wild-

176 **PURPLE ROSES**

Officials ruled a fumble by Brian Musso on this second quarter play, even though his left knee is clearly touching the ground. Daylon McCutcheon took advantage of Sammy Knight's tackle to score on a 53-yard fumble recovery for a 24-7 USC lead. (Scott Strazzante/ Daily Southtown)

cats reminded him of, center Ron Johnson said, "Goofy."

"That's just you, Rob," said injured placekicker Sam Valenzisi. "Just you."

For Valenzisi and injured linebacker Pat Fitzgerald, the week was a bittersweet experience. They could enjoy the sideshows on the trip, but not the action. The closest either came was Valenzisi's hitting 20-yard field goals at each end of the Rose Bowl before the teams began to warm up on game day.

"It's been hard (to stay part of the team) because I'm not used to standing on the sidelines," said Valenzisi, a fifth-year senior whose season ended with that injury-producing jump for joy against Wisconsin. "You bite your tongue and try to make sure the empty feeling you feel in your stomach doesn't make you sick. It hurts because I'm a competitor, not because I'm jealous in any way or because I think I'm missing out on something. It hurts because I want to be out there playing."

Fitzgerald, at least, would be able to play again in 1996.

"It'll be better than the Purdue game where my leg was in a cast and I was on crutches and couldn't get around," said Fitzgerald before the Rose Bowl.

The Thursday before the game, Northwestern's Hollywood connection was displayed for all to see. Charlton Heston, one of NU's own, reprised his role as Moses in "The Ten Commandments," parting Universal Studio's version of the Red Sea during the Wildcats' tour of the back lots. Just to prove anything can happen in Hollywood, it was the Purple Sea. Here was Heston, wearing a reddish-purple shirt, holding a staff, and intoning, "Behold the power of the Lord! The very waters shall honor thee, turning to our school colors, purple and white."

Yep, purple water with white foam. Corny? Of course. And Friday night, when the Wildcats visited "The Tonight Show," things got even cornier. The waters parted and the players ran through, save for Fitzgerald, who was carried across the chasm. Barnett was the guest, and gave host Jay Leno, whose jaw was the model for George Washington's on Mount Rushmore, an extra-large chin strap.

All week, the Wildcat faithful were partying it up in and around Pasadena. By game time on Monday, at least half the crowd would be wearing purple. In the days before, Wildcat fanatics prowled the shops and restaurants. Some got tickets to the big bash at the Pasadena Center, where the band played, the cheerleaders cheered, and Wildcat swells reveled in the glory of being somewhere warm for the holidays.

The frenzy was carried back to Chicago, in part by a large media contingent. On Michigan

Honor Without Glory 177

Avenue, the John Hancock Center's halo was switched from holiday red and green to NU purple after Christmas. Even the Rose Bowl program was on sale in the Chicago area.

About the only thing the Wildcats didn't do was visit the Playboy Mansion. Hugh Hefner, a Chicago native and Illinois grad, had the Fighting Illini over for milk and cookies prior to the 1984 Rose Bowl, and extended the same invitation to the Wildcats. Barnett, perhaps thinking again about the "evil" of halter tops and shorts, turned the invite down, much to the chagrin of sportswriters eager to do more sightseeing.

Eventually, the sightseeing and celebrity schmoozing and the endless interviews by reporters who began to run out of questions, save for those questioning Barnett's plans for the 1996 season and beyond, came to an end, as did the old year.

Pasadena police estimated a million people were in town and watched the 107th Tournament of Roses Parade on New Year's Day morning. The *Pasadena Star-News* questioned that figure, based on research by a physicist from the Jet Propulsion Laboratory in town, who said a million people couldn't fit on the streets. However many saw the floats and the bands, either in person or on television, on that Monday, they were treated to a spectacular show, one that was rivaled by only two things: the glorious weather, the temperature reaching 75 degrees by mid-afternoon with clear skies, strong overnight winds having scrubbed the air to grant all a glorious view of the San Gabriel Mountains, and the 82nd Rose Bowl Game itself.

The pregame festivities included the appearance of grand marshal Kermit the Frog and the two school bands. When the NU band, led by director of bands John Paynter, who had played clarinet at the 1949 Rose Bowl, played the school's alma mater, and half the crowd sang along, it became clear the Trojan contingent was outnumbered.

Fan favorites or not, Northwestern would not win the Rose Bowl. The fairy-tale story that began in winter workouts, gained momentum on Mount Trashmore and at Camp Kenosha, went public at Notre Dame and reached epic proportions at Michigan and against Wisconsin and Penn State, would not have a perfect ending.

This Hollywood tale ended with the last reel spliced in upside down. The Wildcats nearly pulled off one of the great comebacks in Rose Bowl history, and indeed took the lead after trailing by 17 points late in the second quarter. Hampered by a pair of turnovers, Southern Cal's surprise offensive strategy of using three wide-receivers and two running backs in a no-huddle attack, and an inability to thwart the talented play of someone who first became attracted to

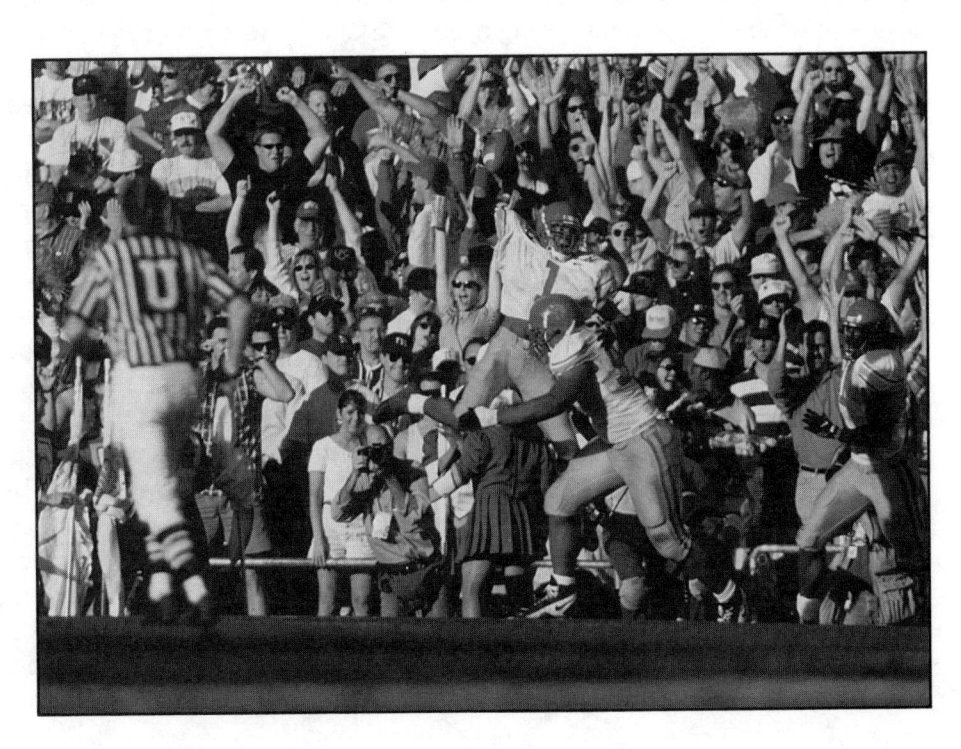

Daylon McCutcheon celebrates his fumble recovery score in front of the USC faithful. (Scott Strazzante/Daily Southtown)

the Trojans by watching their open practices as a kid, Northwestern wasn't able to sustain the momentum it built.

The Trojans rallied in return, winning 41-32 to capture the Rose Bowl for the first time in six years, and for the 20th time in all.

The Wildcats, three-point underdogs, played valiantly in what became a Rose Bowl shootout on the scale of the USC-Wisconsin game of 1963, which ended with Badger quarterback Ron VanderKelen throwing touchdown passes in the moonlight in an effort, eventually futile, to overtake the Trojans.

This time around, the moonlight was aided by the stadium's lighting system, which was installed a few years ago, and just in time. Both the Wildcats and Trojans would score in each quarter, with NU scoring more points than it had in all but one game, and allowing more than it had in any contest all season.

That it would turn into a last-scorer-wins game played into the hands of the Trojans, even though Northwestern's offense, revitalized at Cal-Irvine and Citrus College, was more effective through the air than it had been since the early stages of the year. Darnell Autry ran for three touchdowns and 110 yards, and was overshadowed by the career-best 23-of-39, 336-yard showing of NU quarterback Steve Schnur.

But those figures were overshadowed and rendered nearly meaningless by what Trojan quarterback Brad Otton and receiver Keyshawn Johnson — the kid who had hung around 'SC's Howard Jones Field years before — accomplished.

Otton completed 29 of 44 passes for 391 yards, two of the throws for touchdowns. Twelve of the catches were made by Johnson, who went for a Rose Bowl-record 216 yards, most of them after making the catch. All 12 of his receptions were good for first downs, and seven of them came in third-down situations.

In short, he was unstoppable. No matter what alignment the Wildcats tried to contain him — and they double-teamed him most of the afternoon — Johnson would spring loose for a key reception at a critical time.

"I thought they were a little above everybody else on the field," said Barnett. "We weren't able to put enough pressure on Otton to get him out of rhythm, and when we did, he always found another receiver to go to."

Or found Johnson, usually the No. 1 option. That Johnson even made it to Southern Cal, given his recent past history, made Johnson's personal life a success beyond his considerable on-field accomplishments. He and other neighborhood kids began to hang around USC practices in the spring of 1980. The players and coaching staff — Robinson was in his ultra-successful first stint with the Trojans then — took to them, especially Johnson.

Johnson became semi-officially attached to the Trojan program. He'd shag balls in practice, and even in games. He'd work in the sports information office. He'd do the dirty work most go-fers do, and more, all the better to keep occupied in South Central L.A.

The neighborhood eventually got to him. Not able to watch new coach Larry Smith's closed practices (Ted Tollner, like Robinson before him, had left the door open for anyone to watch), Johnson hung around the neighborhood, becoming "affiliated," he said, rather than joining, a gang. He started to sell drugs at age 13, did it for three years, and, while in eighth grade, was arrested for and convicted of possession of marijuana, cocaine and possession of a concealed weapon, a handgun. He served nine months in a state youth correctional facility.

That record is hardly uncommon for South Central L.A., which makes the worst areas of Chicago look like a picnic grove. What was uncommon was Johnson turning his life around. He said he never used drugs himself, and still loved football. A prep standout at Dorsey High School, he garnered a scholarship to Miami, but when his SAT scores were subpar, had to take the junior college path, playing at West Los Angeles College in 1991 before getting thrown off the team for failing to go to class.

Motivated by a chance to play in 1993, Johnson worked his tail off in the classroom all through 1992, got back on the team, and proceeded to become not only a fine player — catching 55 passes and scoring 12 touchdowns in nine games — but a team leader.

Southern Cal, his dream team, with old friend Robinson back in charge, offered him a scholarship. This time, his grades were acceptable. That, in turn, accelerated Southern Cal's return to the top of the Pac-10 heap, for while Johnson started slowly in 1994, he was at full-throttle by season's end. Texas Tech found out in the Cotton Bowl a year ago, when Johnson caught 222 yards of passes.

"He's one of the great players I've ever been around, and one of the great players for rising to the occasion," said Robinson. "His story, what he represents to college football, everything about him is fabulous."

During the 1995 season, he averaged 110.7 yards a game. Johnson knew he'd get the ball. The Wildcats knew he'd get the ball. Hey, everybody from Fresno to San Juan Capistrano knew Johnson would get the ball.

What nobody knew was how hot Otton, the starting quarterback, would be. He usually yielded to Kyle Wachholtz for the second and fourth quarters. Not this time.

Otton went the distance, Robinson eschewing the usual switcharoo when Otton hit on seven of eight passes on the game's first drive.

"One of the great performances I've seen in my time," said Robinson. "There were so many times when he got rid of the ball, they took his No. 1 choice away and, because of his superior intellect — right? — he went to the No. 2 or No. 3 guy and a lot of times, got it away just as somebody was about to hit him.

"Brad was so effective, and dramatically effective, in the game, I felt I couldn't take him out. I feel very bad that Kyle Wachholtz couldn't play. That's important stuff to us."

"Even when we knew they were going to throw it to Keyshawn," Barnett explained, "we were not able to prevent him from catching the ball or able to put enough pressure on the quarterback to keep him from getting it off to his second or third read.

"It's about the best job of quarterbacking I've seen in a long time. Kudos to him, and to Keyshawn for the kind of catches he made. We put our best players on him, and it just wasn't enough."

Who was doing the throwing didn't bother the Wildcats as much as how well the throwing was being done, to say nothing of the catching. The Wildcats' trouble with Johnson stemmed from his size (6-foot-4), his speed (a 4.5 40-yard dash), and his agility, which cannot be quantified statistically. Other than that, he was a pushover.

"He's the best guy we've played against this year, I'll tell you that," said Barnett. "I'm glad he's out of here."

If Johnson wasn't enough of a load to deal with, by lining up a third receiver, the Trojans gave NU's suddenly-porous pass defense that much more to deal with.

"We were well-prepared, innovative," said Robinson. "We had ideas that worked. It was a great football game, one of the best I've ever been in. The tide of battle went back and forth. We got up, they came back, and we finished it."

"We were forced to pressure a little more than we wanted to, and they did a great job of calling good plays and taking advantage of the opportunities we gave 'em," explained Wildcats defensive coordinator Ron Vanderlinden. "We couldn't get the ball back.

"Early on, we could not get pressure out of a four-man rush, and the three-wide receiver, two-back set, they only used that 13 percent of the time during the season. We didn't have as complete a package on it. They caught us a little bit off guard there.

"And the no-huddle, that was a surprise."

It meant Vanderlinden, who shuffles his lineup constantly, depending on the situation, couldn't always get the defensive alignment he wanted on the field, notably in adding defensive backs. There was one more surprise.

"I really, fully expected them to come out and run the ball," said Vanderlinden. "They didn't ever attempt to."

The Trojans threw from the start. Otton's first two passes were good for first downs, as was his fourth, a 7-yarder that got Johnson the ball for the first time, and also got it into Northwestern territory.

Then the show truly began. Otton hit Johnson for 31 yards over the middle to the Wildcat 14, and the NU defense saw what it was really up against. Six plays later, LaVale Woods jumped into the end-zone on a 1-yard plunge, and the Trojans led 7-0. Thanks to a penalty and lost yardage rushing, USC had to move the ball forward 93 yards on their 83-yard drive. Otton threw for 90 of those yards, most of which came with the Trojans running the no-huddle, sometimes with Otton in the shotgun.

"We wanted to tire them out," Robinson said, aware that the Wildcats had six misting fans stationed behind the home bench, compared to none for USC. "It was a nice warm day out there, a typical California winter day."

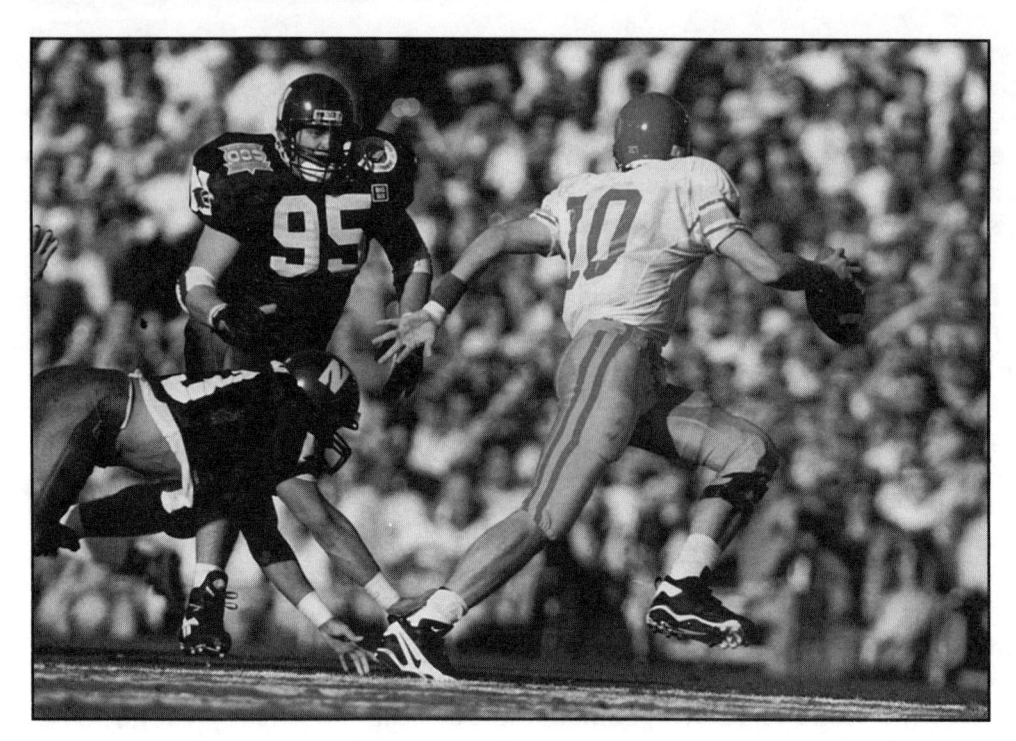

Matt Rice (95) and Eric Collier go after USC quarterback Brad Otton, who threw for 391 yards. (Scott Strazzante/Daily Southtown)

"Otton did a good job scrambling and giving (Johnson) the rock," said safety Eric Collier. "It was just a combination of things. A lot of passes just came out of nowhere. You thought he was going down, he got the ball off, and Keyshawn made something out of those plays."

Additionally, USC was three-for-three on third downs on the first drive. The Trojans would eventually go 12-of-17 in that situation.

"We have not been good against third down all year," said Barnett. "They led the Pac-10 in third-down conversions. They held true to form and we held true to form."

Northwestern came right back with an answering touchdown of its own before four more minutes had elapsed. The Wildcats moved 68 yards in 10 plays, including three passes from Schnur to D'Wayne Bates. Brian Gowins' extra-point kick tied the score at 7-all with 6:15 left in the first quarter. The game was afoot.

It was soon almost out of reach. Southern Cal scored the next 17 points.

"After they scored that first time, I went to (offensive coordinator) Mike Riley and said, 'Just let me and Brad take over this one together,'" Johnson said. "Then I said to Brad, 'Let's do it together.'"

Otton came back two possessions later with three passes to Johnson, the longest for 24 yards, and capped the drive with a 21-yard strike to fullback Terry Barnum, who was uncovered and hanging on by his toes in the right side of the end zone, for the score.

The Wildcats drove to the Trojan 19, but Gowins, off a low snap, missed a 37-yard field goal attempt. When a 30-yard field goal by Josh Abrams on the next Trojan possession moved USC ahead 17-7 with 9:42 left in the first half, it was obvious to all in the sellout throng that both defenses were in for a long day.

While the Wildcat defenders were in up to their necks trying to slow up USC's passing attack, the Trojans were beginning to have trouble with Autry. He was alternating small gains with big chunks of yardage. At the same time, Schnur wasn't seeing a huge pass rush.

Three snaps after Abrams' field goal came the game's first critical play. The Wildcats started on their 26, and Schnur missed connections with Brian Musso on first down, his diving attempt to catch the pass going in and out of his hands. Schnur hit Autry on the right sideline for five yards on second down, then went back to Musso on the left on third-and-5, as the NU crowd shouted "Go, Cats, Go."

Musso caught Schnur's pass and turned upfield, getting as far as the 50 before Trojan strong safety Sammy Knight stripped the ball from Musso as Musso's left knee hit the turf. There was no whistle, the ball bounced around on the grass, and freshman cornerback Daylon McCutcheon, the son of the NFL notable who played for the Rams, picked it up. He weaved his way through traffic on the far sideline, in front of the Southern Cal bench and most of the Trojan cheering section, eventually traveling 53 yards en route to a touchdown.

"I'd like to think my knee was down," said Musso, correctly. "As much as I think about it, I can't change it. The refs called it as they saw it, and had to call it in a split-second. I've got to deal with it.

"I'm always trying to get as much yardage as I can, and it kinda turned against me this time. It'll be hard to swallow for a couple of days."

Barnett, likewise questioning the call, thought it could have been a 14-point swing "with Musso's fumble, quote-unquote."

Now, Northwestern trailed 24-7, and was up against it. The Wildcats caught a small break with 12 seconds left in the half, when linebacker Tim Scharf forced a fumble by Woods, Hudhaifa Ismaeli recovering. But with so short a period of time to work with, Schnur could call only one play, a 22-yard completion by Bates, before Gowins came in to kick a 29-yard field goal.

That, at least, restarted the Wildcat hearts, and shaved USC's lead to 24-10 at the half.

"We decided to pressure more, try to bring more heat (on Otton)," said Vanderlinden. "I think we had turned the momentum around."

Northwestern's comeback had begun with Gowins' kick, and reached full speed in the first seven minutes of the third quarter. The Wildcats drove to the Trojan 11 after Ismaeli returned the opening kickoff of the second half to the NU 43, and Gowins hit a 28-yarder to pull the Cats within 11 points at 24-13.

Then came a shocker, especially to the Trojans. Gowins, who had pooch-kicked a kickoff at the end of the half, lined up for the kickoff, and barely tapped the ball. The Trojans, 25 yards downfield, couldn't adjust, and Josh Barnes recovered the unexpected onside kick at the Northwestern 48 with nary a USC player within 10 feet of him.

"We saw that in film study," said Barnett. "We went into the game knowing we'd use it. It was great execution by Barnes and Gowins."

This drive didn't end in another Gowins field goal. Instead, it concluded with Autry snaking around the right side for 9 yards and his second touchdown of the day with 8:17 left in the third.

The Wildcats had trimmed USC's lead to 24-19. Barnett decided to go for two points on the conversion, setting up the potential for a game-tying field goal later on, but Schnur's pass went between Bates and Dave Beazley in the right-hand corner of the end zone.

All season, save for the debacle against Miami of Ohio, the Wildcats defense stiffened in the second half. That wouldn't be the case against the Trojans, for USC commenced its offensive activity in the third quarter the way it began the game.

Otton to tight end Tyler Cashman for five yards. Otton to Johnson close to the left sideline for 19 yards and a first down. After a penalty, Otton to tight end Johnny McWilliams for 11.

The Cats were reeling, but it seemed they had finally begun to reel the Trojan defense in on second-and-10, when Ismaeli, brushing off Otton's bodyguards, sacked him. It was only a loss of one yard, but it set up a third-and-11 on the USC 44.

In the first half, Otton had connected on seven-of-10 third-down situations. Nothing was going to change. Otton had time in the pocket, then spotted Johnson breaking open in the right flat. Otton threw the ball, Johnson caught it, and then fairly flew into the end zone, his 56-yard touchdown reception consisting of 16 air yards and 40 ground yards.

How, though, could the man Northwestern wanted most to stop get so open?

At first, it appeared that Ismaeli had gone for the interception, because he was diving when Johnson caught the ball. Actually, he had collided with linebacker Don Holmes a split-second earlier.

"We had double-coverage, with Hudhaifa inside," said Barnett. "As he tried to catch up (after running into Holmes), he probably got too much momentum. Keyshawn swam underneath him. He parted the seas like you-know-who."

182   PURPLE ROSES

What had been a pair of Wildcats ready to converge on Johnson and stop him for a 16-yard gain instead turned into a pair of Wildcats scrambling to recover. They couldn't.

"I just blew it," said Ismaeli. "I played him outside and I should have played him inside."

"He musta caught 100 balls, but the one catch is the one that killed is," Barnett figured. "If he doesn't catch it, this is a different game. It's the big play we had to prevent, and we didn't do it today."

That gave USC a 31-19 advantage, and would have broken the hearts of a lesser team. To their credit, Northwestern did not give up. If anything, the Cats played even harder.

Ismaeli returned the kickoff out to the Wildcat 26, and on the first play, Schnur, off a play-action fake reverse, found Bates open behind safety Jesse Davis and cornerback Brian Kelly for a 46-yard gain. It would be Schnur's longest completion of the day, and, combined with a roughing-the-passer call against the Trojans, moved the ball to the USC 13. From there, five running plays were needed to get Northwestern's third touchdown of the day on the board. Schnur did the honors, sneaking in from about 1 inch away seconds after officials ruled he'd been stopped short from a foot. After Gowins' kick, USC led only 31-26, and the Wildcats had all the momentum.

The turn in fortune became even more pronounced on USC's next series. The Trojans went nowhere, Otton's only completion going to offensive lineman Norberto Garrido when Matt Rice applied serious pressure. The Trojans were back on their 7 when John Stonehouse punted.

The Wildcats would get the ball back on their 43 with 1:35 left in the third quarter. After a long comeback, they had a chance to go ahead.

Again on this occasion, NU was most effective through the air, especially early in the drive. Schnur hit Autry on the right for nine yards, Mike McGrew on the right sideline for 11 more, and Musso in the right flat for 23 yards to the Trojan 14 on the first play of the fourth quarter, immediately after the Northwestern band played "High Hopes."

It was third-and-13 when Autry went off left tackle for just nine yards, but was the beneficiary of a face-mask call that moved the ball to the USC 4. Two plays later, he bulled his way into the end zone behind bruising blocks by McGrew and Ryan Padgett, who had been helped off the field earlier but couldn't stay out for long. Autry's 2-yard score, his third touchdown of the day, gave the Wildcats a 32-31 lead with 13:01 to play.

Again, Barnett called for a two-point conversion try, for the logical reason that leading by three points is far better than leading by two.

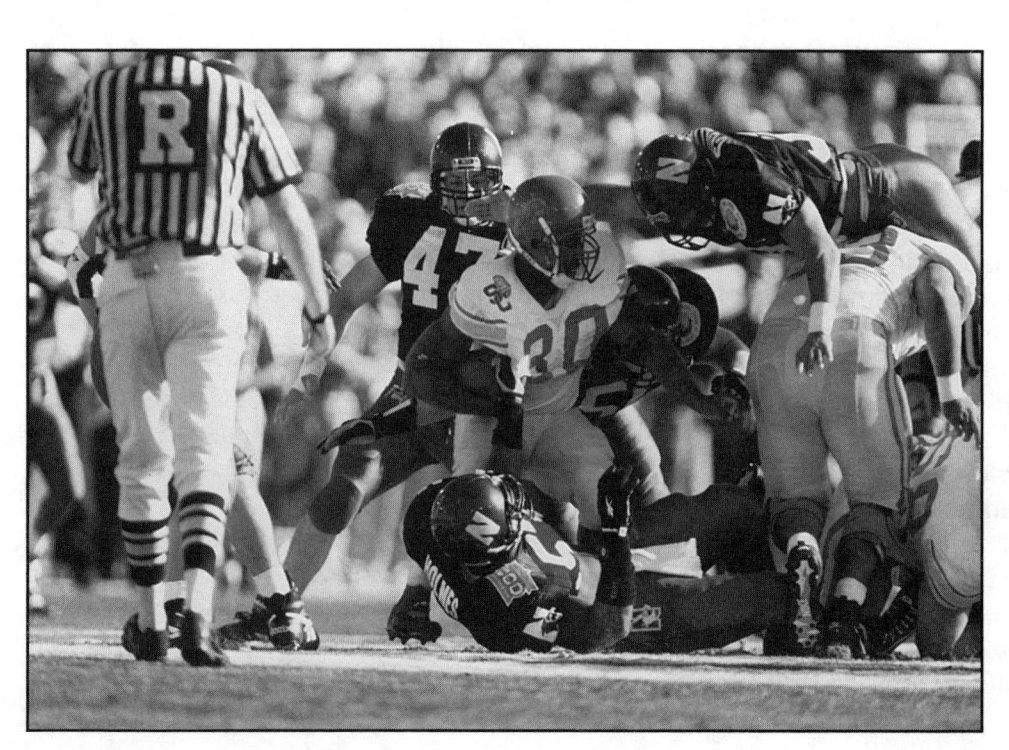

Southern Cal's LaVale Woods is swarmed by Geoff Shein (47), Danny Sutter (50), leading NU tackler Don Holmes (on ground) and another Wildcat defender. (Scott Strazzante/Daily Southtown)

Injured linebacker Pat Fitzgerald consoles linebacker Tim Scharf near game's end. (Scott Strazzante/Daily Southtown)

Schnur went for tight end Darren Drexler, who was five yards deep in the end zone on the left side, but couldn't make the connection, thanks in great part to free safety Micah Phillips' excellent coverage on Drexler. Nevertheless, Northwestern, which had not had the advantage all day, was leading by a point. What seemed unlikely just before the half was now reality, brought about by Northwestern scoring on five straight possessions.

Unfortunately for the Wildcats, the next lead change of the game would be the last lead change. As darkness closed in on the Arroyo Seco, the Trojans closed in on victory. A workmanlike drive that featured a pair of third-down conversions, both on Otton pass completions, culminated in a career-long 46-yard field-goal by Abrams with 9:09 remaining to give the Trojans a 34-32 lead.

"We weren't good enough on defense today to stop the bleeding," said Vanderlinden.

In college football, nine minutes is just short of an eternity. Northwestern, then, had time to play catch-up. What the Wildcats didn't have time for was a mistake, and six plays into their next drive, the mistake occurred.

Schnur had hit Bates and Beazley for 10- and 16-yard gains, respectively, and a three-yard run by Autry moved the ball to the USC 44. There was 6:54 left in the game when Schnur, trying to force it while under pressure, threw across his body from near the right hashmarks, trying to find open fullback Matt Hartl. Because he threw across his body, he couldn't get much on it, and Davis picked it off at the USC 29.

"He threw it right into my arms," said Davis, who wasn't hauled down until getting to the Wildcat 31, a 40-yard return.

Unlike Musso's fumble, there was no question that was a turnover, and the kind of mental error Schnur had studiously avoided making almost all season. He'd thrown only five interceptions all year.

Once again, Otton and his band of receivers was too much for the NU defense to corral. Twice, he completed passes for first downs in third-down situations, the second time hitting Johnson at the NU 7. Two plays later, sophomore Delon Washington did his best Sam "Bam" Cunningham impression and vaulted across from the 2, giving the Trojans a 41-32 lead with 2:55 remaining.

Still, the Wildcats wouldn't give up. Schnur was looking at third-and-10 at the NU 42 when he found running room and gained first-down yardage. With 1:42 left, it was fourth-and-1 when Autry plowed through the line for six yards to the USC 31.

One play later, it appeared as if the Wildcats were within an onside kick of challenging for the lead again. Bates got free down the left sideline, and Schnur lofted a 26-yard pass to him in the end zone.

Touchdown!

Penalty flag. No touchdown. Back at the line of scrimmage, Wildcat tight end Shane Graham had held defensive end Israel Ifeanyi. Now, Graham was holding his head, looking for a deep hole to crawl into. What appeared to be a touchdown with 1:07 left that would have brought the Wildcats within a field-goal at the least was, instead, nothing.

"I didn't even know there was a penalty until I walked back to the huddle," said Bates, deflated.

A Schnur-Musso collaboration on second-and-22 got the ball back to the USC 31, and after a pass to Bates was caught out-of-bounds, Gowins came in to attempt a 49-yard field goal with 41 seconds left.

If he connected, the Wildcats would be within six points and line up for another onside kick. If he missed, Southern Cal would run out the clock.

Paul Janus snapped the ball. Paul Burton teed it up. Gowins kicked it. And it hit the left upright, caroming back onto the field.

Otton kneeled down to kill the clock, and Northwestern's dream season was over. The Trojans had won, and, ignored even by their hometown press for the most part, would have the last laugh.

Johnson, who would be named the game's MVP, would dance for joy in the purple-and-white Northwestern end zone. Once, in 1985, he'd caught field goals behind the end zones in the Rose Bowl. Now, he was the star of the show.

"It was my last football game as a Trojan," he mused. "I stayed up late last night thinking about that. Past curfew, in fact. Thinking this is it. But I told the guys, 'We go out tomorrow, and it's 12 midnight. And their dream is over. It's a new year. It's our time.'"

The Trojans, who finished 9-2-1, couldn't stop talking about Northwestern's Cinderella reputation.

"I officially want to say that Cinderella is dead," said Trojans tackle John Michaels. "The glass slipper is broken, and we've sent her back to Chicago in rags."

Hah, the Wildcats said.

"The proof that we're no Cinderella will be when we come back with games like this next year and do what we have to do to get back to Pasadena," said center Rob Johnson, his 45-game career completed.

Robinson, still stinging from the criticism he took for losing to Notre Dame and UCLA, finally had ammunition to fire back at his detractors. Asked if beating Northwestern saved the Trojans' season, he had his opening.

"It doesn't save our season," said Robinson, now 4-0 in the Rose Bowl. "This win is this win. We were the Pac-10 champions. We've stumbled twice during the season.

"No other opinion from somebody else, saying we're saved or not saved, makes any difference. We've won more games with this group of players than any other Pac-10 team over the last three years. We screwed up twice this year, bad.

Gary Barnett in the final seconds. (Scott Strazzante/ Daily Southtown)

"We 'saved' our season today, so you go ahead and write that."

Some people even believed Robinson had saved his job by beating the Wildcats. Such is the pressure at a football powerhouse.

What Robinson did like about the pre-Rose Bowl festivities was the relative lack of attention paid to the Trojans. It was a built-in motivating tool.

"We didn't feel (NU's getting the attention) was that way," he said. "We were left out of it. I got bruises, and most of our players have injuries on their toes from you people stepping on our toes and shoving us out of the way to get to the other guys.

"We had a great time. We had a lot of fun. We have fun when we go to the Rose Bowl, and we do not associate being occupied by you as, by any stretch of the imagination, being fun. Your ignoring us was certainly OK with us."

Barnett, in charge of the instant powerhouse, one that finished 10-2, placing eighth in the final vote of writers and broadcasters for the AP Top 25 and seventh in the *USA Today/CNN* coaches poll, was more reflective.

"Overall, I'm really proud of the way our kids just kept fighting back," said Barnett. "It's typical of the kind of adversity we've come through in the last three —21 years — 24 years. We played just the way we'd been all year, from the first game to the last game. I thought we handled all the hype and publicity and hoopla with a lot of manners and grace and poise and class. We handled this game the same way.

"What we did today was have to play against two opponents, against ourselves and also USC," Barnett added, referring to the turnovers. "Normally, when you have to play against two, you don't win.

"We'd had trouble getting to the quarterback all year. We'd just been able to cover receivers enough to where we've gotten away from it because our coverage had been so good, or else we haven't played against a receiver of Keyshawn's quality, or the kind of scheme USC has.

"We don't see that scheme where they throw it 90 times a game. It was the combination of good players, a good (USC) scheme and a couple turnovers," Barnett continued.

"It was a great game, with two good teams. We turned the ball over and lost. That hasn't been our M.O. We were second in the country in turnover margin. We hadn't committed those kinds of errors. People have committed those sort of errors against us, and we've taken advantage of them, lived by that, more or less, all year.

"You do that, you're just not going to win in bowl games."

Southern Cal's only turnover of the day resulted in Gowins' field-goal late in the first half, but that wasn't nearly enough to make up for the two NU turnovers that turned into 14 USC points.

"It was a wonderful season, and sure, we'd all like to go home with a win, no question about it," said Barnett. "We played well enough to win, but we just turned the ball over. Our kids fought hard enough. There isn't anything I'd do over. I thought our kids played as hard as any time all year."

It was suggested that losing the Rose Bowl tarnished the Wildcats' amazing season. Barnett disagreed.

"Does it tarnish it?" he said. "Well, it's not what it coulda been. We're a good football team. We came from nowhere and did some great things. I'm really proud, we're proud of each other.

"Does it tarnish? We didn't win the Rose Bowl. So we're going to have to come back and win it. That's the way we'll have to approach it."

THE 82ND ROSE BOWL GAME

Monday, January 1, 1996 at The Rose Bowl, Pasadena, California
Weather: 75° Wind W 5 Sunny
Attendance: 100,102

SCORE BY QUARTERS	1	2	3	4	SCORE
USC	7	17	7	10	41
Northwestern	7	3	16	6	32

First Quarter

		NU	USC
USC 10:02 L. Woods 1-yard run (Abrams kick) (12 plays, 83 yards, 4:53 TOP)		0	7
NU 6:05 D. Autry 3-yard run (Gowins kick) (10 plays, 68 yards, 3:51 TOP)		7	7

Second Quarter

USC 13:05 Barnum 21-yard pass from Otton (Abrams kick) (8 plays, 78 yards, 2:29 TOP)	7	14
USC 3:29 Abrams 30-yard field goal (11 plays, 68 yards, 6:13 TOP)	7	17
USC 2:56 McCutcheon 53-yard fumble return (Abrams kick)	7	24
NU 0:02 Gowins 29-yard field goal (2 plays, 22 yards, 0:10 TOP)	10	24

Third Quarter

NU 11:01 Gowins 28-yard field goal (11 plays, 46 yards, 3:50 TOP)	13	24
NU 8:17 D. Autry 9-yard run (pass incomplete) (6 plays, 52 yards, 2:43 TOP)	19	24
USC 6:08 K. Johnson 56-yard pass from Otton (Abrams kick) 5 plays, 79 yards, 2:05 TOP)	19	31
NU 2:58 Schnur 1-yard run (Gowins kick) (6 plays, 74 yards, 3:02 TOP)	26	31

Fourth Quarter

NU 13:01 D. Autry 2-yard run (pass incomplete) (10 plays, 57 yards, 3:34 TOP)	32	31
USC 9:09 Abrams 46-yard field goal (12 plays, 39 yards, 3:36 TOP)	32	34
USC 2:55 Washington 2-yard run (Abrams kick) (8 plays, 69 yards, 3:47 TOP)	32	41

TEAM STATISTICS	NU	USC
First Downs	23	22
Rushing	10	1
Passing	11	21
Penalty	2	0
Rushing Attempts	39	27
Yards Gained Rushing	152	58
Yards Lost Rushing	13	29
Net Yards Rushing	139	29
Net Yards Passing	336	391
Passes Attempted	39	44
Passes Completed	23	29
Had Intercepted	1	0
Total Offensive Plays	78	71
Total Net Yards	475	420
Average Gain per Play	6.09	5.92
Fumbles: Number-Lost	1-1	1-1
Penalties: Number-Yards	7-72	11-86
Interceptions: Number-Yards	0-0	1-41
Number of Punts-Yards	2-77	2-89
Average Per Punt	38.5	44.5
Punt Returns: Number-Yards	0-0	2-18
Kickoff Returns: Number-Yards	8-225	3-31
Possession Time	30:13	29:47
Third-Down Conversions	8 of 15	12 of 17
Sacks By: Number-Yards	4-21	0-0

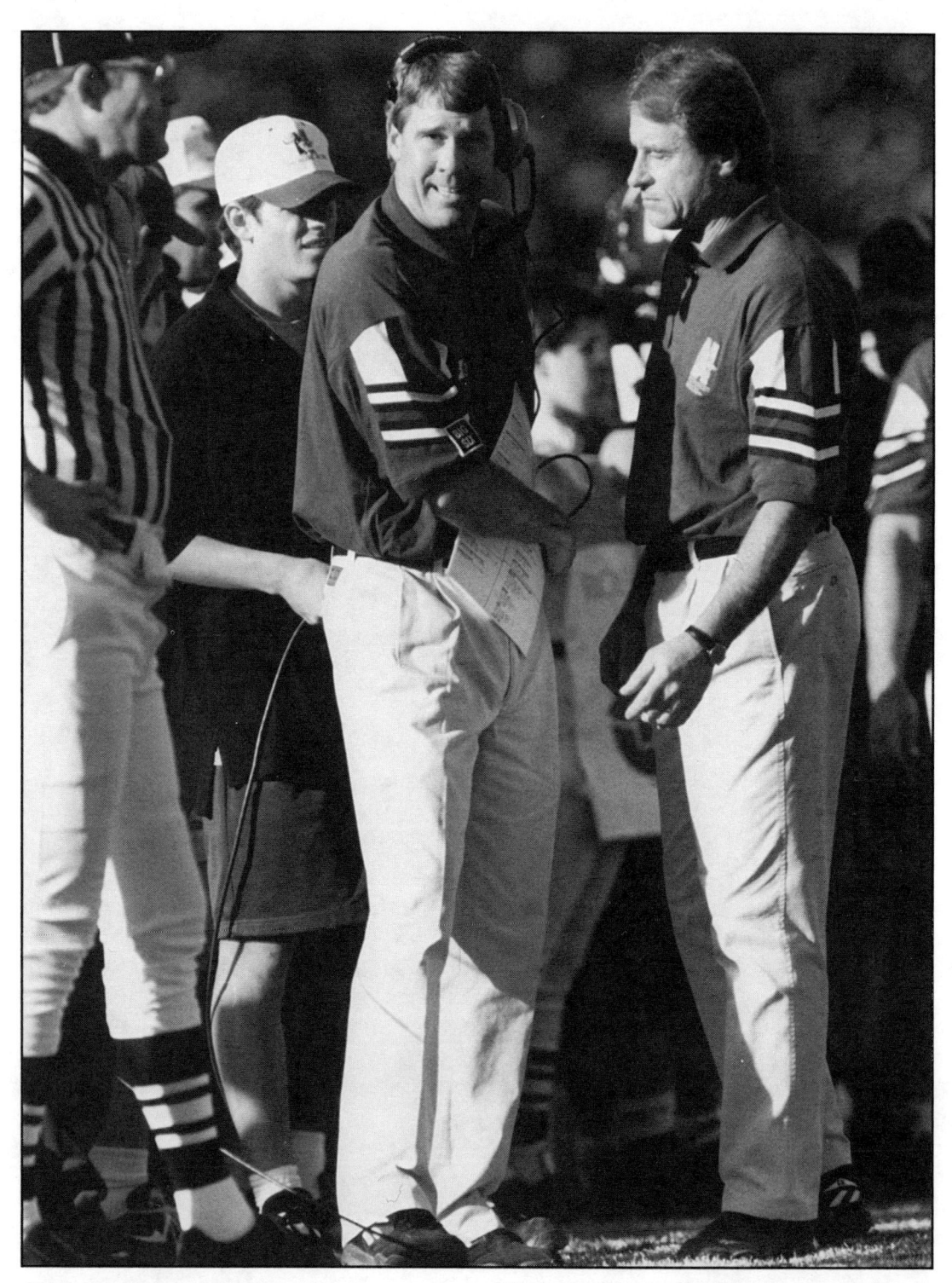

Until Gary Barnett announced he was staying at NU, speculation made defensive coordinator Ron Vanderlinden the leading in-house candidate. (Scott Strazzante/Daily Southtown)

Chapter 20
A BRIGHT FUTURE

"We going to go out and dominate it."
—Gary Barnett on the Big Ten

"LOOK AT ALL the seniors in their lineup," people sometimes said of Northwestern this season. "They can't do this again."

Yes, they can. Northwestern's seniors aren't all seniors in the athletic sense. Though a full analysis is impossible to make, this appears to be one of the youngest championship teams in Big Ten history. Perhaps no team since Ohio State's 1968 national championship squad, which had a covey of key sophomores, has been so youthful.

Northwestern, in its media guide and on its offense-defense flip charts, doesn't do what most schools do, and note what year of athletic eligibility a player is in. NU denotes what academic year he's in, even if he's been red-shirted.

For instance, starting quarterback Steve Schnur, listed as a senior this season, was a junior for athletic purposes. He had company.

The Wildcats lose only two offensive starters, guard Ryan Padgett and center Rob Johnson. Granted, losing a pair of All-Big Ten first teamers isn't a help, but look who's coming back.

Darnell Autry, the only offensive starter who wasn't red-shirted, will be a junior, and, as the Big Ten's leading rusher in yards-per-game average (152.3 to Eddie George's 152.2), a Heisman Trophy hopeful from the start. Receiver D'Wayne Bates (42 catches, five touchdowns) and fullback Matt Hartl will be listed as juniors, but have two years left to play after 1996. Tackle Paul Janus will be a four-year senior eligible to play in 1997.

There will be five fifth-year seniors closing out their careers: wide receiver Dave Beazley, tight end Darren Drexler, guard Justin Chabot, tackle Brian Kardos, and Schnur (54.1 percent completion percentage, nine touchdowns), who'll be back in a battle with the redshirted Tim Hughes for playing time, not to mention Chris Hamdorf. Both will be in their senior year, and able to come back for more in 1997.

Six starters depart on defense: end-outside linebacker Mike Warren, corners Rodney Ray and Chris Martin, safety William Bennett, and inside linebacker Danny Sutter, Geoff Shein.

Five regulars return: tackles Matt Rice (who'll be a fourth-year senior in his last season) and Joe Reiff (a fifth-year senior), right end Casey Dailey and safety Eric Collier (seniors also eligible in 1997), and Pat Fitzgerald (13.0 tackles per game, the best average in the Big Ten), who'll be a fourth-year senior, and like Rice, in his last campaign.

The biggest losses are Ray and Martin, three-year starters at cornerback. But even there, NU has depth. Hudhaifa Ismaeli earned All-Big Ten second team honors, while Josh Barnes was the team's defensive newcomer of the year.

The preponderance of returnees—in all, only 12 players graduate—means Gary Barnett's recruiting will have to be selective.

"Right now, I'd have 13 scholarships if I brought all the fifth-year seniors back," he said at season's end. "Those are things that have to be talked about with the fifth-year seniors, guys who want to come back.

"Everyone will be dealt with individually. If they want to come back is the first consideration. Two, their role on the team this year and projected role next year comes into play.

"We're in a position where most of our guys graduate in four years, so if there's guys who want to move on, that would be another scholarship for us."

Barnett knew that no matter how many scholarships he had, he had to find the right people: risk-takers.

"We have a little different deal here in that we had to find a good match as far as a recruit goes," he said. "A much better match, a fit here than most places have to look for a fit. As long as we're able to go out and (find players who fit), then we'll be OK."

Barnett knew winning the Big Ten was a major accomplishment, indeed, at Northwestern, a monumental achievement, but he was as humble in victory as he had been gracious—and ticked off—in defeat. Asked if he'd built a dynasty, he couldn't help but laugh.

"Four months ago, I said we had a chance to have a significant season and you guys thought I was smoking weed," Barnett said on November 20. "Now, you think I'm going to say we're going to have a dynasty here? A guy can only set himself up so many times. Let's do this a little bit at a time. In 15 years, we'll talk about dynasties and consistency over a period of time."

As NU moved up in stature—and in the polls—through the course of the season, Barnett's name began to come up as a likely candidate for other head coaching positions.

Some people in the Wildcat athletic office even believed he might leave for Michigan, but that became impossible when Lloyd Carr lost the "interim" tag from his title. Likewise, Wildcat fans breathed easier when Notre Dame announced Lou Holtz could coach the Fighting Irish as long as he wanted.

Then the annual coaching silly season began. George fired Ray Goff. Terry Donahue left UCLA for CBS, with Colorado's Rick Neuheisel quickly rumored to be going to UCLA, his alma mater. That would leave an opening at Barnett's old stomping grounds.

The Buffaloes were ready to offer Barnett a

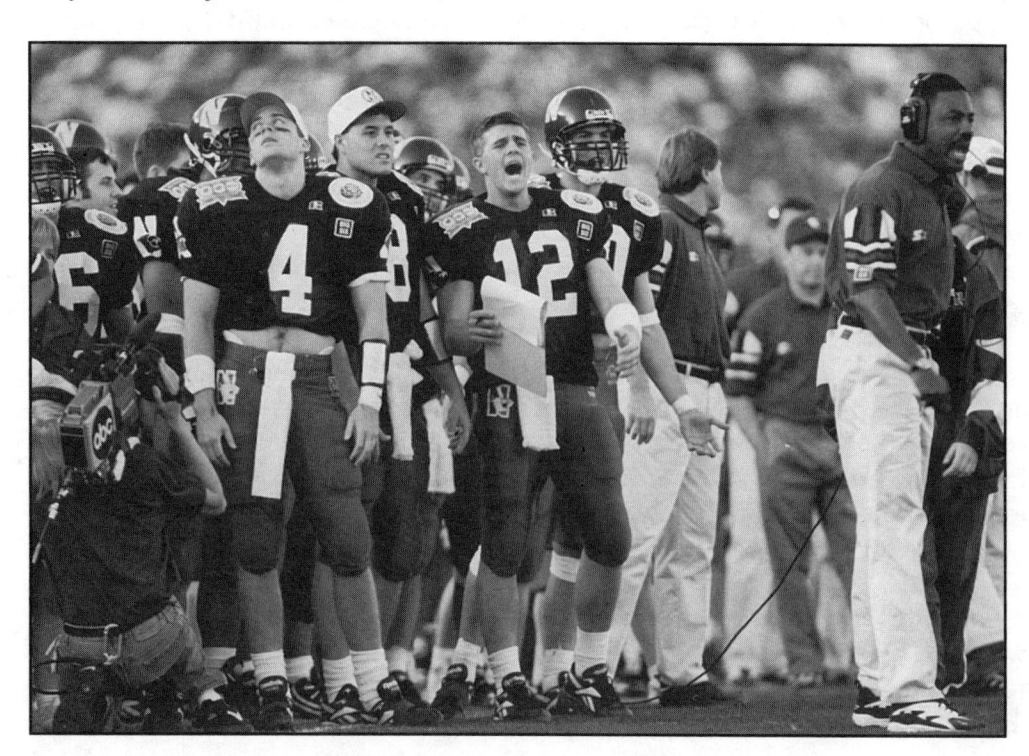

A trio of quarterbacks, Chris Hamdorf (4), Tim Hughes (8), and Mark Broxterman (12), will challenge Steve Schnur for the starting job next year. (Scott Strazzante/Daily Southtown)

deal, but Neuheisel stayed, and with NU and Barnett's lawyer, a man he has identified only as "Rocky," already talking about a new pact, Barnett seemed anchored in Evanston. The university wanted to keep him, and initiated talks to extend his contract, which had been extended through 1998 the year before, around the time the Wildcats beat Michigan.

Then December 1 came, and the deadline Barnett had given NU to present him with a firm offer passed without an offer. Barnett began to look around.

The Georgia situation heated up first. On December 8, Barnett called on Georgia athletic director Vince Dooley, and Dooley promptly told the *Tribune* that the chat was to see "if there was enough mutual interest to have future discussions."

In the end there wasn't, but that move woke up NU's administration. Their offer finally hit Barnett's desk, and on December 15, when Barnett told a few reporters huddling with him in a corner of the Nicolet Center that he and Northwestern were close to terms on a long-term deal, the possibility that he would bolt again seemed put to rest.

The pact would boost Barnett's salary to well above the $200,000 he had been making. It would give significant raises to his assistants. And it would be for 12 years, keeping him at NU through 2007, when he would be 61, unless he chose to invoke a buyout clause.

"You see why I feel good about where Northwestern is on this deal?" Barnett said on December 15. "I think if I asked for 15 years they'd give me 15. If they offered 15, I'd take it.

"We're beyond the blow-up stage. We're working on the language."

Four days earlier, however, UCLA athletic director Peter Dalis called NU AD Rick Taylor.

"What on earth are you calling for?" said Taylor when he picked up the phone. He knew. Like Dooley before him, Dalis wanted permission to talk to Barnett. Taylor granted it.

"When UCLA called and asked permission to talk to Gary, I granted it without hesitation," Taylor explained on January 4. "I think that's the way to go in this environment. I would never even think of withholding permission for someone to talk to somebody else."

The UCLA rumors surfaced in the days before the Rose Bowl, where the Bruins play their home games, and got stronger and stronger as game time approached.

By now, Wildcats fans hearing Barnett say he wasn't a candidate for any other job had to believe him even as the players believed they'd get to the Rose Bowl. The theme for the season was Belief Without Evidence, and it was working both ways.

If Barnett was staying, why didn't he come out and say he wasn't interested in the UCLA job? Because he was interested. Barnett and Dalis met early on December 30, a short chat that, said Barnett, didn't involve money. Dalis and Barnett's lawyer talked on the phone, once before the Rose Bowl and once after, about contract terms. The *Los Angeles Times* even reported that Gary's wife Mary was looking at housing.

Finally, on the morning of Tuesday, January 2, Barnett and Dalis met again, scant hours before the Wildcats flew home. Dalis faxed final contract terms to Barnett back in Evanston that night.

On Wednesday morning, Barnett went off on a two-day recruiting trip to North Carolina. For him, it was the middle of a 36-hour decision-making process. He decide to stay and called Taylor that night.

"This is what's best for my family," Barnett said at a packed house in Nicolet Center's auditorium on Friday, January 5. "Every decision I've made in my professional life has been driven by those things. When I made a decision to move from Colorado to Northwestern, it wasn't popular with my peers, but it was the best move for my family.

"At that time, my family consisted of four. My family now has grown to include nine or 10 (assistant coaches) with their families as well as 100 or so athletes. What started off as four is now about 135.

"If a person's going to have integrity, then he needs to stand up for and make his decisions on the things he says he's about.

"So, I made a decision not to go any further with the University of Georgia because it was best for my family. I pulled out of the UCLA position because it was the best thing for my family.

"It really is about as simple as that."

Barnett, who has a daughter, Courtney, who is a junior at Northwestern, and a son, Clay, a

Northwestern fans, heretofore ready to celebrate a mere winning season, will set their sights higher from now on. (Scott Strazzante/Daily Southtown)

senior at Loyola Academy High School, said that if he was making the decision based only on his own desires, or strictly on money, it would have been different.

"If this was not going to be as good a place as UCLA or Georgia, then I would have gone to UCLA or Georgia or wherever. But it is, and I deem it so based on what the university has offered me and my coaches.

"It's not just about money. If it was just about money, I wouldn't be here. There's a couple places out there that throw around a lot of money.

"It's about where you live, it's the quality of your life, how happy your family is.

"As I put myself in both positions, my family in them, and everybody involved in them, this was better for us."

"Us" being the whole football family.

"It might have been easier for the four of us to go than for the other groups to go," Barnett explained.

Barnett also decided to stay at Northwestern because of the massive interest the program attracted as a winner.

"It's been overwhelming what happened," he said. "It's important here. If it weren't important here, I wouldn't stay, because this is my job. This year's proven the success of the team is important to not just Evanston, but the whole Chicago community, and that is huge for me."

Even before the Rose Bowl, defensive coordinator Ron Vanderlinden, architect of the third-ranked defense in the country, had withdrawn himself for consideration for the head coaching job at Northern Illinois a few days after interviewing for it. Vanderlinden, though, was considered the most likely assistant to take a post elsewhere.

Inevitably, players change, as do coaches, but the physical structure of an athletic department is more permanent. Northwestern's athletic facilities had trailed the rest of the Big Ten for years, and football's facilities were farthest behind of all.

Barnett was fond of saying, "All kids want is to be like everybody else." He meant in quality of support, from the amount of people in the stands to the ability of their coaches to coach, to where they did their work.

It was the latter that hadn't been addressed often.

A lack of commitment to upgrade facilities was one of the many reasons Dennis Green quit a week before spring practice in 1986. A football office that was on the drawing board never got off the drawing board until after Green left.

That building, the $3.1 million John C. Nicolet Football Center, opened in the summer of 1988, and had all the modern accouterments needed in big-time athletics: separate offices for each coach, a big meeting room, the works. Compared to the cramped offices on the west rim of Dyche Stadium the football staff previously had, it was the Taj Mahal.

Except for one little thing, which was actually a big thing.

Northwestern had no indoor practice facility. A decade ago, when Green was grousing, that was no big deal, but in the intervening years, it became a big deal. The Big Ten's "arms race" saw every other school in the conference, plus Notre Dame, build an indoor facility. Indiana's was the last to go up, completed in the late fall of 1995.

That left Northwestern without a roof over the heads of its players, save for a 25-yard strip of old, old Astroturf in the back of McGaw Hall. North Arena, it had been optimistically named. And that was hardly useful, either for full-scale practices or as a recruiting tool.

At the Big Ten meetings in early August, Barnett had revealed that NU was finally going to get the football building. The plans were unveiled on September 27, and included a surprise: a full-scale renovation of Dyche Stadium.

The indoor facility, to include an 85-by-60 yard practice field under a 55-foot ceiling, will be attached to the north side of the Nicolet Center, and was expected to be ready for the 1996 season. Bids were being taken in the fall of 1995.

The improvements, to include new practice courts in the North Arena for the basketball and volleyball teams in the old indoor practice area, would be funded by a $20 million facilities-improvement campaign, of which 39 percent was already subscribed at the time of the announcement.

"You can't have an excellent university if only two or three departments are excellent," said Raymond Farley, a Northwestern board member and the chairman of the fundraising campaign. "If you're going to be in athletics, you can't be poor at it. You can't be mediocre at it. You have to be excellent to be an excellent university. If you have a poor athletic program, you won't attract good students and good teachers. You begin to get a malaise."

Indeed, the school reported a rise in applications in the late fall, coinciding with the Wildcats' on-field fortunes. Other private schools, notably Boston College in the Doug Flutie years, had seen the same trend.

"In 1985, we found there was very profound support all around the country for Northwestern," said Patrick Ryan, vice chairman of the

Darnell Autry, shown here scoring his third Rose Bowl touchdown, would become NU's all-time leading rusher with another 1,675-yard season. (Scott Strazzante/Daily Southtown)

NU board of trustees. "They said we'd raise $2 million and we raised $21 million."

Ryan backed up his words with a major donation to the new campaign on behalf of his family. He'd also done so in the past. McGaw Hall's interior was renamed Welsh-Ryan Arena in honor of his and his wife's parents after they donated much of the cost of the 1985 refurbishment.

Improvements to Dyche, built in 1926 at a cost of $1.2 million, would take about $16 million of the $20 million project. And Dyche, while in no danger of falling down, needed help. Peeling paint and cosmetic cracks in the concrete walls shouted at visitors that the whole program was run down, not just the stadium.

"The structure of Dyche Stadium is intact," said Northwestern president Henry Bienen. "Dyche isn't falling down, though occasionally it chips off a bit."

However, the stadium's seedy look, something no amount of ivy could cover up, is what prodded Bienen to take action.

"When I took a tour of Dyche, it was an eye-opener," Bienen said. "In many ways, it was not an appropriate facility for the university. If you're going to have a major football program and bring people into your stadium, you really want that to be the place which lots of people have contact with Northwestern. To me this was a facility that definitely needed renovation."

Northwestern is in the midst of facilities changes. The Lindheimer Observatory on the lakeshore, deemed to have outlived its usefulness, yielded grudgingly to demolition teams, who thought they could implode it and eventually had to pull it down. Perhaps prophetically, it could be seen listing to the south from the Dyche Stadium press box, about 1½ miles away, during the home opener with Miami of Ohio.

A refurbished Dyche, it was announced, would be more fan-friendly. There would be new seating, three times the restrooms, far more concession space, a new press box, and, perhaps, luxury boxes to go alongside the administration's box. An entertainment center, something to replace the tent behind the north end zone, was also slated.

Not on the drawing board: lights or an expanded seating capacity. It would still be about 49,256.

Asked if expansion was contemplated, athletic director Rick Taylor said, "That's in somebody else's lifetime. I'd want to fill it for four or five years first."

This, of course, was when Northwestern was 2-1, when the Wildcats were unranked, were still stinging from the loss to Miami, and before the sellouts began to pile up.

Dyche had been renovated in 1975, 1981 and 1987, and new AstroTurf installed in 1994. All the renovations would be stopgap measures compared to the new construction.

"It's almost a new stadium life," said Taylor. "We wanted to get a 40-to-50 year life out of it."

Aside from the new press box atop the west stands, Dyche wouldn't look much different.

"The towers will stay," said Taylor. "I think it's unique."

"We're not going to change the basic structure," said Barnett of the exterior arches, which complement the towers.

"Northwestern's commitment, in the founder's words, is to the highest order of excellence," Bienen said. "That's what we're about. That's what we're known for, and I would like that to also obtain for our athletic programs."

Bienen called the new building "critical to the success of our student athletic programs and pivotal to the success and continued improvement of Northwestern's varsity football program."

In August, Barnett compared the forthcoming practice building to facilities improvements at Colorado and remembered the time-frame in which success followed.

"When (Bill) McCartney went to Colorado, he was asked how long it would take to build the program, and he said from seven to 10 years. Wisconsin did it in four years, but they started with the same things as everyone else.

"We're trying to make it a level playing field. Then it'll be four years after that."

As it turned out, success, in its most overwhelming form, came four years early. When the artist's renderings were first displayed, Barnett may not have been completely sure the Wildcats were on the fast track to success, but he knew they were on the right track.

"We have now heard the commitment, seen the commitment," said Barnett. "Skeptics should be responded to now. The questions were do we belong in the Big Ten and should this university stay in the Big Ten?

"This is an overwhelming answer, and it's you're dang right we do. And we're going to do more than just be a part of it. We're going to go out and dominate it."

1995 ALL-BIG TEN FOOTBALL TEAM

(As selected by Media Panel; players in ALL CAPS have 1996 eligibility)

Offense

First Team		Second Team
Bobby Hoying, Ohio State	Quarterback	Darrell Bevell, Wisconsin
Eddie George, Ohio State	Running Back	Mike Alstott, Purdue
DARNELL AUTRY, Northwestern	Running Back	TSHIMANGA BIAKABUTUKA, Michigan
Rob Johnson, Northwestern	Center	Todd Jesewitz, Minnesota
Ryan Padgett, Northwestern	Guard	Matt Purdy, Iowa
ORLANDO PACE, Ohio State	Guard	Joe Marinaro, Michigan
JON RUNYAN, Michigan	Tackle	**BRIAN KARDOS,** Northwestern
Rickey Dudley, Ohio State	Tight End	Scott Slutzker, Iowa
Bobby Engram, Penn State	Receiver	Mercury Hayes, Michigan
TERRY GLENN, Ohio State	Receiver	**D'WAYNE BATES,** Northwestern
Sam Valenzisi, Northwestern	Placekicker	BRETT CONWAY, Penn State

Defense

First Team		Second Team
Simeon Rice, Illinois	Line	MATT FINKES, Ohio State
MIKE VRABEL, Ohio State	Line	WILLIAM CARR, Michigan
Jason Horn, Michigan	Line	**MATT RICE,** Northwestern
TAREK SALEH, Wisonsin	Line	NATE DAVIS, Indiana
PAT FITZGERALD, Northwestern	ILB/OLB	Terry Killens, Penn State
Kevin Hardy, Illinois	ILB/OLB	PETE MONTY, Wisconsin
JARRETT IRONS, Michigan	ILB/OLB	Bobby Diaco, Iowa
Shawn Springs, Ohio State	Back	Antwoine Patten, Illinois
Chris Martin, Northwestern	Back	**HUDHAIFA ISMAELI,** Northwestern
BRIAN MILLER, Penn State	Back	RODNEY HEATH, Minnesota
CLARENCE THOMPSON, Michigan	Back	CHARLES WOODSON, Michigan
NICK GALLERY, Iowa	Punter	Brett Larson, Illinois

Honorable Mention:
Tyrone Washington, Illinois; Eric Smedley, Alan Sutkowski, Aaron Warnecke, Indiana; PLEZ ATKINS, Casey Wiegmann, Iowa; REMY HAMILTON, ROD PAYNE, Jay Riemersma, AMANI TOOMER, Trent Zenkewicz, Michigan; FLOZELL ADAMS, Yakini Allen, Tony Banks, DERRICK MASON, Michigan State; Mike Chalberg, Mike Giovinetti, RYAN THELWELL, Minnesota; **William Bennett, ERIC COLLIER, Rodney Ray, STEVE SCHNUR, Northwestern;** GREG BELLESARI, LE SHUN DANIELS, Ohio State, LUKE FICKELL, JUAN PORTER, Ohio State; Todd Atkins, Keith Conlin, KIM HERRING, Andre Johnson, Marco Rivera, Penn State; MARK FISCHER, CHIKE OKEAFOR, DERRICK WINSTON, Purdue; Jason Maniecki, Matt Nyquist, Eric Unverzagt, JAMIE VANDERVELDT, JERRY WUNSCH, Wisconsin.

Offensive Player of the Year:	Eddie George, Ohio State
Defensive Player of the Year:	**Pat Fitzgerald, Northwestern**
Freshman of the Year:	Curtis Enis, Penn State
Big Ten-Dave McClain Coach of the Year:	**Gary Barnett, Northwestern**

POSTSEASON AP TOP 25

1. Nebraska
2. Florida
3. Tennessee
4. Florida State
5. Colorado
6. Ohio State
7. Kansas State
8. **Northwestern**
9. Kansas
10. Virginia Tech.
11. Notre Dame
12. Southern Cal
13. Penn State
14. Texas
15. Texas A&M
16. Virginia
17. Michigan
18. Oregon
19. Syracuse
20. Miami
21. Alabama
22. Auburn
23. Texas Tech.
24. Toledo
25. Iowa

1996 NORTHWESTERN SCHEDULE

Sept. 7	at Wake Forest
Sept. 14	at Duke
Sept. 21	OHIO U.
Sept. 28	at Indiana
Oct. 5	MICHIGAN
Oct. 12	MINNESOTA
Oct. 19	at Wisconsin
Oct. 26	ILLINOIS
Nov. 2	at Penn State
Nov. 9	at Iowa
Nov. 16	PURDUE